THE WILLERS
OF THE WILL

THE WILLERS OF THE WILL

V. H. Ironside

When you are the willers of a single will, and you call this dispeller of need your essential and necessity: that is when your virtue has its origin and its beginning.

Truly, it is a new good and evil! Truly, a new roaring in the depths and the voice of a new fountain!

It is power, this new virtue; it is a ruling idea, and around it a subtle soul: a golden sun, and around it the serpent of knowledge.

Nietzsche, *Zarathustra*

The Book Guild Ltd
Sussex, England

The Book Guild Ltd
25 High Street,
Lewes, Sussex

First published 1995
© V. H. Ironside
Set in Times
Typesetting by Raven Typesetters, Chester

Printed in Great Britain by
Antony Rowe Ltd.
Chippenham, Wiltshire.

A catalogue record for this book is available from the British Library

ISBN 1 85776 013 1

CONTENTS

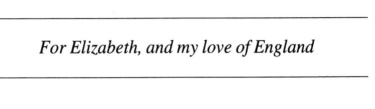

For Elizabeth, and my love of England

INTRODUCTION

The prophet, however, shall eat and drink beside
me: and truly, I will show him a sea in which he
can drown!

Nietzsche, *Zarathustra*

THE PROPHET

I have a terrible fear that one day my name shall
be pronounced Holy!

Nietzsche, *Ecce Homo*

'Holy be thy name to all future generations! In the name of all thy
friends, I thy pupil cry out our warmest thanks to thee for thy great
life. Thou was one of the noblest and purest men that ever trod this
earth.'

The year is 1900, the occasion Friedrich Nietzsche's mid-
summer funeral, the speaker Peter Gast. There is no doubt that
Gast was sincere when he delivered this obituary oration at the
poet-philosopher's burial-place, for he had already given him
some twenty years of the most loyal and unswerving devotion.
But his epitaph yielded nothing. In the popular imagination
Nietzsche has always remained the arch-exponent of racial
hubris, and the cause of the *Superman* its most combative agent.
As determined by a completely false set of references, the
prospect was that of a legacy haunted by guilt and recriminations.

When we first encounter Nietzsche's 'philosophy of the
future', it is an inspired and prophetic conception. As it stood,
however – left to sink or swim in the titanic convulsions of the
succeeding century, the century of the holocaust and the first full-
scale global wars – it became increasingly turned upside down,
good and evil proceeding in opposite directions. In fact, it is probably no exaggeration to say that no other cause in the history of

ideas has been so tragically, so perversely and so assiduously mis-represented by friends and foes alike than the cause of the Superman. Having created what was to all outward appearances an utterly elitist doctrine about the necessity of man's having to be replaced by some species of *Übermensch*, it was perhaps inevitable that the reaction of those who misunderstood Nietzsche's admiration for the Overman – and the idea of self-overcoming – as a deliberate subversion of the prevailing moral order, should have been one of downright execration. The idea is indeed a complex and a fascinating one. For one thing, Nietzsche himself seems to have appreciated that failure, under the present timetable, was almost implicit in the sheer extravagance of his conception, in the sense of cosmic scope behind the gospel of the Superman: 'It seems that, in order to inscribe themselves in the hearts of humanity with eternal demands, all great things have first to wander the earth as monstrous and fear-inspiring grotesques.'[1]

For him the destiny of humanity was not a political one. He pre-ferred the observances of a world he diagnosed as decadent, its follies and infirmities, to those more definitely associated with the socio-political philosopher. The striving to surpass rather than a socially sanctioned equality was to determine the merit of one's actions. And in the general idea of the Overman, the idea that 'mankind's fate depends upon the success of its highest type', he raised a clear-cut moral issue which overrode all other distinc-tions of nation, custom, creed or race. Too few, perhaps, read his works now, but seeing how maliciously he was libelled and how unfairly he has been treated, justice, it seems to me, demands acknowledgement of these facts. One is aware, of course, that for as long as there is a single chauvinist left in the world, or the ves-tige of a nationalist creed, the term 'Superman' will always have its racial connotations; but the true Nietzschean meaning – distin-guished as it is by the ideal of surpassing oneself, by the striving for the highest and the necessity for evolution – can never be refuted. No careful reader of his works, moreover, is likely to dis-pute that the imperative for Nietzsche was predominantly the moral question; that they bear witness above all to his profound integrity as a teacher and a moralist. To the almost obsessive intensity of that execration of 'self-righteousness' which, far beyond any detestation he may have expressed for Christianity, is the essence of his philosophy.

There is irony, perhaps, in the fact that he who was a moral fundamentalist of the most passionate kind should have proclaimed himself the 'Antichrist' and been thoroughly devoted to establishing a reputation as an 'Immoralist'. Indeed, we can say with perfect safety that there will always be those for whom Nietzsche is, and ever has been, the Devil's mouthpiece. Perhaps. But although the creator of the Superman set up an unorthodox moral problem, inasmuch as he became a great Immoralist by what he once contrived to call his Hell: 'his love for man'[2], nothing but moral passion, that element in him which sought the highest, could possibly have sanctioned it. This may come as a surprise to all those who have viewed him as the archetypal dissenter whose deprecation of values which had been held dear for centuries inevitably made him the great apostate that he was. But above all he valued humanity. And the almost superhuman intensity with which, by a supreme effort of unending self-discipline, he remained indissolubly attached to one object and one intention alone is the most consistent feature perhaps of his entire philosophy: the elevation of the species of man to new values before it would succumb to the sickness of its age, to the inescapable relativities of a moral life under easy material conditions.

The problem, as it stood then, is the same a hundred years on. Nietzsche, of course, had his own teachers and precursors. Great thinkers such as Heraclitus, Empedocles, Spinoza and Goethe were among them. Thinkers who, in various forms and degrees, directly and indirectly, influenced profoundly the life and outlook of this remarkable philosopher, scholar and poet. Nietzschean apostles there have been not a few. Indeed, the distorted doctrine of the sovereign breed was carried by the Nazi cult to a grotesquely ruthless pitch, miscarried almost beyond recognition. But, taken at his own evaluation, he has had no successor to lend nobility to his cause, no new begetter of value-judgements rather than ignoble purveyors of the racial theories of Gobineau, no modern incarnation of that spirit of Promethean hubris which created the Superman – one cannot help feeling to mankind's irreparable loss. Nor is it necessary to invoke a new spirit of mastery, or to create a new mood of intellectual pride in respect of a moral order which would favour hierarchical ambitions at the expense of 'the meek and the poor in spirit'. But too much, at the same time, should not be made of the postulate which is still maintained in some quarters, that only the poor, the impotent, the lowly and the discriminated against, are pious, reasonable and just. I believe, on the contrary, that mankind, though permanently and undoubtedly human, is motivated not by a socially sanctioned equality, and its concomitant the so-called morality of the mass, but by the striving to surpass which has seemed so very significant to Nietzsche's own philosophical inquiry, based as it is on a thoroughly transcendent foundation.

There is no reason to suppose that hierarchy does not exist intrinsically in nature. Before Nietzsche natural evolution was but a specific concept concerning the origin and development of the species (of man). But in his case we must ignore all the precepts of Darwin, Lamarck, de Vries and others, of species transformation by natural selection or by the inheritance of acquired characteristics. Nietzsche had his own plans for the destiny of the world. He prophetically foresaw the genesis of a Superspecies, the species most congenial to him. Extravagant though this genesis may seem, it has a considerable appeal to common sense nevertheless. But is it probable?

The reply to this question reveals the whole dichotomy of the modern material world, the deep ideological split of the kind discussed in Part One of this book between Men and Supermen. Between the single-minded representatives, in other words, of a classless, narrow and static ideal of culture and the men – or their successors – for whom history has essentially meant evolution. Taking the latter kind first, we can recognize something of the make-up and disposition, even the purpose of a 'superior species' in that sense of enterprise and application which first revealed itself in commercial forms, in trade and maritime expansion; which found continuity in the great motive force of geographical exploration and which achieved its highest culmination in what has more usually been maligned as the 'imperial idea'. Our knowledge of the former kind is essentially of the successful representatives of a socio-political ideal whose closest humanitarian loyalty happens to be an egalitarian one. They never have, or so it seems, felt the thrill of great and greatest things. They are in fact the very men who are prepared to trade unmitigated genius for arbitration between equals. For even though one is naturally concerned with the context of ethics from which the 'Superman' is going to emerge, I for one have yet to be convinced of the excessive optimism of those who wish to solve every problem life has to offer by the pathetic stratagem of material happiness and complete equality of income for all.

It has never been my intention to write for a converted, or even well-meaning, audience. Even though I have no dispute with those who disclaim Nietzsche's doctrine of the Superman so long as they have grasped its profounder significance, what most of its critics will find is that there is no substitute whatever for the force and the ability of mankind to aspire to something that is greater than itself. Given that Nietzsche had nothing but ridicule and contempt for the Englishman's inalienable faith in the power of democratic ideals, it may seem surprising, moreover, to discover that the preponderance of historical evidence throughout this book will essentially be Anglo-Saxon. There is, however, nothing especially surprising in the way the Anglo-Saxons coped with the problems presented to them throughout the formative centuries of modern Western history. Unlike Nietzsche, I am not personally an unqualified admirer of the great Corsican conqueror and the Napoleonic conception of the dominion of the world which flourished for its brief day. But then, we all have skeletons not our own which we seem to be carrying with us, and even though Nietzsche's master philosophy does not immediately concern us here, my own historical method of abstraction will predominate in terms of the Anglo-Saxon approach to problems of supremacy and – which comes up for comment next – of the means whereby the imperial idea and the *pax britannica* proved their worth under all conceivable historical conditions.

Although in point of fact this idea may have established itself among the Greeks, the Romans, and other civilized nations of antiquity long before the Anglo-Saxon conquests, for the Englishman a recognition of the rights of others, indeed, of their humanity, was a thing peculiarly inalienable. The British never were leaders of the mob, of the 'impotent, the poor and the lowly'. If anything they were the first and the finest of free men, scarcely more than first among equals rather than a class of masters. Their *imperium* implied compromise and striking a balance between self-restraint and the restraint to be imposed on others. Here indeed were the 'Lords of the Earth', heralding a humanist enlightenment of the Western make. The culmination of that unbroken succession of kings, soldiers and generals, of seafarers, discoverers, conqistadores and empire-builders to whom from antiquity onwards it was given to explore, conquer and hellenize the world and who, some three thousand years later, now stand

13

between the achievements of a truly great past and the challenges of a future to which one of the major impediments is precisely that it seems to find itself incapable of rising to greater heights.

Hence the reaction, the spiritual retrogression and Decline of the West which, induced as the direct result of the frustrating cessation of the great fight for power, constitutes the subject matter of the Second Part of this book. Certainly, some very conspicuous changes have been taking place in the course of this century; changes, which have been deplorably for the worse. Much good, admittedly, has also been done, especially in terms of law reforms and long-lasting programmes of social legislation, decreeing equal opportunities for all and setting their seal upon constitutional forms of government which proceed by common consensus. Here, though, is the cause of the change. Suddenly enriched, as part of our nineteenth century social inheritance, with all the gradually accumulated wealth of remedial legislation, the aim and purpose of twentieth century policy makers has been to teach the mass of society how to be socially responsible and prepared for collective action. This is, in fact, the obvious intent. To organize and facilitate their highest aspirations into what they seem best designed to produce: the creation of material wealth, and at the same time to exploit the profit motive which is always a dynamic mode of ambition, as a means of initiating better welfare for all and of making social services more amenable to the poor.

The conclusion is inescapable: 'Nothing could be more chimerical than the notion that Man is the same thing as Economic Man and that the problems of life, Man's life, can be solved by any merely economic arrangement. To suppose that the equalization of income could solve these problems is only slightly less absurd than to suppose that they could be solved by the universal installation of sanitary plumbing or the distribution of Ford cars to every member of the human species.'[3] Thus Aldous Huxley, the exasperated author of *Brave New World*. He detested *homo economicus* as much as Nietzsche did and was as adamant in proclaiming it. To him the 'complete practical realization of the democratic ideal' was but a social danger, a psychological catastrophe of the most petrifying kind.

The problem, therefore, is to create new values, new conceptions of greatness, before the increasing polarization of good and evil in human society and its various institutions turns into an inexpiable social war, like that of Hobbes, waged by all against

14

all. Nor is it a return-to-basics that we must look to for a happy issue. Only new objectives and altered motives can make a regenerate world. 'The richer, the more materially civilized we become, the more speedily it will arrive', as Huxley remarked in a prognostic passage, 'this great orgy of universal nihilism: Destruction for destruction's sake. Hate, universal hate, and an aimless and therefore complete and thorough smashing up of everything.'[4] The facts speak for themselves: violence has become an end in itself, sought chiefly as a stimulus to the exercise of itself. Moreover, unless such objectives are created, 'the races of the industrialized West are doomed', to quote his own description, 'to self-destruction – to a kind of suicide while of unsound mind. The first symptoms of mass insanity are everywhere apparent. A few years more, and the patient will be raving and violent.'[5]

And so he has proved to be. The world is a madhouse to him, and he himself has made it so. Some years ago it might have been profitably argued that the world was better off provided for with sanitary plumbing than with the gist of great ideas. But, looking back, one cannot say that the mission most often most loudly proclaimed has been instrumental in promoting either universal happiness or the spiritual development of modern man. Caught in his self-made egalitarian trap, all that can be said with definiteness is that it has helped to promote that genius in egalitarian ethics which, as the world approaches its catastrophe, is the twentieth century's perhaps most abiding legacy. With the result, of course, that people will stop at nothing to exploit these particular ethics as a means of personal or material salvation, and never more contemptibly so than when an ethical humanity can be made the pretext and occasion for a self-complacent hedonism. Contemptibly, in the sense which Nietzsche had in mind when he said that 'this latter tends to espouse the cause of the criminal; [its] most pleasing disguise is a kind of socialist sympathy. And the fatalism of the weak-willed is indeed beautified to an astonishing degree when it can present itself as *'la religion de la souffrance humaine'*;[6] that is, as a philosophy of life which makes the lower appear the higher choice of motive.

It would be wrong perhaps, to complain at length of the strange culminating perversities which seem nowadays to have ended in the struggle for human rights. One notes, however, that there is a remarkable similarity between the misdemeanours of a previous era and the thoughts and manners of a new social and legislative order based on the Rights of Man. Sexual conformity has taken on a new meaning. A new liberation has been the catalyst for the social and psychological transformation which has made the freer sexual life of a great commercial civilization at once fascinating and confusing. One cannot help feeling, on the other hand, that we have advanced rapidly enough, possibly too rapidly, without some form of criterion to guide us, in what its apologists call the struggle for human rights. For when it is put to the ultimate test, it is obvious that we are found wanting, that we lack the conviction, the resolve, and the tempering equanimity to be redeemably and hopefully human. As Tacitus said of the Britons: 'Step by step they were led to practices which disposed to vice – the lounge, the bath, the elegant banquet. All this in their ignorance they called civilization, *when it was but a part of their servitude.*'[7] (my italics).

Tacitus never lost his faith in the curative effects of martial activity; nor was he speaking of Britons 'whom a long peace had not yet enervated'. Masculine women are bad enough to endure, but the effeminacy of manhood in a society whose stability of character is only assured by the stability of anthropological codes of behaviour which themselves constitute a congenital if unwritten convention of ethics, would have been too much for this confirmed admirer of the Roman *virtus* which may or may not antedate the *mores maiorum*, or manners of one's ancestors but which, according to some authorities, were 'among the most potent forces in Roman history'. Nor were they being confounded with those virtues which lead to the highest possible good for the highest possible number and, paradoxical though it may sound, to the worst kind of social illness – material solicitude with its unmitigated vices and moral forfeits.

And so we come to the Sayers of the Law, 'the good, the true and the just' with their great statesmanlike humanity and their pious fiats. But the lawgivers and priests, peace-makers and social reformers who rally the masses so readily and subserviently to their vision of social happiness have brought with them no means – none, at any rate, that I can conceivably discover apart from 'equal opportunities for all' – to mitigate the truth which one feels, which comes back so obsessively, again and again, as one contemplates human history: that it is not to them, not to their social service philanthropy, that we owe our conception of human success. *This* Brave New World, so humanitarian and admirable

with all its kindliness and good will, its plethora of social legislation, its harvest of human rights (including the right to pornography), its emancipated and even absurd, carnal prodigality, is a
stagnant world – as we may realize when we consider any of history's great or late civilizations – precisely because in all the
flurry of endeavours there is no flow of great ideas.

All this is obvious enough. But what H. G. Wells was after
when he wrote *The Island of Dr Moreau* went deeper than mere
contempt for the Sayers of the Law, such as the Ape Man or their
ape-like propensity to chant with the crowd. The details of this
propensity need not concern us for the moment, since they will be
discussed in a subsequent chapter. But in spite of everything else
Wells may have said of the problem of the relation of science to
culture, he still drew the inevitable conclusion that there can be no
field of endeavour more important than the conquests of natural
science in our time. Which is especially true of the principle of
nuclear energy, always supposing of course that it will be harnessed for constructive ends. Science has produced many acci-
dents and synchronicities, so many indeed that the progress of the
civilized world has frequently depended upon them. Fifty years
on it is almost hard to remember that it was the atomic bomb
which opened up the nuclear age, and even though other great
improvements have since been made in human methods of
destruction, as Freeman Dyson said: 'Our purpose and our belief,
is that the bombs which killed and maimed at Hiroshima and
Nagasaki shall one day open the skies to man'.[8]

It was impiety, perhaps, but with a difference. Nuclear science
is now a means and not an end, a passage and not an impediment –
and so indeed is Gravity. We may think ourselves fortunate that
we are possessed of the Earth, the flourishing garden of the Solar
System, a jewel among planets and a natural paradise. But what is
an ever decreasing circle of green and pleasant earth compared
with the whole of the Solar System, indeed the whole of the
Universe, for men who see themselves about to be possessed of a
desert instead of a terrestrial paradise, a slagheap of the Industrial
Age rather than an Eden of tranquillity for people, animals and
plants. It is beside the point to suggest that the cause of what is
hardly an unexpected development lies not with the constitution
of the Earth, but with man himself and with his material values.
The result, in any case, is the same. For this planet, unless it is
very gently and carefully treated, is bound to have the serious

imperfection of holding back the progress of the human race and of human evolution very considerably indeed.

For all our promises to reform ourselves, for so long as our economic basis remains harnessed to current demographic and social trends, even visionary circles in human government will be loath to squander public investments in so remote a region as space. Yet, it is precisely within these remote, unknown cosmic realms that lies the secret, the awesome, inspiring, unifying vision of the human soul. It is bound up, perhaps with a certain gathering sense, only dimly apprehended as yet, of belonging to a world which has passed its prime. And it would probably be exactly on this ground that the idea of penetrating into distant, inaccessible, even mythical regions of our vast solar system and the Milky Way galaxy, would create a major thrill and a novel source of inspiration for all possible segments of human society, particularly, one imagines at a time when the demographic saturation of the planet Earth has fully exceeded its sustainable limits.

The challenge is not simple. But in all one feels that whenever humankind has reached the highest point of social and material ascendancy and when, as part of the logic of events, the symptoms of her success become those of her decline, she must needs strive for something greater and more important than Life, Liberty and the pursuit of Happiness. Something that calls for self-sacrifice, for the most deadly sacrifice that men can make: the surrender of life for Life. In actual fact, there is no more active principle of life than the struggle for destiny and existence. Progress lies only in the rough-and-tumble of conquest, of all conquests, including that of self-overcoming. Nor can the struggle cease until its hard, inexorable principle, its power to surpass, has been tested against overwhelming odds, calling for the highest qualities of courage, vitality and resourcefulness.

Thus, at any rate, were laid the foundations of the New World. The story of this magnificent struggle on the part of 'the lowly, the poor and the worthless' to establish themselves as a true class of masters, cannot be told here. Yet, it is to these men that I make my appeal, to the highest and the lowest, to all who have earned the gratitude of posterity and borne the brunt of the worst the history of the world has had to offer. Noble values, it has been said, make noble men! I have no concern with prejudices of religion or race, with divisions of class, cast or ethnicity. A hierarchical society, replete with rank and ceremony, is not what I am after. Nobility is a term to apply to all levels. What I have tried to do in order to make this appeal plain and unmistakable is to be discriminating rather than comprehensive in the choice of my subjects and themes. Hence, there will be little chronology in these pages, no attempt at consecutive narrative, but much circumstantial history. Nor is this an academic treatise in any impartial sense, but a work of exacerbated contemplation. It is a testament to the truth.

To bear witness to the truth and to succeed in doing so, one needs to have faith not only in one's own moral integrity, but faith in one's own intuitive judgement as to what this truth may be. Indeed, if any man desires to be elevated at all, to possess and treasure veracity, no blind struggle, no lack of integrity in his own sense of purpose will ever achieve that end. Yet, it is impossible to overlook that the definition of truth is very largely, perhaps crucially, of our own making and, besides being ambivalent, that it can also be very misleading. No matter how deeply one immerses oneself in the contemplation of facts, facts in any exact sense have ceased to be verifiable. All that can be known about facts is that they give definition to what is chaos.

Of course, there is another sense in which, as part of the mental process of the physicist, facts convey a truth which no one can doubt. The classical physicist did not speculate about what was manifestly apparent. His notions of cause and effect were traditional and predictable and they were set out with great precision. Twentieth century physics makes a different appeal. It is not just about laws but concepts. The emphases placed upon effects and their causality have been amended and physical knowledge, besides being more perplexing, has become more ambiguous, much less precise and much more uncertain of interpretation. The prevailing mood is one of introspection. The whole is more than the sum of its parts. In fact, as one traces out the events which lead by steady progressive steps from Planck's fundamental physical 'constant' to Einstein's 'mass-energy' equation and Niels Bohr's principle of 'complementarity', one is led to review the creation of almost the entire universe. Physical theories, once believed to be final and recognized as absolute and fundamental, have since become obsolete. New inferences are drawn, inferences which are derived not so much from new discoveries and disclosures as they are based upon new dimensions and perspectives. Their significance lies not in data and details, but in the general affirmation of the principle that the human mind may in fact generate what it has more commonly been thought to discover, and not only in the broad sense in which this is applicable to the general physics of relativity but in the special sense in which quantum physics complements a view of reality which philosophical idealism has been formulating for perhaps the past four hundred years.

To want immortality and to begin aspiring to it, we need to have confidence in our capacity to achieve it. We must also forget all previous attempts made by fundamentalists to trace the genesis of man from beyond the genesis of natural evolution. Because it really explains nothing, what absolutely fails to convince is the mythological aspect of the matter. No man, in any case, can be born of woman and not be divine – or consecrate at any rate. Clearly, it is only one small step from idealism to fundamentalism, and insofar as this idealism extends to an understanding of what it is that twentieth century physics has added to modern thought, it is, insofar as I am able to understand it myself, 'the germ of our highest hope', to adopt a Nietzschean expression.

And hope, precisely, is my reason for this rather roundabout introduction to the legacy of the man whom I have chosen as a spokesman for the particular body of opinion to which I adhere. The reader will notice the intention. For the guiding idea of this book, with a somewhat different requirement for each chapter, is the Nietzschean frame of captions under which it appears. Nor can I conceive of a truly great thinker to equal that profound inner passion of Nietzsche's own undying faith in himself or, indeed, the compelling nature of its underlying 'immortal' assumptions. Clearly, these are very delicate matters to state with certitude, and, traditionally, the verdicts on Nietzsche have ranged from 'madness' to 'megalomania'. But whilst the various reasons behind such promulgations may or may not be debated, if I were asked to sum up, I should scarcely consider myself lucid enough to fathom the mind of this genius, if I did not believe that his exposition of the Overman belongs to subsequent centuries or that the future is going to be made according to superhuman specifications. In addition, I happen to think that both these culminations are intimately bound up with the laws which regulate the course of human evolution, for the human experiment might as well be dropped as an experiment not worth going on with if 'the higher man' were not recognized as its natural and desirable consequence.

'My task is tremendous;' Nietzsche said, 'but my determination no less so . . .', as indeed emerges plainly enough when he announces, 'and if I achieve all *I desire to achieve*, I shall die in the knowledge that future millennia will take their highest vows in my name'.[9] To his contemporaries as indeed to the inheritors of 'their insignificance and miserable little individualities', these words might well have seemed totally incongruous. Genius, in other words, is far less perceptible to those who live in the midst of dwarfs and midgets than it appears when the outstanding individual of an epoch is isolated and exhibited. Who but a small man would deny Nietzsche a linkage of circumstances as 'decisive and fateful as that of standing between two millennia'? Call it madness or megalomania, one is simply compelled to salute the man's lucidity, along with his prophetic foresight, for it is very likely that the future and the prophet who predicted it will one day be seen to provide the context for each other; very likely indeed that – if it must be said, and I suppose it must – future generations will cast their highest vows on the altar of his name. For the plain truth of the matter is that the great superhuman genius invoked by Nietzsche can be denied only by the denial of either truth or hope itself.

PART ONE
MEN AND SUPERMEN

I am writing for a race of men which does not yet
exist: for the lords of the [Universe] . . . Live
dangerously!

Nietzsche, *The Will to Power*

1

CHILDHOOD'S END

> The present and the past upon earth – alas! my
> friends – that is *my* most intolerable burden; and I
> should not know how to live, if I were not a seer of
> that which must come.
>
> Nietzsche, *Zarathustra*

*'He has multiplied his numbers to plague proportions, caused the
extinction of 500 species of animals, ransacked the planet for
fuels and now stands like a brutish infant, gloating over this mete-
oric rise to ascendancy, on the brink of a war to end all wars and
of effectively destroying this oasis of life in the solar system.'*[1]
Or, let us put the matter in a different way: Man is the most dangerous of human enemies, the first force of destruction.
Dangerous not only to himself, but to the environment over which
he lords in a state of increasingly hostile symbiosis, almost as if
his breed alone ought ultimately to prevail on Earth. Humans exist
everywhere. Moulded into a vast, fearsome, irresistible and all-
consuming force, they virtually cover every accessible part of the
globe. They are more universal than the teachings of Christ and
more widespread than the doctrines of Karl Marx or, passing from
the former to the latter, equally as moribund.

The reasons for this are obvious and obviously perpetuated.
Human beings, it has been pointed out, are contributing to the
greenhouse effect not only because of power-stations, chloro-
fluorocarbons, the destruction of the rainforests, the production of

toxins, or because of the widely ramifying results of wasteful consumption, whether these be water pollution, desertification or ozone depletion, but – as trustworthy people assure us – because of the waste products of the human metabolic and digestive systems. If the relevant calculations are correct, the human metabolism emits a quarter of a ton of carbon dioxide every year. Industry, it has been estimated, produces 3.3 tons per annum for every person on Earth.[2] We are given no hint as to the annual output of the less dignified equivalents of the bodily greenhouse gases, except perhaps to say that this is not a commonplace worry about atmospheric pollution but a firm indication that, however life-sustaining, what Freddy Hoyle once called man's 'excessive reproductive vigour' has now effectively reached non-sustainable and even catastrophic proportions. Indeed, since nothing can induce the combined millions of billions of human beings to compromise in matters of the most rudimentary metabolic activity, the danger is really less substantially abstract than that which inspired Sir Fred to calculate that if the present rate of demographic expansion continues, 'within 5,000 years the total mass of humanity will exceed the mass of all planets, stars and galaxies visible with the 200-inch telescope on Mount Palomar.'[3]

Still, one must not exaggerate. Perhaps the most conclusive aspect of the demographic crisis when perceived as a fundamental problem underlying the very triumphs of a humanitarian, moralist and altruistic society, is the destruction of the human community, at least in its original form, by that exorbitant representation of its own inherent genius: the Megalopolis. Inevitably, the Megalopolis is the most artificially protracted of self-generating of human constructs. It is also a characteristically Western product. Indeed, that its very existence bears witness to the inherently terminal nature of all organic processes is a fact which can be demonstrated out of Western history. First of all as a mass movement from a rural to an urban mode of living which completed a development that began in ancient Greece with the appearance of the first *polis*, and in the second place, (however life-destroying) as an entirely new form of life; a cybernetic organism, a cumbrous evolutionary carcass whose only certain and possible future lies in its total commitment towards the transformation of life from an inherently organic development to an artificially protracted and inorganic one.

Appropriately enough, it was Aristotle who seems to have suggested that 'no city could be well governed if its citizens were so numerous that they did not know each other, and its size so great that the herald's voice could not be heard throughout'. How instructive then, when judged by these standards, is the comparison with what is to all intents and purposes but a gigantic death-trap, an artificial mass-culture which corresponds to nothing whatever in the world outside its own metropolitan precincts; or, differently expressed, which prescribes for men a way of life, particularly in terms of the life and ideals of a single individual, that is more and more of such an assimilating or constraining tendency that it becomes quite impossible to disengage one's personal activities from the levelling impact of a whole anti-cultural, or post-modern way of life.

Certainly, even Babylon, the Great Mother of Harlots, had her defenders; chiefly kings and devils, if the Biblical admonition is correct, drinking of the wine of the wrath of her fornication. Nor is it necessary for me to insist at length on the wrath of her fornication, merely to avoid the implication of saying that the latter is something emphatically not to be over-indulged in. Turning from the Biblical prediction to philosophical reflection, however, what interests us here is the fact that pessimistic forecasts and apocalyptic anticipations about the death of a civilization (or, as is presently the case, about the demographic trauma of a complex, sophisticated and highly artificial society of men moving from the blessings of the industrial and technological revolution towards potentially the greatest ecological disaster in modern terrestrial history), are generally considered in conjunction with the advent of a new birth, an impending New Age wherein mankind will attain a new and higher state. With, shall we say, promises of a new dawn and hopeful missives of universal redemption and the belief that the millennium is at hand.

It is a remarkable fact, as one can see, that from the late-nineteenth century onwards, when the impact both demographically and economically of the Industrial Revolution was beginning to take far-reaching effects, we have been confronted with a global situation that, literally, has existed at no time before. What is ironical about it is that the negative effects of economic growth have far outstripped the positive, and not just in the industrial West. Thus, there is a curious, although doubtless quite natural, significance in the fact that whenever the historical destiny of mankind has served to intensify perceptions of 'death and decline', it invariably marked the stage where an impassioned and ennobling

27

mystique of moral, spiritual and cultural revivalism has begun to form the opposite element. And that, in a number of ways, is what is happening now. As has often been said, we aspire in circles, and rise and decline, at least on the accepted historical interpretation of its cyclic interaction, are the two fundamental ingredients whose periodic return in the evolution of human society can always be traced to the same seemingly immutable law.

It is certainly the case that a philosopher of history like Oswald Spengler whose masterpiece *Der Untergang des Abendlandes* originally appeared in 1918, was neither the first nor the only one to have applied the theory of historical recurrence, albeit that *The Decline of the West* was a pioneer work of originality and genius. The issue had frequently been raised in earlier times in one form or another, notably in Plato's *Republic* and by a good many of the classical historiographers. Vico developed his own theory of *ricorsi*, or recurrence, and Johann Gottfried von Herder, thinking perhaps in 'environmental' terms, the so-called *Organismus-Gedanke,* to account for the rise and fall of civilizations. Nietzsche himself thoroughly informed by Heraclitus, called it 'the most scientific of all hypotheses.' It was this hypothesis at any rate, and his incessant preoccupation with the great crises of the age at a time when the total extinction inflicted upon Carthage had already been known to history for more than five generations, which inspired Sallust's vision of decay and death as the fundamental, enduring law of creation: 'Everything', to use his own naturalistic metaphor, 'that is born must die.'

Sallust, one would have thought, all but arrived at an impressive historical truth. For him, as for so many others, this formulation meant the final and irreversible birth-and-death cycle of an evolution of life whose by-product is historical change. Above all, it conveys a sense of inevitability. Nor, to return from a philosophical digression, would it be inappropriate, in its contemporary terms, to read into this formula something of a reversal of the original historical process, an anticipation, no less, of one certain and ineradicable end. Metaphors, on the other hand, are not literal declarations of truth. It may be difficult to resist the conclusion that there have been few periods in the long history of human thought and endeavour which have offered a greater variety of apocalyptic possibilities than ours (perhaps the foremost being the possibility of man's first real scientific defeat), but it is a mark of the quality of man's recuperative powers nevertheless, that the crucial aspect of Nemesis for him has essentially been what surmounts it. It is, in fact, difficult not to overstate how acutely his defects have conditioned man's strength. Indeed, if there is no period in the entire history of civilization that was as close as ours seems to be to either death or immortality, it is with the narrowness of the margin that tragedy lies.

The significant fact is that for the first time in history the problem of evolution can be approached from a predominantly scientific and technological point of view. Indeed, for the first time ever the course of human evolution is no longer determined, as Sallust was convinced, by the predictability of history or subject to inevitable and ultimate collapse. Whatever point of departure one cares to choose, and the Roman historian's analogy appears to accommodate about as severe a qualification as one can possibly make, the problem no longer lies with Sallusts's historical law requiring that everything which is born must die. The contemporary evolutionary debate, in other words, is no longer just one of gradual organic development or of the cyclical interpretation of history as a struggle of life and death. It concerns the entire technological destiny of mankind. Although one cannot possibly encompass in mere words the sheer magnitude of the extraordinarily comprehensive exertions required to literally make the technological leap into Space, to make of it anything less than a magnificent transfigurative vision, a supreme conviction capable of any conceivable effort, is to ignore the hopes, beliefs, longings, dreams and visions that millennia of human genius and imagination have already erected upon it.

What amazingly improbable universes, what profoundly dissimilar orders of existence, what reverent and thoughtful perspectives may be attributed to the same genius and imagination, to the same powers of analysis and judgement, at different phases of men's scientific evolution? Yet, for all their astonishing differences, to turn to evidences of them is not to say that those various universes which men have constructed out of such multifarious materials as religious doctrines, philosophical systems, mathematical theories, and scientific facts, were either true or false in any absolute sense of the term. On the contrary, the universe does not get truer and truer; its connotations merely change. In fact, it may almost be said that conceptual differences between different universes are as real as differences between different civilizations. And who can doubt that in the long history of the universe there have probably been as many different ways of viewing the cosmos as there have been cultures and civilizations, each applying its own characteristics, its own science, philosophy and religion; each investing it with a higher set of values,with the highest and most important of spiritual and intellectual virtues, psychological as well as scientific, each casting it in its own image.

'In ancient times', Isaac Asimov has noted, 'man tended to accept himself very literally as the hub of the Universe. The Universe was not only geocentric, with the Earth – man's home – the immovable centre of everything; it was homocentric, with man the measure of all things.'[4] It is, moreover, one of the radical facts of the history of modern science that, having first made nonsense of the idea that man is in any sense central to his cosmology, scientific professionals have turned full circle once again and placed the anthropocentric view at the heart of cosmic perception. In Newtonian cosmology, for instance, everything that happened could be predicted from an examination of any one of its parts. Indeed, a complete representation of one of its parts would practically yield the whole of the classical universe. Today, it has been said, 'the Universe is incapable of computing the future behaviour of even a small part of itself, let alone all of itself.'[5] This view, advanced from about the mid-20s onwards, was in fact the real basis of the present quantum mechanical models which have raised nature's intrinsic unpredictability to the rank of a principle. There was no mechanism known to classical physics that could account for such dynamics. Nor is it inconceivable any longer that the activity of interpretation itself performs the function of knowledge as a conceptual force. Indeed, it seems likely that the extraordinary arrival of that body of general ideas which followed Max Planck's introduction of discontinuity into the physics of radiation, is evidence less of an uncanny and intimate relationship between the subject and the object of its knowledge, as it is the logical point of reference for the dynamics of spontaneous anthropic conditions.

It is not enough that the stars are as immovable as ever. What matters is that as its complementary nature gradually reveals itself the universe is governed by laws which are essentially unpredictable rather than laws which are supposed to be necessarily true. The universe, in other words, always remains subordinate to the grounds of its most searching knowledge. Rationally, it is obvious that only one universe can be real, recognizably our own.

Ideally, it is apparent that there are an infinite number of possible universes present to the human understanding. Yet, what finally distinguishes one universe from another, what makes one more real than all the rest, is the sense we have of our own response to it as a legitimate and essentially inescapable aspect of human existence. And it is in this enormous, retrospective subjectivity that the unrivalled conceptual power of the human mind, weak though it may be in other respects, is ultimately vested. To an outstanding degree, therefore, it gains point from the structure of the universe in all the mystery of its beauty: from the ages of the stars and the precision of their movements to the power that warps space and time; from the profound scientific mysteries of black holes to the astonishing physical processes of relativistic astrophysics and, finally, and most conclusively of all, from the almighty procreative force of the atom. All this, in short, with its epic, auspicious nature, gives the universe a grand, prophetic quality; prophetic not only on account of its timeless structure, infinite dimensions and hidden meanings from which countless cultures and civilizations have derived purpose and inspiration but also because of the incomputability of its outcome which is that of some great and awesome intention.

One may perhaps let it go at that, but again the indeterminacy intervenes. Whether as a primordial fact of human psychology or as a fact of cosmic structure, there is an awesome ambiguity about the mighty, measured movement of the stars. Indeed, it will be found to be pretty generally accepted nowadays that man is no longer a stray incident on a very small and temporary planet orbiting one of the hundred billion stars that make up our spiral galaxy, some accident of circumstance in the plane of the Milky Way, as lost and lonely as time itself. Despite his overwhelming isolation I prefer to believe that, regardless of the magnitude or the vacuity of the dimensions involved, before the riddle of man's psychology or that abstraction called his soul, the implications are practically the same. The only ultimate solution, therefore, is to go back, through space rather than time, and to try and identify clearly and precisely the source and origin of a destiny which now inevitably devolves on him.

Time and the stars pervade the universe. The ostensively dependable flow of time is not, however, absolute. As the interesting case of a black hole suggests, time slows to a halt at its event horizon. Of the stars it may altogether more safely be said that they are powerful transmitters of radio-waves and high-energy radiation at virtually every wavelength of the electromagnetic spectrum. Here, the far-away voices of the universe become audible from beyond the limits even of the observable universe. Much of such information derives from satellite observation of x-ray sources, gamma-ray astronomy and emission processes that are invisible at optical wavelengths. In point of fact, given the extreme faintness of pulses ranging over distances of the order of billions of light-years, neutron stars, until fairly recently, were only hypothetical artefacts of the scientific imagination. Today, of course, there are increasingly sensitive optical telescopes and great advances in 'invisible astronomy'. There is the use of increasingly powerful computing facilities, of highly sensitive low level light detectors instead of film, and highly improved resolution on extended satellite instrumentation orbiting above the Earth's atmosphere in order to maintain a constant watch on the sky. Among the latter are the two US High-Energy Astronomical Observatories launched in the late 1970s, and the International Ultraviolet Explorer (IUE) and ROSAT satellites. Again, in 1983, the joint European and United States Infrared Astronomy Satellite (IRAS) was launched. The Hubble space telescope, too, with its restored primary mirror, has opened up possibilities never even dreamt of a few years ago.

Meanwhile, on an ever larger scale, new generations of computer-controlled giant telescopes may hearken to the faint, attenuated echoes from the great soliloquy of the stars. From stellar winds whispering eternal things, from giant glowing nebulae, incandescent mists, cosmic dust-storms and great swirling star clouds at the far ends of the universe. From stars that are still unborn. From visible and invisible light, whether infrared or ultraviolet, hot or cold. From cosmic rays, whether known or unknown, highly energetic light quanta and, we may suspect though we cannot be certain, from gravitational waves. In short, chaos need not necessarily imply disorder. More likely, it is but a small step to assert that the seemingly irreducible conflicts we experience at the outer frontier of knowledge, are irreducible only from our side. The implausibilities scarcely matter. They are inconsistent perhaps with observed reality, but not flawed in themselves. Besides, it is the weakest of all contentions to hold that there is a rigorous and consistent body of physical laws which it is our business to be rigidly and permanently bound by, when in fact the distinction between the real and the ideal itself becomes a function of matter in its last stages of disintegration.

But then, even this is not an exact formulation. When one order of existence is allowed to impinge upon another the reality with which it deals is conflicting and baffling. It is apparently a fact that black holes, insofar as they may be independently constituted at all, are both spurious *and* real. In other words, one of the greatest astrophysical enigmas of our time can only become intelligently explicit at a certain critical radius, the event horizon which virtually excludes from existence all other events but itself. Nor does the event stop there. It has given birth to a whole new aspect of astrophysical science in terms of its departure from the classical laws of mechanics and gravitation. Any attempt to explain how is to set oneself a problem in chronology. For in what has to be considered one of the most astonishing of all astrophysical theories, the density of matter and the curvature of space-time become infinite as they undergo a complete gravitational collapse of the commonsensible view of the world, and that is both limited and circumscribed in time.

Anthropomorphic concepts, then, introduce epistemological contradictions. As an ambiguously rationalized but mathematically precise way of saying that space-time has turned inward upon itself, there is, very clearly, a conflict in the genesis of the black hole as a self-contained material entity. Of course, nobody is saying that it is contained within the same sidereal system. But one may certainly question whether the principle which determines the chronology of events is the outcome of a real occurrence or whether it is a mathematical and therefore theoretical convenience whose real function it is to assist a predetermined conceptual cause. For if the black hole is at once of and outside the universe, nothing is more immaterial than a bodiless abstraction which is forever potential but never actual – even if sometimes it is both. After all, its condition being such that it is incommunicable, the black hole is also an abstract non-spatial entity that we cannot directly observe. Yet to describe it simply as the embodiment of a principle, an auxiliary mathematical projection, is to fail to take into account the nature of information as a conceptual medium whose significance is both veritable and mutable. Analogously expressed, the black hole thus recapitulates the logic and inherent uncertainty of the Quantum Factor, the factor which is as resolving as only conceptual images can be, the factor which is the triumph of mind over matter.

To discuss the black hole as if it were creating an illusion of itself, generated by a conceptual clash of radically matched and mutually exclusive geometrical relations is of course to ignore that it involves affinities and structures which are to be understood as physical tensions rather than being attributable to any particular model of the conceptual relationship by which it is determined. On the other hand, because at this stage of theoretical knowledge inherently abstract relations cannot be sifted from facts with any certainty at all, facts specify nothing. In many ways, to formulate a cosmic theory of knowledge is rather like appealing for *habeas corpus* on behalf of Proteus. Indeed, it is precisely because an invisible astrophysical happening remains as protean and indeterminate as ever that it has become one of the most allegorical and transfigurative symbols of our time, the product of an enormously fertile and introspective experience of the human mind. One of the great scientific limits, it may be said, or a sort of conceptual arcanum which in its turn both conceals and unveils the conscious motive of its makers.

Some day perhaps, when it has become more generally serviceable, students of space, time and causality will come to consider in more transcendent ways the enormously fruitful configurations inherited from that arcanum. Meanwhile it may well serve to stimulate the imagination of those who can read the magic formula. In that, moreover, it proposes a major question to the age it may also become a catalyst, and a portent even, for an era in science which – if there really is to be another 'dawn' – must needs find a new set of terms for what would essentially constitute a new *cycle*, that of successive cosmological evolution.

Today, at any rate, the world appears to have become a kind of dialectical contradiction for everything suggests its opposite, is bound together by contrasts rather than complementarity. In the geocentric cosmology of Ptolemy everything was eternal, indivisible, inevitable and perfect. Above all perfect. And if it did not easily coincide with our own definition of physics, at least it was straightforward. Now everything is operating against its own nature, continually on the verge of becoming the opposite of itself, so that even ordinary time relationships have come to be represented mutual-exclusively. In short, the continuum which is without the conceptual intelligence alluded to above, is not the continuum we know, if indeed such a concept could ever exist.

And here one may agree with Protagoras, whether informed by Heraclitus or by his own good sense, that man is the measure of all things, 'of those being that they are, and of those not being that they are not' – a kind of moving influence, one might say, whose nexus is the dynamic impulse of the universe itself, the enduring form of all the processes in which its force is manifest. I would rather suggest a force – and doubtless this has been suggested before – which does not represent the observable universe as intrinsic and imperishable instead of as a transitory cosmological flux that has no self-defined or finite existence, so that we might expect to find a continuing ontological process in which the cosmic evolution, with all its generic complexity, is in some way a consequence of the human.

It is not necessary to explain either, or reduce the one to the other. It is enough to say that there are riddles which the physicist is not called upon to solve. The universe, in other words, is first of all a concept and only then time and extension. Oddly enough though, it can be satisfactorily explained only if it is contemplated at the molecular level or considered in terms of atoms rather than rendered by way of propositions which neither assert nor require the existence of anything divisible. Or so we fatuously go on believing. Hence the relic: *atomos* – the safe and sound remainder of another time. Meaning 'indivisible', the word was first used by the Greek philosopher Leucippus to define the basic units of the material world and subsequently, among others, by Democritus, a leading exponent of the material school, to develop his own atomic theory. We can measure the success and the validity of their materialism by the fact that it seems to have stood the test of time and, as a basic principle of modern theoretical physics, even acquired something of the status of dogma. Nor is it easy to deny the wisdom of these skilled observers, or indeed the foresight of their observation, arriving, as it did, so far ahead of its time. On the other hand, though really of universal application, no one would invent if he were inventing it all over again, a universe made up entirely of atoms. For all their ingenious mechanisms operating a complex and highly determining cause, arguments of substance and utility, causality and number, derived from earlier and more elementary conditions, are simply not enough. Atoms may be called specific, functional, or even primary and indivisible, but something never entirely communicated is the essence of the secret itself.

Thus, in looking for a completely satisfactory synthesis of the universe's constituent parts, the modern physicist has become a worker of miracles. No idle spectator of the cause of events which was once believed to exist independently of man, but a determined builder of his own utopias, wiser than the ancient sages and second only to the gods. And yet, we should be mistaken if we saw in this development of a unifying tendency throughout science as a whole evidence that the physicist's creative imagination can solve the problem of causality. With the success of scientific theories in dividing up the atom, it has become easy enough, at the one extreme, to measure the electric charge of a single electron or, at the other, to accurately compute the total amount of pressure inside the core of a supernova. It is more complicated, however, to recognize one's own presumption. And not the least of our difficulties, in speaking about the creative powers of human presumption, is to give them a fitting ideal and to suggest our future intentions.

Science requires motives as well as methods. And since no ideal is worth the destruction of the human species, the ambivalence of this aspect of nuclear science can easily be put into terms of the contradictions of the contemporary age which are not so readily reducible to the humble scale of an atom's constituent parts. When we consider that science today is so potent a force, and its power and influence increasing with such enormous rapidity that it practically involves every important query which has ever stirred the mind of man, it is essential that we should take full cognizance of the nightmare that could ensue if we are not entirely clear in our own minds precisely where we wish to go. I, for one, remain yet to be convinced that when the future is put solely into the context of our planetary ecology, or what is essentially a *sense unique* or 'No Exit' situation, that science can do anything but give the final disaster its ultimate and inevitable issue.

We may never tire speaking of a safely humanitarian world; of the elevation of the species of man into something altogether more noble than the mere sum total of its reproductive capacity. The logical conclusion, however, is this: anyone who accepts that both the aims and the methods of modern social utopias under just laws and fair democratic processes bear a certain resemblance to those first enunciated at the beginning of our Christian era, must also acknowledge that humanity's rise to a global civilization and

36

the welding together of its various and variegated societies into an all-consuming and irrepressible demographic force, can in part be ascribed to those methods, laws and ideals.

Considered, then, as a statement of ideals, or, at a less exalted level as a set of social theories, there is of course no question about the worthiness of Greek philosophy, Roman law, Mosaic monotheism, Christian theology, the humanism of the Renaissance, the rationalism of eighteenth-century enlightenment and nineteenth-century democratic revolution or, as a wholly admirable concern, of joint action on the scale of humanity as a whole. As a generally acknowledged hint of the nightmare that could ensue by an entirely different line of reasoning, however, it could be as usefully argued that its organizing ability, reforming zeal and social sense of responsibility have also, and perhaps more so, brought us to the brink of a war on two fronts. A war, it may be said without counting sporadic occurrences, against *inhumanity* on the one hand, and on the other . . .? Against the kind of humanity that might emerge if its concomitant materialism, its excessive demographic congestion and insensate technological overgrowth, have a chance to combine in producing the kind of conditions that have their own utterly logical and inescapable conclusion.

It is unnecessary for me to recapitulate the arguments. But to anyone who takes the trouble to study all of the conflicting facts of human existence, it will be apparent that, like everything else that has reached its culmination, the species of man is now in eclipse; a victim, ironically, of its own success as well as being at the mercy of its own reproductive recklessness. Hence, there is a great deal of truth in the remark made by Heraclitus of Ephesus some two and a half thousand years ago, that 'Homer was wrong in saying: "Would that strife might perish from among gods and men!" He did not see that he was praying for the destruction of the universe.' And this precisely is what Aldous Huxley had in mind when he charged the Christian humanists, the moralists, and the altruists with, in a word, 'aspiring towards annihilation'.[6] 'Luckily', as he remarks elsewhere, 'the majority of nominal Christians has at no time taken the Christian ideal very seriously; if it had, the races and the civilization of the West would long ago have come to an end'.[7]

One may of course envisage this process of combining an increasing density of population with maximum economic growth strategies as continuing indefinitely, its basic democratic motive unaltered. Indeed, it is perfectly proper to say, with more or less Christian assurance, that 'man is being called upon by God to subdue the earth by his labour'. It is a simple and at first a satisfying call. Appearances, however, can be misleading. For it is also open to the objection that for all our efforts spent on the increase of national wealth and other desirable social objectives, nothing could be more utterly calamitous to a future society than the ecological burdens it imposes on the planet Earth, the last sanctuary of man, in the name of its poor and regrettable inheritors.

In actual historical fact, the broad possibilities which will determine the future are no longer the special utopia of the social variety of genius, now seated in democratically elected parliaments and concentrated on reducing the scale of potentially uncontrollable and tragic events. To put it another way, the concept of genius, whatever else it may be, is essentially a surpassing one. As a matter of fact, unless we make a rather more comprehensive and far-reaching attempt (and the opportunity to do so now is utterly unique in history) to purposefully mobilize all of the powerful technological means of history-making now at our disposal, the regeneration of the species of man, let alone its elevation to new values, new objectives, new aims and ideals, in short, to everything that is purposive and creative in human affairs, may be difficult to accomplish.

The fulfilment of such an undertaking is not, of course, a mere technological issue, nor the work of a moment. A sense of cosmic enterprise and the prospect of a plurality of potential futures belongs to a surpassing and forward-looking sense of destiny, precisely – as far as the record shows – where the intellectual pride of man would most wish to deploy it. To me, at least, science makes obvious the fact that no other development would be more fitting to men's superior conception of themselves. I cannot go here into these developments as fully as I should like to, since they will be discussed in subsequent chapters. But enough has been said in this chapter to show that already across the world – in research laboratories and scientific institutions – a race of 'supermen' is gradually evolving; a race, I am convinced, that can see visions, read riddles, dream dreams, talk to the stars, learn their language and even – and it would be disingenuous to avoid the subject – communicate with other beings.

It was a happy childhood. Ever since the world began men have misjudged the irrational forces of history, whether evolutionary or revolutionary, but, in any case, inspired and ridden by paradox in much the same way and as part of much the same everlasting process that makes death the first condition of renewal. This is not a prophecy of course, but as anyone wishing to pronounce judgement on the future of the species can foresee, there is a fateful and increasing inevitability about the deadly inertia of a living system which, literally, cannot escape its own gravity. Having long since fallen into a pleasant routine of life under congenial material conditions, men's whole treatment of history seems to be the expression of precisely that materially congenial method of living a philosophy, a single idyllic system of social permanence, which, in its necessarily consistent way, commits them implacably and inescapably towards some final and inevitable state of certain petrification.

Now larger and more populous than ever, humankind began in a small way, coincidentally, almost inadvertently, one might say, though with a more prolonged infancy perhaps than any other species. 'The history of mankind is the history of the attainment of external power. Man is the tool-using, fire-making animal. From the outset of his terrestrial career we find him supplementing the natural strength and bodily weapons of a beast by the heat of burning and the rough implement of stone. So he passed beyond the ape . . . So slowly', as H. G. Wells tells us in '*The World Set Free*', 'did humanity gather itself together out of the dim intimations of the beast.' To say therefore, as we certainly can, that it made a phenomenal ascent, broke into ever higher conceptual levels, launched out into the solar system, mastered every other species and, with or without compunction, even created some additional ones of its own, not only tells us practically everything about the long history of man, it tells us all but everything about the enormous potential of the future evolution of man. But such is man's inertia, such his intellectually retentive love of system and rigidity, of social organization and material accomplishment, that the majority of human beings simply refuse to accept these facts or subscribe to that philosophy.

It is, of course, more than just a method. But whatever the processes by which modern man has emerged in a haphazard way, gradually at first and then with almost extravagant acceleration, from several different strands of primitive Palaeolithic society, looking back, it is almost possible to see something like an inner selective principle, an abiding perception it might be argued, of the necessity for something surpassing in the affairs of man. Something which we might well rationalize as a guiding evolutionary principle, as a quest for truth no less, or as a progress towards genius. Towards realities so unreal, one feels, that we may not even recognize them as such. What can be said for certain, however, is that our planet is a blue and fragile jewel, and if it is ever to assume a surpassing role instead of merely passing over it like a flight of locusts, humanity's future, on the basis of this necessity, unquestionably lies in close and creative cohesion with its inherent genius, the enduring force behind the awesome, unsuspected, almost supernatural power of the human mind. The Power, in the language of its prophecy, which 'doomed the mammoths, and began the setting of that snare that shall catch the sun!'[8]

2

DEAD MEN'S DREAMS
– THE EPITAPH –

> Whether one be servile before gods and divine
> kicks or before men and the silly opinions of men:
> it spits at slaves of *all* kinds, this glorious selfish-
> ness!

Nietzsche, *Zarathustra*

When Karl Marx devoted himself to the formulation of his famous doctrine of the materialist conception of history he was – in total contradiction, incidentally, to his own stated view[1] – decisively, and thus radically, informed by the 'dialectic' method of Friedrich Hegel. A method which, as suggested by 'that mighty thinker', consisted as a perpetual conflict of wills between old and new forces. In a word, between contending principles of social order as the eternally creative source of the historical life. And ultimately, owing to this emphasis on contending forces, the main thrust of Marxist socialist thinking has undoubtedly come from its doctrine of the class struggle, the mechanism *par excellence* by which the Hegelian process was put into effect and for which Marx himself substituted the battle of material forces as constituted by the clash between capital and labour.

Needless to say, Karl Marx was not by any means the first of the socialist theorists. In the context of a growing demand for 'equality of community' or property without distinction of class or privilege, revolutionary aims and ostensively socialist or working-class movements already existed throughout much of nine-teenth-century Europe, notably in Great Britain, France and Germany, which saw the rich grow richer and the poor grow poorer simply as a consequence of the peculiar social conditions which concentrated the so-called economic means of production essentially in the hands of the classes in which political power was vested.

Of the suffering which this situation caused the poor there can be no question. Without a political voice of their own and con-demned by the dictates of exigent economic circumstances to work long hours, often under inhuman conditions and for pitifully inadequate wages, they were held down by an arrogantly exploita-tive system of social injustice and political abuse from which there was no escape – as Karl Marx was to argue when he wrote his famous *Manifesto* – except through insurrection. And insur-rection – since no democratic emancipation seemed possible, was used very effectively – for a short time at any rate – to precipitate the struggle against the political institutions of capitalist property which led to the revolutionary excitement of 1848 and – a unique distinction – to the discovery of a new type of man: Proletarian Man.

The inflammatory effect of poverty and social injustice on the birth of revolutionary movements is, of course, well known. What may seem surprising is that Marx, who not only had every occa-sion to encounter abject poverty and squalor at close quarters but who himself was to know destitution – indeed, drastic destitution – in perhaps its shabbiest form, nonetheless made something of a distinction between the egalitarian conception of social and polit-ical change which informed the vehement invective of his *Manifest der Kommunisten,* and its actual application. Not only did he plead for extreme solutions (and he certainly did so to excess), but 'nothing prevents us', he also said, 'from combining our criticism with the criticism of politics, from participating in politics, and consequently in real struggles'.[2] But even so, particu-larly after the Hague Congress of 1872, there inevitably arose radicals on the left flank, ideological pamphleteers, brilliant young revolutionaries and dyed-in-the-wool anarchists who were passionately committed to the complete reorganization of society and who did not hesitate to have recourse to assassination and terror for the creation of a class without privilege or property. Nor, indeed, would they have tolerated any other.

'Property' became a synonym for evil, a byword for iniquity, to 'utopian socialists' such as Charles Fourier or Etienne Cabet, and an object of obsessional loathing to Joseph Pierre Proudhon – 'Property is Theft!' – no doubt made all the more malignant for his being denied a share of it. And political specialists such as the apocalyptic Michael Bakunin for whom the very notion of private ownership was an affront, advocated selective assassination and the radical annihilation of society for the abolition of all social ills. Here at long last the 'enlightened' communism of the pre-Marxist idealists and utopian dreamers whose social vision had had little real bearing on the political complexities of their time, was at an end. Before the February Revolution, the Orleans monarchy fell. Louis Philippe, the 'Citizen King', left the throne of France. In November the Hohenzollern Frederick William dissolved the National Assembly and conceded a constitution. Even the reign of the Habsburg dynasty was interrupted by the *annus mirabilis* of 1848 – the year of high hopes and the Communist Manifesto – which saw the fall of the arch-conservative Metternich and the flight of the Imperial Eagle.

The autocratic eagle of the Romanovs' alone was not the sort of fowl to have his talons pruned. Ironically perhaps for a nation whose ultimate vocation in history was the total abolition of all classes, whilst a community of French, Germans, Italians, Magyars and Slavs could not be kept down, Russia remained the leading reactionary power in Europe. Incomprehensibly to the century of Marx and Darwin, Nicholas I, by his own aristocratic self-assurance, was still sealed off from the rest of Russia as was Russia from the rest of Europe, and almost as aloof from it. And until the Emancipation Act of 1861 which conceded the liberation of the serfs and, for a brief period, ushered in a new era of enlightenment, the most stagnant oppression continued to reign in Tsarist Russia, the very nation where the single most important social development of the age was going to take place. With its settled traditions and long dilatory history of the peasant communes from which, ultimately, communism was to grow, serfs remained a species of livestock rather than thinking individuals. Their only equality lay in their common submission.

Thus, with one or two exceptions, one can affirm without fear of contradiction the public spiritedness and personal disinterestedness of the large, assiduous coalition of men who believed in the State as the highest manifestation of the people as a con-

43

stituent power and who only too well understood the need for protective labour legislation which had so impressed Karl Marx and Friedrich Engels. Yet, no review of the history of the great socialist doctrine of reciprocal communist justice can fail to give considerable thought to the fact that because a concern for social justice and the application of essentially egalitarian methods has been far more enthusiastically maintained in the capitalist West and, indeed, been markedly more favourable to the concept of a social contract which we see so admirably expressed in communist doctrine, there appears to have been an ineradicable conflict between Marx's political philosophy as an urban revolution and the materialist conception of history he had first seen as a rural revolt.

Certainly, communist theories lend themselves peculiarly well to the illustration of economic principles, including the material emancipation of the individual. But facts have a way of defying preconceived ideas. Of all the copious illustrations, systematic analyses, reviews, theses, and disputations, there had yet to be one with the merest allusion to the fact that any institution is only as good as the men who represent it and that whether or not the socio-economic laws which Marx believed to have discovered, would prove to be sound depended not so much on economic factors as upon the men and women upon whom they devolved. Nor does it make any difference that Marx was noted for consistency of thought and attention to detail (which was in any case perfunctory), for by the time he had finished a theory running counter to every plausible inquiry into the nature and causes of wealth, it had failed to stand up against the singularly exacting test of human nature.

With the crisis atmosphere brought on by the great Chartist demonstration in London, Lord Palmerston commented on the general fight 'between those who have and those who want to have,' as he put it, 'between honest men and rogues,'[3] or, as Marx preferred in his Communist Manifesto, those 'who have nothing to lose but their chains.' Such divergent comments by two men who were ideologically worlds apart, leave no doubt about the type of impulse each felt to be operative in the bitter struggle marked by the ebb and flow of revolutionary action and antidemocratic reaction. Despite the lip service Palmerston paid to certain revolutionary movements abroad, his refusal to recognize the domestic problem at home by confounding a type of social protest with an essentially misunderstood conception of law and order certainly helps to clarify, if it does not explain, the difference between legislatively ordained laws and the unimpeded operation of natural laws. Laws, it will be noticed immediately, which Karl Marx too was flouting when he objected that the workers' 'right to the whole product' was not the right of any individual worker to his own product, but a social right of all the workers to the whole product of their collective and co-operative labour.

Max Weber puts it well: 'Man is dominated by the making of money, by acquisition as the ultimate purpose in his life.'[4] And this, baldly stated, is what is meant by 'greed for gain', or, more euphemistically perhaps, by the inspired 'egotism of profit'. There can be little doubt that it is by far the most powerful of the perhaps less agreeable manifestations of the 'struggle for existence'. Especially when sustained by that peculiar intensity found in people who have nothing but their chains to forfeit. People who are hungry, it has been well said, cannot be punctilious about virtue. Nor, as an attribute of the instinct for self-preservation, can 'greed' be anything but entirely to the taste of the masses with their insatiable appetite for procurement, if not as powerful as the need to love. 'We address ourselves, not to their humanity, but to their self-love'; the astute Adam Smith did not fail to note, and as the causality principle of a capitalist economy the egotistical drive of the human personality seems perfectly healthy to me.

Can we condemn it realistically? Though Max Weber was also to write that 'unlimited greed for gain is not in the least identical with capitalism, and is still less its spirit',[5] the economic function of greed nevertheless subserves a profound necessity in the political economy of the West which has never intended to forfeit the benefit of its drive out of mere considerations of morality. Nor does it diminish with the moral pretensions of any one ideology. Max Stirner, apostle of anarchy and a contemporary of Karl Marx, found it impossible to accept the proposals of democracy, pacifism and class-cooperation which are associated with the moral traditions of classical Marxism and its more idealist doctrinaire hypotheses. To him the very notion of morality was a farce, an impediment to the freedom of the individual whose sole concern lies with self-gratification and the satisfaction of his needs. And even though one would hesitate to accept such sweeping declarations as defining the human personality with any measure of precision, Stirner's *The Ego and His Own* is yet a remarkably perceptive analysis of the central psychology of the self which has never been fully grasped even yet by the revolutionary humanism of proletarian ideologies.

In a sense, the whole humanitarian argument may well be said to have begun with Jean Jacques Rousseau's revolutionary faith in the natural goodness of men and the philanthropic ideals of the *philosophes*. Men such as Voltaire, Helvetius, Diderot, d'Holbach, and d'Alembert were the future apostles of liberty, equality and fraternity. Their free-thinking precursory ideals appealed powerfully to the Utopian Socialists and radical intelligentsia of the early nineteenth century as the philosophical *summa* of the Enlightenment, and decisively shaped their conception of justice, toleration, and the true moral sovereignty of the people. Admiration of the Common Man became almost a religious dogma. But what its apologists chiefly admired about the people, some of us may be relieved to know, was in fact their own idealized notion of it as the vessel incarnate of natural justice, humaneness, and inherent moral power, while the great magnitude of its flaws went completely unnoticed. Virtues that had apocryphically emerged from the revolutionary phases of European culture contrasted with a dissolute, degenerate upper class, worshipping the demon of selfishness, at the same time as the unspoiled moral pretensions of the common throngs – 'they are the only ones who have courage and feeling' (Marat) – were absurdly idealized as somehow immune from the corruptions of their oppressors.

Echoes of this can be found in the social thinking of such precursory socialist thinkers as Robert Owen and William Godwin as well as in the socio-populist ideals of the Compte de Saint-Simon, Fourier, Cabet or Lamennais and, with a later reference to the French social novel, in the pen of Victor Hugo and George Sand with their idealized portrayals of the uncorrupted moral instinct of the common people. Before long, it appears, this almost mystic infatuation with the meek and the humble as thoroughly idealized archetypes became widely disseminated in mid-nineteenth century thought and, notwithstanding the flimsiness of the evidence, appears to have been a highly seductive argument, if not one of the most important and leading themes in the populist recruiting campaigns envisaged by proletarians and internationalists who, in all good faith, saw themselves entrusted with a mission of enlightenment similar perhaps to that of the French *Encyclopédistes*.

In Tsarist Russia Alexander Herzen was by no means the only one who firmly believed that the morality of the Russian peasant was purer and – on what seems better evidence, perhaps – more Christian than that of the rapacious European bourgeoisie. 'God will save Russia.' wrote Feodor Dostoevsky, 'Salvation will come from the people, from their faith and their humility.' Kropotkin reinforced this sanguine statement, musing in characteristically populist tones, 'what treasures of goodness can be found in the hearts of the Russian peasants.' Pleasing words, to be sure, and full of genteel eloquence, but it is certainly not easy to imagine that the common *muzhiki* were accessible to such homage. Truth to tell, the peasantry had no love for the populists. Nor did they wish to be martyrs in a cause they were very far from admiring. But even if they did improbably mistake the uneducated mass of rustics for their moral superiors, the liberal intelligentsia in the Russia of Alexander II, in their general self-identification with the oppressed, could hardly fail to be affected by this new mood. Dostoevsky's *Poor Folk*, in accordance with this attitude, was imbued with the sanctity of its moral power, while the whole problem of servitude was comprehensive enough to assume a distinct socio-political cast in the writings of the most promising young authors of the day. Although Nicolai Gogol, himself neither a liberal nor a progressive, had never carried the argument as far as men like Visarion Belinsky, foremost literary critic, or the poet and publicist Nekrasov, he was, almost in spite of himself, loquacious on the subject. So was Chichikov, speculator in dead souls and main protagonist of the book by that name which drew attention to the flaws of an iniquitous social system and went on to lampoon the whole extraordinary world of Orthodox Russia. In his own unmistakable fashion, Turgenev carried it even further. Sharing a common revulsion against serfdom with the exiled Herzen, figurehead of that articulate minority which expressed a profound disaffection with the ancestral and stubborn backwardness of the inveterate social class-antagonism in Russia, he gave all his domestic servants their freedom even though it was not with any serious hope of solving the actual problem of serfdom itself. And the monkish latter-day Tolstoy in his celebrated peasant shirt, matched by the features of the common rustic, longed to inspire people all over Holy Russia by his famous example. So perhaps did Maxim Gorki, fast building up a reputation for his Marxist affiliation and banished to the Crimea where Tolstoy confronted him with his adoration: 'I am more of a muzhik than you are and my feelings are more like a muzhik's than yours!'

When, for the first time in history, constitutional communism began on November 9, 1917, the day the new Soviet Order was formally inaugurated, it elevated an international conspiracy to the status of a government. Faced with an event of such consequence, the concept of freedom and harmony within a communist commonwealth, breathed its last. What had started out as a bold revolutionary experiment in social renewal ended as a sordid political exercise in totalitarianism. An entire conspiracy vanished. Triumph was but momentary, a guide to future disasters. In fact, it was more than a disaster for the rights of man as a new liberating force and for the social contract of government by the governed. The proletarian revolution had been no revolution at all, even though more than half a century would pass before that fact became public knowledge.

If it had been an orthodox truism that political tolerance bred independent action, the new trustees of the common weal were heedful of the stability which orthodoxy imparted and, anxious to centralize all power in the Soviets, swiftly established themselves as the very forces of reaction. Finding themselves in the minority in the National Assembly, they simply did away with it. It was part of the price that had to be paid by the many to the few. Clearly, for the majority of the governed the form and nature of Bolshevik power meant little more than a change of masters possessed by the notion that all aspects of communist life should be sanctified by the Holy Trinity of Marx, Lenin and Engels. And never to permit itself to be dispersed by democratic action it enjoined the monolithic unity of the Communist Faith, thus restoring – without a trace of moral regeneration – the whole of Orthodox Russia.

Party rituals replaced religious observances in this otherwise indistinct reincarnation. Conceit passed for humility. Intellectualism became treasonable. Spiritual problems invited administrative responses. Mediocrity became institutionalized, poverty collectivized, and power an end in itself. And to force every aspect of government and officialdom, of administration and judicature, of legislative and executive, into one narrow, rigid, centralized framework which recognized no political alternative and which was composed of the world's most heavy-footed, irrational and secretive bureaucracy perpetually on the look-out for anything subversive, that, indeed, appeared to be the most important need for this anxiety-ridden doctrine, terrified as it was into acts of repression by its inveterate distrust of popular sovereignty by responsible citizens such as were forbidden to think for themselves and whom it ruled, unequivocally, like Robespierre's Committees of Public Safety.

In historical terms, however, Soviet inspired Marxism was already at that critical stage when, after the first full assessment of Communist Jacobinism, a gnawing anxiety about the anachronism of autocratic government began to conflict ever more powerfully with a deep inner reluctance to take the gigantic step of admitting that it was progressing in the wrong political key. And in terms of the tensions created by the interaction of these contradictions, it was its passionate anti-intellectualism, its assiduous and indeed desperate refusal to acknowledge default and to admit how completely the Marxist failure had in fact turned out to be, which effectively revealed – if it did not actually prove – the traumatic character of the ensuing Soviet crisis of confidence which clearly sprang from something more personal than mere doctrinal conflict and ideological uncertainty.

For all its latent inability to go directly to the truth and call an end to the Communist experiment, for all its hereditary stubbornness, its cynicism, its facetiousness and its human element, this uncertainty thus contained another, a powerful and disturbing quality which united potentially all the aspects of the trauma of Bolshevist revolution. Whether they were the boundless absurdity of irrational biological principles, of abstract economic theories, the abrogation of natural or 'inalienable' rights, the strains and stresses of preposterous social principles, of internal dissensions, they all, phenomenally, explain the doctrine – and its tough committee-men, to whom the amelioration of social injustice meant little or nothing at all and who, whilst maintaining the illusion of a prosperous body politic, were in fact leading an anachronistic backward-looking doctrine to its eventual surrender in a contest of economic power with the West.

It has been rightly observed that 'When the Bolsheviks seized power in October 1917, they found a country on the verge of economic collapse'.[6] What remains to be added, in establishing this fact, is that when in 1991 they finally relinquished power they left the country in much the same state that they had first found it. And difficult though it is to turn without some lapse of continuity from a vast supra-national Soviet Empire to what was once the grand Empire of all the Russias, it is still possible to see a certain resemblance between the current repeal of the very structure of totalitarian power, and the emancipation of the serfs in the Russia of the early 1860s. For that too, as an event affecting the lives of millions, had raised new hopes after the harsh and exceedingly autocratic reign of the old Tsars.

There is, in truth, a certain historical identity between Alexander II, one of the more enlightened of Russian autocrats, holding the balance of power between reformers and reactionaries, and Mikhail Sergeyevich Gorbachev whose own contemporary role was the most nearly analogous. Obviously, the situation in Tsarist Russia was somewhat different from that of the counter-revolutionary Soviet Union a hundred and thirty years later. But it is intriguing nevertheless to comment on the role of Tsar Alexander as the one figure in nineteenth-century Russian politics who was completely, and perhaps tragically, aware that the country needed an entirely new moral basis if it was to be governed in any meaningful way. 'When Alexander II followed his father Nicholas on the throne,' the Slavonic scholar Lionel Kochan has pointed out, 'he had the wellnigh unanimous support of all groups of Russian society and even of political exiles such as Herzen. A few years before his death,' he then goes on to say, 'the Tsar was isolated from the Russian people, unpopular with the educated public, and cut off from the bulk of society and the Court. His fate had become a matter of indifference to the majority of his subjects.'[7] Though he refused a National Constitution, a sort of climax to his reign came in 1861 with the emancipation of the Serfs who constituted the large majority of the Russian population, 23,000,000 souls in all, and again in 1865, with the establishment of elective representative assemblies in the provinces. And that, for the time being, was that: 'The reign which began with high hopes ended in – assassination.'

To some extent, of course, even more relevance – in the context of our time – attaches to the enlightened despotism of Tsar Peter the Great whose own ruthless reforms, at a far less advanced stage of historical evolution, were perhaps the most thoroughgoing piece of westernization known to Russian history to date. To Peter, the benefits to be reaped from the technologically more advanced countries of the West lay essentially in the form of knowledge. He gathered to himself the best expert advice he could attract, recruiting naval and military specialists and inviting various experienced Western scientists to Russia. From this time onwards Russia ceased to be a closed and xenophobic land. The enormous and altogether unprecedented influx of highly skilled foreigners of all kinds increasingly began to determine national affairs, not only embracing and releasing Russia's great maritime development but eventually even leading to the large-scale reconstruction of Russian cultural life, under the auspices of a ruler who saw fit to clip the wings of a hereditary aristocracy and for whom the term 'reform' would essentially have meant what Mikhail Gorbachev called *perestroika.*

Expressed baldly in this way it is tempting to see in perestroika, as a creed of the times, and in *glasnost* as one of the most widely used terms of the period, a statement of the case of the reformers against the hardliners. Which is to say of those who came to power on democratic anti-totalitarian programmes, against the old party faithfuls, who shared, or perhaps still share, a general kind of wrong-headedness against everything that is progressive, enlightened and informed by a genuine sense of openness, with the old pre-Petrine Slavophiles who stubbornly clung to their established ancestral backwardness. For it was precisely on this showing, as Lionel Kochan also observes, that Peter the Great not only became 'the most unpopular of all the Tsars during his lifetime but also the most controversial afterwards. Did his reforms wrench Russia from its natural path and force the country into an alien mould? Was he a calamity for his country or its saviour? Did he introduce a split in Russian culture, for ever afterwards setting a Westernized upper class against an unregenerate mass of peasants?'[8] Nor would it be far wrong to suppose that former President Gorbachev's haphazard but fateful commitment 'to abandon everything that led to the isolation of socialist countries from the mainstream of world civilization' not only created a new class of persons who no longer belonged with the old established socialist system, indeed, whose functions now included the egalitarian exercise of democratic power, but entirely succeeded in overturning old hierarchical relationships.

It is true that Russia's immediate pretensions to joining the main stream of world civilization have to be interpreted with some caution. But although her economic claims are well and truly scattered, central Russia's immense and enigmatically latent power, despite all the incipient disadvantages of a prolonged crisis of readjustment, still remains compact. Indeed, on the further horizons of historical visibility, now tentatively tinged with the hues of real freedom and equality, one can even discern the dim outlines of true values in Russian life, some of them – cultural, ethnic, religious – of no uncertain significance and now gathered together, half-way between anarchy and a free market democracy, within the thinly prevailing dogma of a 'confederate' unity, to create an entirely new, one might say cosmopolitan, instead of Communist, force. That said, it is obvious enough that the only real bond between politically confederate but ethnically alien republics with a strong sense of national identity is their common opposition to the centralizing ambitions of the old Kremlin diehards and the now defunct Supreme Soviet.

This is hardly surprising. On the contrary, it is one of the lessons of history, which Aeschylus, on the testimony of Aristophanes, seems to have expressed with the epigram about the Lion's whelp: that it is best not to rear him, but having reared him, one must serve his ways. Whatever Mikhail Gorbachev may have intended when he provided men far inferior in genius with the lion's milk of the free-marketeer, it is not impossible to suppose that when he turned the Soviet Union from a once great superpower into what is now generally acknowledged to be a major social, political, economic, ecological and nuclear liability, he may potentially have compromised the national integrity of the Russian Federation herself. It further appears that nationalism, in every possible version of its basic idea as a community of ethnic values, has always resisted decree. It was unremitting, undying, rebellious and omnipresent among the *federati* of the Roman Empire and necessitated more than mere campaigning or, more contemporaneously perhaps, massive coercive authority. It required supreme statesmanship, something in which successive Soviet Governments appear to have been conspicuously lacking.

This, then, provides the clue for the 'rebellion of the *federati*', [9] which, in interchangeable terms also ushered in the declining phase of Roman imperialism and, finally burst forth in massive waves of barbarian migrations scattering everything before them.

Though in the cathartic perspective of a context so turbulent and traumatic as the age of communist decay this rebellion obviously entails a whole upward movement of social classes, an affray between authoritarian socialism and free market forces, or should I say, and increasingly ruthless entrepreneurs who are undermining the free process by operating illegally or in open defiance of it. One must, in any case, confront the basic issues and make a distinction between a failed proletarian phase in the East which, on its own, cannot be considered purely Russian either in origin or character, and the great world-historical responsibility that Russia might yet be called upon to assume. It has often been suggested, with justice I believe, not only that Russia wishes to become the successor of the old Soviet Empire, but that a new and powerful world culture would emerge from the Slavonic heartland of Russia after Western civilization, already afflicted by natural demographic attrition, has reached the extreme limits of historical possibility. And if some way can be found of saving her from the long-term consequences of Marxist folly, of opening up the greatest agrarian land mass in the world, and of extracting her vast resources in manpower and raw-materials, it seems perfectly safe to assume that what has once been called 'the largest known energy resource in the world' might also become the most formidable nation on earth.

Thus, having long since given way to the singularly precise facts of an economic nature, nothing is more unsound than a theory which, as suggested by Friedrich Engels, 'views modern capitalist production as a mere passing stage in the economic history of mankind'.[10] Now, of course, the tables are turned. Too many variables, in any case, have been left out. But, for all its variability, in looking upon the capitalist mode of production as 'imperishable and final', instead of, as Marx too has reiterated, 'as a passing historical phase of its evolution',[11] it would nevertheless be unfair to Karl Marx not to acknowledge his great pioneering spirit, nor not to point out that the triumphant successes of the Internationalists took place against the background of considerable historical logic. Their joint efforts on behalf of the collectivization of economic and social means, though itself corresponding to a passing stage of historical development, would first of all reflect the fundamental legitimacy of their historical claim – made good with a vengeance by the Bolshevik revolution – at a time when Darwinism had come to be considered as the basis in natural history for the Marxist view of social evolution. Indeed, Marx himself, in treating the proletarian movement as a process of natural history, had emphasized as early as 1862 the importance of, as he came to view it, 'natural selection for the class struggle in history'.[12]

Here, then, was the preliminary to what subsequently became known as the international proletarian revolution. And yet, whether pure or modified by totalitarian governments, it is hard to imagine two more discordant doctrines than Darwinism, which permanently belongs with the common stock of the natural sciences, and Marxist-Leninism as a political economy which, cut off from practically all predisposing causes, was the very antithesis of the natural laws of evolution. Nor is it any easier to reconcile two such contrasting individuals as Charles Darwin, the amiable, withdrawn country-gentleman in whom ordinarily no one would have taken the slightest interest, and Karl Marx, that half-cynical, half-compassionate apostate, possessed by an icy-cold will and cracking the whip over the various problems and principles of political economy which fired his brain.

He may well have distinguished himself as an abstract economic theorist, noted for strong and radical ideas. Yet, in concerning himself with practical issues, his real problem was the absence of any natural disposition which would allow him to bring his many diverse and opposite interests into fruitful co-operation with the political process. Trying to stipulate that the proletarian worker existed in rigorous subservience to his collective function was to apply an impossible law. No sensible man, at any rate, would subordinate all the constituents of his economic and private life – such as profit, incentive and enterprise – to its exacting totality. Here, then, lay its true anomaly. In making a statistical abstraction out of political economy he achieved a marvellous flexibility in forcing the facts to fit his vision where Darwin reduced facts to laws. In a word, Darwin grasped social behaviour such as it was, Marx understood the world such as it was supposed to be. And in the end it all adds up to one thing: that Dialectical Materialism is to Communism what theology is to religion – the prerogative of fools and saints.

If nobody, on that last point, can pretend that modern religion is anything but a posthumous conclusion to an inspired ideal, the same is true of contemporary communism which has neither battles nor purposes left. There is, moreover, in a historically posthumous conflict, no essential need for contriving new value judgements for a long-dead doctrine. Nothing, in the circumstances of our time, is more true than Oswald Spengler's observation that 'if we allow that Socialism (in the ethical, not in the economic sense) is that world-feeling which seeks to carry out its own views on behalf of all, then we are all without exception, willingly or no, wittingly or no, Socialists'.[13] Or, as Bertrand Russell said of Social Democracy, it 'is not a mere political party, nor even a mere economic theory; it is a complete self-contained philosophy of the world and of human development; it is, in a word, a religion and an ethic'. Elaborating further, he even objected that 'to judge the work of Marx, or the aims and beliefs of his followers, from a narrow economic standpoint, is to overlook the whole body and spirit of their greatness'.[14]

The point is well made. Nevertheless, even if we do accept with Bertrand Russell that one of the great mortals of our time, that immensely bold and confident, proud and disdainful, wilful, intense, energetic and so imperial Karl Marx of the Communist Apologia, was humiliated and betrayed by one of the greatest and most stirring of dreams when it was at length resolved into the ultimate non-entity by the monopoly of political mediocrities in positions of absolute power, it still goes to show that it does not become us to dream of a perfect human idyll, suddenly and miraculously at hand; of an exclusive never-never land with its millennial character, its farewell to spontaneous individual action, its violation of every natural principle and its false claims to objectivity. Some forms of idiocy are circumstantial perhaps, but considerable nevertheless. One shudders to think of a world where each individual consents to serve in his assigned place, of a time when everything is available and all things are possible, of a future when all of society's ills are mysteriously taken care of by a most fortunate propensity for infallible leadership, by a ubiquitous sense of moral probity, by an admirable unity of purpose; a world where there are no rich to envy and no poor to weep for, perfect, sufficient and intransitory, causing loathing by its bounty and surfeit by its abundance. A dummy of a world, neither certain nor even likely, but a place in any event in which men would soon have difficulty in defining their reason for living – difficulty, if such a thing were possible, ever to dream again.

3

FOUNDATION TIME

'I would annex the planets if I could!'

Cecil Rhodes (Empire-Builder)

To redeem the past and to transform every 'it was'
into an 'I wanted it thus!' – that alone I call
redemption!

Nietzsche, *Zarathustra*

In all likelihood, no two great men, set side by side, have ever
existed who were in sharper contrast to one another than Karl
Marx and Cecil John Rhodes, the communist and the imperialist.
Rhodes I shall for the present neglect. Marx, as we have seen, was
a dreamer at heart. His utopia, it has often been claimed, was not
an end in itself but the end of the beginning. The beginning of a
new chapter in the history of mankind, and a far more enduring
chapter indeed than any which had preceded it. Most importantly
of all, it was to provide a new definition of history, of, given ver-
batim, 'where pre-history ends, and history begins'.

The notion of the end of history, epitomized by Oswald
Spengler's *Decline of the West* (which he wrote to describe its
cyclical processes), is only now beginning to occupy the versatility of professional historians, but for some two decades or so it
has been the prevailing mode of social thinking and the fulcrum
for aesthetic doctrines in support of post-modern man, the last
man, as definitive and final as the society he serves. In fact, the

whole question of the end of history is much more profound than so far it appears. Its initial appeal, of course, is understood easily enough. Indeed, it is likely that the charge of post-modernism is largely a reflection of the social aspirations of academic intellectuals, futilitarian philosophers, fashionable ideologists and politically correct social theorists. Hence it comes as no surprise that as we are approaching the end of the second millennium we are rewriting its history. The past is being abolished. In fact, we are probably engaged in the most radical overhaul ever to alter any retrospective reading of the history of human civilization, preoccupied as we are with the very rejection of the values upon which it was based. It is interesting to speculate on the conflict between the two ways of thinking. The more particularly since on it also depends the type of value which we will ultimately choose to preserve. For the current preoccupation with the post-modern condition, as understood by many modern academics, indicates not so much a condition where the future no longer appears as a manifestation of the past but as the manifestation, to express an opinion, of our own exhausted impulse. It is possible, of course, to bring forward other causes for the post-modernization of history than the poverty of its intellectual purposes. But it is possible also to suggest that the promulgation of a new-fangled post-historicism may be accounted for – linked indelibly as it is with the nadir of imperial power – by what seems to me our failure quite to compensate for the loss of a more elitist conception of history's grand objectives.

I am well aware, of course, that it is no longer fashionable to be an imperialist. Needless to say. Post-colonial reaction has been total and unmitigated. In fact, the remarkable story of Western imperial expansion, once endowed with a grand and epochal meaning, is today so universally maligned as an unprincipled if highly successful history of money-grubbing and profit-making, and its massive civilizing force invested with so many different, ambiguous and frequently detrimental and abusive meanings that, for all its unsurpassed rapacity, nobody seems to want to notice anymore how decisive, indeed conclusive, the pursuit of geographical discovery, through conquest and settlement, has been for the very future of human civilization. Nor would I question for a moment that it was an insatiable and predatory movement, characterized by the liberal use of force and the appalling neglect of civil and human rights. But to consider an ideal as perverted or, in all tragic seriousness as unobtainable in execution, does not, in my opinion, justify the extent to which the historical value of a geographical movement that conferred incalculable benefits upon human civilization has been vindictively, and often very incompetently, vilified and disparaged.

Five hundred years ago Christopher Columbus discovered the New World. If nothing else, to have shown in the teeth of almost universal benightedness that the earth was round, is this master mariner's abiding merit. By any standards, it is remarkable enough. And yet, whether universally acknowledged or not, to this very day an unparalleled navigational feat occupies, indeed torments, the thinking of those for whom the results were, as they see them, a complete reversal of everything that stood for America's own autonomous indigenous evolution. Which is quite true of course, so far as it goes. Nor is it easy for us to imagine the intense cultural shock that America's various, and indeed variegated, indigenous cultures and civilizations must have received at the hands of their first invaders. But when, increasingly to the detriment of historical sense, posterity recapitulates and reviews itself by a continuous act of recrimination, we come to a most decisive parting of the ways. It is the crudest of all preoccupations but not, it may be protested, a very likely explanation for the phenomenon we have seen repeating itself over millennia rather than centuries: the rise and decline of civilizations.

Or take the case of Cortez and Pizarro. The one common single preconception in the timeless, archetypal, order that unites the whole of mankind, it has often been said, is the attainment of external power. If we read, for example, W. H. Prescott's *The Conquest of Mexico* and *The Conquest of Peru,* we find a plausible and convincing account of the cupidity of the Age of Discovery. An age, it is true, peculiarly given to the attainment of a new consciousness, a new awareness of the meaning of power. Nor was it by chance that the would-be conquerors of Mexico and Peru were tackling the problem of the attainment of power in the most intensely archetypal manner possible: the quest for gold. With Columbus, however, the case was different. His sense of the extreme necessity of distancing himself from the appalling cultural and geographical superstitions of an age that still retained an almost medieval obtusity and lack of vision, is the source of his greatest merit. He had nothing to guide him but his own genius. In fact, it is important to underline its significance and its scope. For it is only when we have fully apprehended the sheer scope of his foresight that we get an idea of the true significance, in an era of intellectual darkness, of one of the most seminal figures in human history.

We come to judge Columbus with the benefit of five centuries of history behind us. Now, of course, the tenor has changed, and conquering curiosity has been replaced by moral recriminations. Gone are the ancient notions of the great Age of Discovery as a geographical movement imbued with an historical purpose. History's heroes are struggling to maintain their reputation in an age, it is worth emphasizing perhaps, which has produced no genuinely great heroes of its own. Whole epochs of geographical and imperial history have been vilified and disparaged. The result, in my opinion, has been an impoverishment, a perversion of the massive historical estate of which the discovery of the New World was as inevitable an event as it is now an inescapable part of it.

To expostulate too noisily in the cause of some defunct historicism is as harmful as to expostulate too little. It is worthy of note, however, that the quincentenary of Columbus' landfall had also been chosen to coincide with the United Nation's 'Year of Space', perhaps the most auspicious revival of a grand historical aim. The next 500 years, then, began on 12 October 1992. Nor is it impossible to suppose that history may have descendants capable, in a more distilled medium, of emulating the great mariner's historical deed. Indeed, I am convinced that the most important, as well as the most congenial, function of a living historical legacy is to endow and give stimulus to the momentum of the historical life. This is one of its crucial aspects, and never more so when demographic conditions and the state of the world's ecology are exacerbating precisely all those factors which, at a time when human values seem to deteriorate faster than at any other, put a premium on the need for scientific progress.

Like most of the great fifteenth and sixteenth century navigators Columbus saw himself as an explorer and a discoverer. But he was much more beside. Indeed, to find anyone to equal him we have to wait for the appearance of Einstein, half a millennium later. The connection between two such dynamically distinct types of men may not, it is true, seem very contiguous. But the very contiguity, for me, lies in the fact that they were both, in their different ways, men of vision. This is true, and with Einstein more than with Columbus, even though it is essential to remember that if the world he created was even more transfigurative than that of Columbus, it is not nearly as tangible in its practical effects. The similarities, as I see them, are best suggested however by pointing out that each brought about a revolution in scientific attitudes, for if the history of the previous five centuries has essentially been one of expanding horizons, the world as we know it now has undergone a fearful contraction. This fact, once acknowledged, can hardly be contested. Today we occupy a planet which is going to be of a demographic density far exceeding that imagined by even the most inflationary Malthusian theorists.

It is a matter of historical convention that from the very moment when the transplanting and reproduction of European society on foreign soil had become standard imperial doctrine; 'that we might inhabit some part of those countries and settle there such needy people of our country, which now trouble the commonwealth . . . through want here at home',[1] it inevitably meant not only that European demographic and intellectual *diaspora* would be universal and, hence, permanent, but it also indicated the beginning of the most comprehensive and most far-reaching human migration ever to revolutionize the history of the world. It is true, for Sir Humphrey Gilbert, who was thus expressing a view which had the authority of the leading Elizabethan minds behind the quest to 'discover and occupy remote heathen lands not actually possessed by any Christian prince or people', the question of *Lebensraum* within the definition used in the modern sense had only an academic interest. Now, however, with the planet reeling under the weight of some five billion human beings, before long destined to be twice that number, we have a suggestion, to say the least, of the enormous demographic force which is being compressed into its ever decreasing circumference. And in considering how matters stand ecologically even before the twenty-first century gets into its stride, it is indeed easy to be persuaded that the age old need for living-space, albeit entirely emancipated from what is historically indicated by Anglo-Saxon imperialism or the *furor teutonicus* with its connotations of racial superiority, has lost none of its urgency and importance.

Five hundred years have passed now since 12 October, 1492, the date generally assigned to the discovery of the Western Hemisphere. And the very fact that ever since then world society has been in a process of change that would inevitably relate population increases to economic and social accomplishments, cannot of course indefinitely frustrate the belief that the logic of this process is the war of all against all rather than permanently sustainable economic growth. Nor are we dealing with an exact science. But one cannot possibly fail to be impressed with the thermodynamics of what approximates a mathematically precise formula. Particularly as its probabilities grow higher. The question of finding an answer to an inescapable global problem and of determining what solution, if any, can be found is of course another matter entirely. Yet, it is undoubtedly the case that all civilized life depends on it. The simple fact of the matter is that rather than assigning large numbers of people to the predetermined conflict between demographic growth and global capacity, the conquest of Space, too, ought to be viewed as a continuation of the great era of geographical discoveries, as an outlet in effect which might have been invented with demographic expansion in mind, or as a fresh pioneering adventure even, as well as of profitable commercial enterprise.

The last, moreover, is true of all major geographical discoveries. The impulse to explore has been largely economic. Indeed, the remarkable fact is that virtually all of the great maritime developments of the sixteenth and seventeenth centuries were due, in no small measure, to the *economic* promise of overseas trade and to the unceasing efforts of the great Chartered Companies which, as one of the major instruments of European demographic expansion, gave the Age of Discovery such a widespread commercial appeal. In our own day, of course, such corporations are organized on an even larger scale and often combine national research (as of the US government's space and defence laboratories for example) with privately funded enterprise. I believe that in this respect America's industrial strategy is compelling enough to furnish the contractual element for an entire space economy, at once increasing revenue and decreasing public expenditure. Of course, proceeding on this basis, it even seems natural to believe that the exploration of a Solar System, too, can largely be funded from the private sector, or that, at some distant date, planetary colonies might generate their own resources if not altogether be made self-sufficient.[2]

Inevitably, no such attempt to open new frontiers in space could possibly hope to be profitable at this early stage of planetary exploration. Nor is it difficult to believe that fundamental problems of astronautical science are first requiring solution before any worthwhile returns are to be expected. In fact, the logistical problems already under development seem stupendous enough. But on such an important issue as this we have to look beyond yesterday and today. Most important of all, we must acknowledge a further obligation, and that is the obligation of our responsibility to the past. This may seem extravagant, but it is exactly the kind of debt that ought to be honoured before any other debt. Not just because we all belong to one and the same civilization. Nor because we will be hard put to justify its continued existence if the heroic tasks which our ancestors accomplished are not in honour redeemed. But precisely, in my view, because we ourselves should have to enter a plea of guilty on behalf of posterity if posterity were to refuse redemption of its own continued existence as a debt which is owed to us. And certainly, if such an obligation prevails I can perceive, not the death of a species, but the forthcoming establishment, by multinational consortia, of colonial foundations in space, indeed, of colonial Empires – and once again there is a close parallel with the systematic expansion of corporate enterprise in past geographical history – powerful enough to rival the future even of the planet Earth itself.

However, this is conjecture, something that has a nice pioneering ring about it, if hardly an extravagant allowance. This does not necessarily mean that one need not be urgent about this. It simply means – and this is probably the conclusion of most astronautical theorists – that it is possible, indeed even certain, that for at least another century or so we shall be nothing but fleeting visitors in a sky that never looked so far. Men inspired perhaps, but quite literally out of our depth before the advancement of astronautical science or, *mutatis mutandis*, innumerable journeys from planet to planet, from orb to asteroid and across the length and breadth of the Solar System will lead to the foundation and occupation, far from home, of delicately extended bridgeheads on its furthest periphery. But men also with the intoxication of a new-found strength. Men, in a popular phrase, who will 'boldly go where no man has gone before'. The sleeping castaway crews who shall be the first to face the silence of the Universe, the first to break out of the Sun's gravitational embrace and come to grips with the stars, and the earliest perhaps to wonder what will be their journey's end?

One wonders, naturally! But there is one outstanding fact about a species of men lifted into that medium of selfless surrender in which heroic deeds are not only still possible but eminently credible. For wittingly or not, these are the men and descendants of men who will give proof of their exceptional destiny by transforming us – and the philosopher who urged transcendence may not have been very far from the truth when he said – 'into forefathers and ancestors of the Supermen' from whom, when examined from the transcendent viewpoint, there should spring a race which will be scattered far and wide across the Milky Way, wondering only as to the limits of their power.

Men's claim to the extraordinary world of the stars might be, at this moment in time, utterly hypothetical and vague in the extreme. But their claim to the planets we need not even trouble to argue. It is not in dispute. Personally, I have always thought the conquest of space a fascinating and deeply exciting prospect, and the conception of Space as a transcendent extension of human consciousness, or as some form of transcendent expression of man's supernatural, eternal, ideals, an inspired situation. As inspired a thing in its way as the actual desire to educate men to a new way of thinking about historical problems and, hence, to make them equal to the demands an impending New Age is likely to make upon them.

Let us bear this in mind, for if it is fascinating beyond measure to watch the now considerably accelerating progress towards the first glimpses of *Gründungszeit* in our Milky Way Galaxy, it is no less fascinating to view the same situation against the background of Foundation Time on Earth. Here we have an almost exact prefiguration of what may consequently be the same future process. It is difficult and, in the event, impossible to repudiate this natural and necessary development. Not only has it been anticipated millenia before our own time by the various migratory periods in the historical life of the human species but, in its most paradigmatic form, by the peopling of new territories with men from the Old World. Which is to say, by the pioneers and explorers who followed on the heels of Columbus with virtually no regard for the safety of their lives and almost no thought for the hardships they would inevitably have to endure.

To study their history is to study the incredible. For nowadays the Earth has shrunk to so pitiful a size at the hands of modern transport and communication technology, that distances are no longer prohibitive. Indeed, it almost requires an effort of the imagination to recall a time when men eager to navigate the oceans were kept at sea for months on end, often not to approach the shores of home again for many a lingering year. Nevertheless, it is still meaningful to compare the existing situation in the Solar System with the long and pioneering search for the Northwest Passage, which not only revealed some of the major outlines of world geography but certainly gave point to the four centuries of continuous struggle it took men to reach the North Pole. Of course, nobody then had the slightest idea about the progress that science was yet to make. By the time Commander Peary had planted the Stars and Stripes on the axis of the world's rotation, Louis Bleriot's almost simultaneous virgin flight just about tore to shreds the myth of its invincibility, even as he was serving notice that in the air men still had everything to prove. The timing could not have been better. But there is one thing neither Bleriot with his all-too brief association with the world of flying machines, nor naval officer Richard E. Byrd with his inspired flight over both the North and the South Pole, could have foreseen: the remarkably short span of time it would take from the first *military* aviators – which were all important for the rapid progress of aerial technology – to full inter-planetary rocket-power. For the notable answer is that it took *less than a lifetime* of aeronautical development from the first heavier-than-air machines to man's first landing on the Moon.

Science has not been idle. Who, even forty years ago would have foretold a landing on the Moon within a single generation? Freddy Hoyle, for example, then took the position – and timidity has never been one of his virtues – that 'within a hundred years it may indeed be possible to leave the Earth'.[3] And that is exactly what happened. Where Sir Freddy was a trifle off was in deducing the number of years. For barely ten years later Yuri Gagarin did actually spark off the great race to the moon. Hence, what really distinguishes the twentieth century from any that has preceded it is the extent to which scientific accomplishments have been capable of surpassing what theory predicted. Nor, for all its unexpectedness, should it be forgotten that it was but little more than a decade after Neil Armstrong's 'giant leap' that, somewhat offstage, the pathfinding succession of Mariner, Pioneer and Voyager probes were already beginning to give very good account of themselves. In actual fact, Venus had been observed by Soviet spacecraft since the 1960s. Meanwhile, of course, all the planets,

with the exception of Pluto have been the object of close encounters with visiting spacecraft; most notably, perhaps, at a
mean distance of nearly 800,000,000 kilometres from Earth,
leviathan Jupiter and the four planet-sized Jovian moons, rather
less than four centuries after they had first been named by Galileo
Galilei.

It is certainly understandable that such encounters should have
inspired an air of visionary excitement. Suddenly the possibility
of space travel has opened up. The Solar System is only beginning
to be investigated. Less than forty years ago the planets were only
known from astronomical observation. A mere four hundred
years ago the belief that the Earth was the centre of the universe
still found an impressive consensus of professional opinion.
Today it is a vapid question whether a theoretical limit can ever be
placed on the manifold ways in which science interacts with
progress. Benjamin Franklin has expressed it perfectly. 'The rapid
Progress *true* Science now makes', he deplored, 'occasions my
regretting that I was born so soon. It is impossible to imagine the
Height to which may be carried, in a thousand years, the Power of
Man over Matter.'[4]

Here perhaps for the first time, is the authentic voice of modern
science and of the developing reason so characteristic of the new
age of Enlightenment. It would come back to haunt H. G. Wells:
'the only trace of pessimism left in the human prospect today is
the faint regret that one was born too soon.'[5] Which can altogether
be taken to mean that we have not, by and large, made an
unpromising start for the triumph over infinity. Even though men
will always manage somehow to create time-consuming diver-
sions by pretending to be very busy otherwise, to me it seems –
and posterity will no doubt agree – that we have already been
making very tolerable use of our spare time by tossing moons into
the heavens and thus providing a convincing demonstration of the
fundamental will and ability of the human impulse to progress
and discover. Frankly, if we can believe that a manned mission
may reach the planet Mars, which at fifty million miles from the
Earth is well over two hundred times further away than the Moon,
say, within a decade or two, there would seem nothing absurd or
incongruous about the suggestion that, by the time Pluto on the
furthest edge of the Solar System completes one more revolution
of its great orbit around the Sun, manned ships will have eased
past perihelion to see their own shadows before them, stretching

all the way to the very stars.

And yet, on the broader question of what our aims and limitations ought to be we cannot permit ourselves to disregard entirely what all this means in practical terms. Considering that those faraway stars do not, as a rule, imply any readiness on the part of the taxpayer to shoulder the financial burdens of a technological thrust into Space, it may yet seem unlikely that the widespread scientific enthusiasm for such future achievements shall ever be gratified, let alone carried through to completion. One can perhaps understand why. Exploration, as a rule, has always been an expensive business. Nor is it irrelevant to say that the conquest of space requires resources far beyond those of any one individual nation. Some even go so far as to say that it is a poor second-best in popularity to the waging of war, and not altogether unjustly. At its most intense, the estimated expenditure of the 1991 Allied offensive against Iraq (not counting the cost in human lives) was said to have run into half a billion dollars a day. And if we glance at US military or defence expenditure which alone is currently (1995) budgeted at an annual 263 billion dollars, we shall be struck by the size of the US space effort which presently amounts to a paltry fourteen billion dollars a year.

It is not, however, the reduction of military expenditures which occupies a central place in the history of geographical discoveries. The one distinctly relevant problem which the explorer of today is called upon to consider is how the bulk of the space programme can be made self-financing by using resources, for example, in the form of investments from the private sector. I have said already that the Age of Discovery and its tremendously accelerating pioneer work in geographical expansion imparted an unprecedented stimulus to maritime commerce and to the great financial corporations whose trading privileges were based on royal charters. Some readers may object, but before emancipating ourselves entirely from its extreme rapacity, we should look more closely perhaps at some of the deeper reasons for the enormous practical success of this remarkable chapter of history as an expensive geographical movement of truly unsurpassed vitality and audacity.

First, it must be realized that it developed into a genuine Joint Stock enterprise at a time when investing money in territories that had barely been placed on the map was thought to be, and in fact was, an extremely insecure investment, even as it offered great opportunities for making a fortune. Nor was it exceptional that, with no clearly defined territorial sovereignties, maritime traders and merchants bent on seeking their fortune should fly their own private pennant for an undeclared war at sea whilst – often on the authority of a somewhat questionable letter of marque – seeking protection in law for plundering with the boarding pike and the sword. That, in token of the low ebb of the treasury, was in fact the Royal commission. And with the possession of qualities more commonly found in pirates than in merchants, the British merchant-adventurer of the period regarded the whole business as little better than a marauding expedition with virtually no regard for the rights and concessions of others as he sought to exercise his own. Even more remarkable were the Crown's financial relations with this odd amalgam of taxpayer, privateer, trader and potential warlord in his own right, whose exploits as 'bagman' for the realm would become the object even of stock-exchange speculations as he returned from the Spanish Main loaded down with plunder. It is said that the *Golden Hind* expedition paid a dividend of almost 100 per cent, whilst Elizabeth I, who could always profit from a favourable enterprise and lose little from its failure, would neither publicly affirm nor disclaim the commissions which had embarked her on a policy of such extreme provocation towards Philip of Spain.

At the same time, however, it should also be noted that Philip himself spared no effort to increase and consolidate his own share of the world, and if marauding on the part of the Elizabethan 'sea-dogs' had been elevated into a tradition of what Carlyle, with a somewhat irreverent melancholy, thought 'long likely to be memorable among the sea-heroisms of the world', the British merchant-adventurer could not, of course, be expected to condone Philip's claims to the New World as an exclusively Spanish sphere of influence which, by stress of circumstances, forced him to become either a smuggler or a buccaneer. For what was perhaps the most bizarre of pontificalia, Alexander VI's Bull of 1493 had allocated all geographical discoveries subsequent upon Columbus' westward voyage, to Spain and catholic Portugal in what virtually amounted to a division of the world along an imaginary line of demarcation that divided east from west and excluded, incongruously, all other nations from a share in it.

It cannot, thus, be said that the British did not have a reasonable case. It being a cardinal point, moreover, with the Protestant queen not to be bound by Papal decree, Elizabeth was hardly likely to countenance an arrangement which seemed considerably more advantageous to Spain than it was to England, to say nothing of France or the rest of the world. And sooner or later it was inevitable that English protestantism should come into a prolonged conflict of geographical jurisdiction with the doctrinaire catholicism of the Spandiards. In effect, by giving a practical demonstration of their presence within the sphere of the Spanish monopoly, in what was certainly a calculated challenge to Spanish prestige, a test of maritime strength between the two powers was made quite inevitable. That this small island nation of less than four million inhabitants came out of it a good deal better than she might have expected was due, we are frequently told, to superior seamanship. Quite apart, of course, from enjoying the remarkably good fortune of God's own patronage – another of those extraordinarily redeemable benefits of being British – which, whether true or false, was central to everything. Had not the winds themselves turned reformist? A large part of the answer, of course, lay indeed with foul weather, blustering gales and contrary tides which saw to it that Lord Howard, Hawkins, Drake and Frobisher always kept the advantage. It also meant that they destroyed a powerful enemy and achieved a famous victory of which so much since has been heard and of which the effects, if not immediate, were indeed far-reaching.

And so the sun set. Broken in body and spirit, the defeat of the Spanish Armada was enormously significant, for the truth of the matter is that the merchant-adventurers of England, perhaps the greatest set of villains that ever roamed the seas, were by no means unequal to the changing patterns of historical justification which looked like producing all the openings for immense wealth, enormous maritime power, and profitable commercial enterprise. But, despite all that has been said above, we can hardly forget that although the reduction of the Spanish naval invasion force was an event which was to have more than a passing impact on the way in which the subsequent life of a small, deeply heroic nation would be shaped, it was only by virtue of the great maritime discoveries which had been made in the name of Catholic Portugal and imperial Spain that it is now possible to rhapsodise in terms of history's inevitable and triumphant progress. Something, therefore, should be said of the brilliant maritime exploits which distinguished the fifteenth and sixteenth centuries, illuminating the Courts of Europe and giving Spain and Portugal an intellectual eminence and a foundation of effective geographical knowledge that became the fulcrum for the entire world.

Nor is it difficult to see why or how the Iberian peninsula should have been faced with the inevitable destiny of any trading nation with a commanding position on the main-lines of communication to India and the spice-islands of Southeast Asia. It is true, they had frustrated a century of Portuguese efforts. But then, success was hard to come by in that part of the world where Bartholomew Diaz had gone in search of fortune. Although unsuccessful in his frustrating quest for the Indies, he was in fact the first to claw his way round the *Cabo de Bona Esperance*, the famous promontory which he had actually christened *Cabo Tormentoso*, or the Stormy Cape, but which is much better known to the world now as the Cape of Good Hope. Soon there followed Vasco da Gama's discovery of the sea-route to Calicut on the Malabar Coast of Southwest India. This came to replace the old medieval trade routes through Arabia, after Columbus' venture had shown his own preferred method of reaching India by the western route to be involved in uncertainty. The first, too, they were to secure a virtual monopoly of the spice trade in an enormous sea-borne empire from the Cape of Good Hope to Goa and all the way to the Celestial gates of China, and the very first indeed, to accomplish the circumnavigation of the world.

At the time, when the science of navigation was still comparatively deficient,and considering that there were no reliable astronomical measures for the determination of direction and position of a ship at sea, it is all the more exceptional that the Portuguese *Fernao Magelhaens* should never have lost heart or wavered in his great resolve to attempt a voyage to the Spice Islands by the western route. For it was not, in fact, until AD 1522, with the return of a few courageous survivers of Magellan's original fleet that anyone had actually completed the first circumnavigation of the globe. Magellan was not among them. Nor is it easy to suppose that any man has ever come closer to being awed than the great global pathfinder as his clumsy, high-sterned ships took leave of the Pole-Star and groped their way towards Centaurus and the Southern Cross.

Since not everything can here be told, it may at least be said that the work of but a few bold explorers, of men such as

Columbus, da Gama, and Magellan, so advanced the calculations of the known world that it was no longer possible to continue the familiar tradition of Ptolemaic geography which had not changed much since the days of ancient cartography. Claudius Ptolemaeus understood the rotundity of the Earth of which the earliest Portuguese navigators still seem to have had a very inadequate idea. And it is an instructive contrast, is it not, nor perhaps in such a context entirely unreasonable that Albert Einstein's discovery of the 'rotundity' of the Universe, of its spherical or geodesic geometry, should here be compared with Columbus' and Magellan's geographical achievements or, at any rate, with the dawning consciousness of a new and unknown world which their astounding deeds then generated.

The parallel and its deeper significance is unmistakable. Of course, if Magellan's circumnavigation could finally be adduced as proof, if proof were still needed, of the argument which was then the subject of so many speculations, that the world was round, the situation with Einstein is rather more complicated. Nor can the question of an intrinsic space-time curvature be solved as comprehensively and, for obvious reasons, is conclusive only insofar as it has been convincingly demonstrated by the bending of starlight through the gravitational field of the sun. In Einstein's universe, however, we already see signs of so final and irrevocable a breach with the prevailing cultural, scientific and metaphysical preconceptions that it is here that a comparison with Columbus becomes eminently possible. Both men stood on the threshold of a conceptual revolution. Both did more, perhaps, than they knew. That this could lead, in Einstein's case, to a physical theory with the power to transfigure the laws of perspective is an education with little appeal to common sense. The question, moreover, of whether or not the treatment of gravitation as something fundamentally geometrical represents an exaggerated rendering of the processes which appear as a natural consequence of its theory, is not important. What matters is the immense perceptivity of Einstein's cosmological conceptualization, the fact namely that he has given us reassurance in quite another dimension. In a world provident out of all proportion to the ever decreasing limits of our own global circumference.

This, then concludes the case. One cannot, of course, say a great deal about it at present save that it has placed our cosmological existence on a much more speculative basis than Einstein himself may ever have imagined. But is there any future? Is there any chance of a new kind of history evolving out of a synthesis of science and philosophy? At the moment it is impossible to tell. Science, of course, is a much more precise art than philosophy and to practise it demands qualities which are exclusive of dogma and dominant ideologies. Nonetheless, the one way by which a cure can be effected is to look to the scientists for a lead. All the indications are that only from them is coming a revival of living, imaginative history. Nor will they assume the post-modern mentality of those androgynous individuals who already conceive themselves to be the precursors of an anonymous world, now that we have entered the last stage of psychological, spiritual and cultural evolution and cybernetic man is about to become supreme. For if history, hitherto, has been understood as a living field of reference, and the important events as a sense of life aspiring to moments of greatness, the next turn of the historical cycle, too, perhaps, can be depended upon to be every bit as important, comparatively speaking, for the future of Foundation Time in Space as was the first geographical circumnavigation for the great Age of Discovery on Earth.

4

HOMO DOMINICUS

Oh blessed, distant time when a people said to
itself: 'I want to be – *master* over peoples!'
For, my brothers: the best shall rule, the best
wants to rule! And where it is taught differently,
there – the best is *lacking*.

Nietzsche, *Zarathustra*

Too much, perhaps, can be made of men's *libido dominandi*, their
lust to rule or, sufficiently extended, of their will-to-power as the
sum total of the instinctual life. To rule, however, is only one
aspect of power. In fact, if we inquire into the nature of power
more deeply, we find that reflection on it leads to an equally
important variation – greed of gain, the one single constituent in
the natural order of things that is common to all of mankind. This
may not have any of the philosophical significance we usually
attach to the will to power but, in its most irresistible form, it is
probably of more significance in accounting for the existence of
the idea of power than any other form of lust or libido whatsoever.
Man is, in fact, incurably self-seeking. If anything, it was his
avarice and greed of gain and not his thriftiness and frugality that
set the great Age of Discovery on its triumphant course. It is true,
virtue as a result of cupidity might well lose some of its inspirational quality. The remarkable thing is, however, that human
civilization would have been quite unthinkable without it.

An unorthodox proposition? Perhaps, but a proposition which

illustrated the universal character of the will to power as a living embodiment of virtually everything that is tending towards social expectancy. When the social philanthropist Robert Owen tells us that men are 'infinitely perfectible', he is summing up a familiar belief in the human ability to rise above the moral confusion wrought by an inherently egotistical self. To be sure, there are a number of grounds upon which this conviction might be assailed. But it is a fallacy nevertheless to expect positive results only from this fictive product of the imagination. For if it has been a transcendent ideal, it has certainly been an ambiguous one, necessarily deflecting in directions other than the quest for perfection and easily changeable for the worst. And this ambivalent fact, throughout man's long and dilatory history, has played by far the greater and the more powerful part.

Clearly then, if nothing can match his 'greed of gain', historically speaking at the very least, no other impulse can match his *libido auri*, the lust for gold which has always been a quest far surpassing in promise the geographical mysteries of the great oceans, rivers and continents of the world. Men's cupidity and love of bullion has often closely approached the pathological, if not – should an ethical justification again be required – without amply having been compensated for with the advancement of great discoveries, both on land and by sea. But all too commonly, in its long and irresponsible history, gold has played such an unprincipled part in the making of enmity that it is almost impossible to imagine a more ubiquitary *casus belli* of all the ubiquitous causes of war with which men have had to struggle, albeit that this has never prevented them from coveting and enjoying it.

Frankly, without human rapacity, greed, envy and ambition, as well as some rather more praiseworthy traits, nothing of any consequence would ever have been started. Not by self-supporting settlers, the descendants of the men who had conquered the lands, nor by tough free-booters, courageous but ruthless men, and neither by the pious, the frugal or the brave. It is true, the great New England Puritan communities were built on self-denial and the 'indubitable certainty of grace', rather than being based on mere greed or the uncertain promise of gold. More significantly, where the gold failed to materialize, as in fact it did on the Northeast coast of America, there was very little activity during the sixteenth century, already in the process of colonial formation, and the explorations of Cartier and the Cabots were only followed

73

at the beginning of the seventeenth by more earnest attempts to settle the land. In actual fact, the earliest large-scale investigations of the interior of the American Northwest was undertaken by the Spaniard Francisco Coronado in a fruitless search for gold and the legendary seven cities of Cibola, and carried on subsequently by the French, most notably by the great Samuel de Champlain who explored the eastern sea-board and the Canadian interior.

Like others of their race, Chancellor and Frobisher sought either gold or the passage to Cathay and the fabled lands of the East, both of which were to prove elusive. In the interim, as I have said, the Continent itself was left largely unoccupied, except perhaps for Gilbert's failed possession of Newfoundland and Sir Richard Grenville's futile attempt at founding a colony on what is now Roanoke Island, between Albermarle and Pamlico sounds in modern North Carolina. Failures which were due not nearly as much to inclement geographical conditions as to the fact that these extraordinarily tough and abstemious pioneers were disinclined at first to take their chance with agricultural settlements hoping, as indeed they did, for quicker returns by retrieving 'whatever gold might be discovered'.

They also, most injudiciously, quarrelled with the Indians and fared not nearly as well as Cortez who burnt his boats before ascending the Mexican tableland with a handful of determined men who could neither give up nor give less than their best. There is something supremely immortal in the history of great and paramount destinies, destinies which count for nothing less than the historic energy that they release. Besides, this destiny involved a man of will. It also involved a natural master of men, and – something a good deal less easily attainable – a master of himself who was well indemnified against any temptation to retreat, having sacrificed his fleet of seven vessels for an ideal – even if *we* cannot defend it – worthy at least of a man's immortality and the name *Conquistador*, for it was in this capacity that he was to make his most enduring claim on history. Cortez, it is true, had been but an adventurer before he became the conqueror of Mexico. But like all great men whose one truly identifiable characteristic is their genius for transcending ordinary human dimensions, *Hernando Cortez*, already regarded as the descendant of the Sun by the remarkable Aztecs he was about to subdue, was nothing if not *homo dominicus*, the man who is lord – truly a man of destiny.

Today he is totally discredited. But is it meaningful to bury the great man under a welter of historical recriminations, to make him responsible for history's development? Cortez may stand for every hard-bitten, semi-literate adventurer of the day, but we must certainly absolve him from the legacy of being a contemporary of his time. The religious and moral qualities of such a man, we must always remember, were not those of an individual but of his time. Of course, we can always describe the time in terms of the individual, but what is important to our argument is that a heroic speculative effort, an almost unfulfillable dream, a fantasy, it would seem, had succeeded at length, and succeeded by means of a persistent personal discipline which fused the man with his fate. Cortez had the genius which is the prerogative of the great. He had the resolve in the conception and execution of a design, that power of the imagination which gives even the simplest man the ability to meet the challenge of his time. That, indeed, was the supreme mark of his quality, one of the chief characteristics of a man with the peculiar power to endure, indeed, to rise above the whole force of circumstances. Besides, no man came closer to defeat.

If the experience was a profound one, it must have been supremely inspiring to him, at the height of his greatest triumph, to contemplate all over again the special laws of history that seemed to have conformed to it, or so one might be tempted to conclude. Indeed, it is hard to explain otherwise the peculiar despondency of what was more usually a warring and autocratic people who slew captives as human sacrifice. It is true, a great empire was overthrown and an entire culture barbarised. But the Aztecs had a different notion of social justice, nevertheless, from that entertained by posterity and might even have been surprised, had they been given the opportunity, to hear themselves described in the equitable, pacific terms applied to them by their moralizing and lineal descendants. Now of course they were confronted with a different type of enemy, untrained as they were in the peculiar duplicity of the devious warfare of those times. Cortez went on to capture the major stronghold of the kingdom of Montezuma. Tenochtitlan, the city on the lake. He then destroyed a dynasty. But his position was extremely precarious. He could easily have been compelled to surrender and his tiny expeditionary force been slaughtered to a man. With the best will in the world, when one considers his extraordinary situation which could not have been reassuring to the bravest of men, one can only marvel at the power of Cortez's resolution; albeit with all the attention focused on an unparalleled promise of silver and gold there seems every likelihood that the perils of conquest remained what I may perhaps call, by analogy, a 'limited concern'.

Call it chance or design, the gold itself proves nothing either way. But who can know? Suddenly everything looked like fulfilling its purpose. When almost every aspect of geographical discovery was directed largely to the acquisition of the means that would pay for its expense, the precious bullion of Mexico and Peru played an almost providential role. In fact, for an idea of the fateful and irreversible changes in sixteenth century Europe that followed from the Spanish conquests of Mexico and Peru, I cannot do better than suggest what many a modern historian has already suggested: that 'it would be hard to name any period in history in which in so short a time so large a part of the civilized world underwent so sudden, so momentous, and so permanent a change.' Actually, T. R. Glover in *The Ancient World* thus referred to the brief but momentous reign of Alexander the Great or, more specifically perhaps, to his great conquest of the empire of Persia and the immense sums liberated from the Persian hoards which so altered the balance of the classical world. But really, as another example of a phenomenon recurrent in history, it cannot be said that his appreciation is much amiss, or that the immeasurable gold accumulations of Mexico and the Peruvian mines did not result precisely in that extraordinary display of Spanish wealth, power and dominions over which they shed their lustre and in which the erstwhile provincial and backward Spaniard soon learned to take the pride which henceforth he was to display in such proverbial measure.

Never before in the Castilian annals had any one king been rewarded so prodigiously for so formidable and lucrative a burden of responsibility as that assumed by Charles V, the grandson of Ferdinand and Isabella, during the proudest period of Imperial Spain. And if it is impossible to tell how the former kingdoms of Aragon and Castile might have fared without the richest source of gold the world had ever known, from the moment the Conquistadores set foot on *terra firma* across the Ocean Sea where Spain would establish her rich western empire, they were no longer the parochial and backward lands the world had known in centuries gone by. The Spain of the sixteenth century had become a world empire, the centre of the universe and – with the notable exception of a time when, according to Polybius 'all the known parts of the world fell under the dominion of Rome' – the greatest agglomeration of power in the history of civilization. Its splendour, prowess, and achievements, both in letters and arms, were second to none and an infinitely redoubtable tribute to the new era and the men who had made it.

The conquest of Mexico and Peru had altogether been a near thing. But then, Cortez's and Pizarro's case would not be measured by its nearness to failure or success nor by its notoriety in the annals of fame, but by the associated coming of the white man who first rose upon the New World in his ceaseless quest for gold. That it has also tarnished the essential humanity of his nature, been the cause of innumerable wars, of bitter colonial rivalry, and directly responsible for the appalling death rate wrought upon the natives of many races, cultures and continents, has never been likely to narrow its appeal to those who were, literally, in it up to their necks and who based their arguments, albeit with considerable freedom of interpretation, on the views of their own time. Though the Conquistadores may have given little thought to subliminal things, neither the conqueror of Mexico nor the destroyer of the Inca empire in Peru was the kind of man to consider himself bound either by moral doctrines or humanitarian precepts which, at any rate, they were unequipped to meet. Indeed, their ability to go beyond the limits of what is ordinarily possible seems nothing short of miraculous, precisely the sort of synchronicity – to give substance to its theory – which only the man of destiny can command.

Nothing could have induced them to abandon their quest for *El Dorado* which was, in essence, the story of the Argonauts recast, I dare say, with a considerable sense of occasion in what is perhaps the most forthright piece of history ever written. It forms that grand design of human destiny, the sort of vision which dreams alone can confer and which, lest it exists for the bounty of poets, has been rendered almost meaningless in this age of supreme detachment, spiritual stagnation, and purely material forces. An age, it will probably be found, where men can no longer dream in that same grand manner nor, consequently, put the same forces of fate into effect. Forces which are pervasive and even beautiful: to observe the transit of Venus across the face of the Sun; to attempt the discovery of the legendary Northwest Passage in the Arctic regions; to locate a sizeable stretch of mythical territory (the fabled Southern Continent) between Good Hope and the Antarctic Circle; to ask for the impossible and yet to press on further, are facts of Western history, of an enormously rich treasure of images, icons, ideas and achievements. There are many other instances seeming almost to defy the distinction between history and myth, between the wanderings of Ulysses, Jason's quest for the Golden Fleece, and James Cook's search of the southern oceans, between the deeds of men and the extremes of fortune. Celebrated instances, to be sure, of the wonderful momentum and great immortal impulses given to the minds of men who lent vitality and visionary force to the culture, idealism and heroic heritage of the West which goes back – to give point to an antithesis – to as long ago as Xerxes and Thermophylae.

This may well have been the happiest period in the history of Western nations; the Golden Age of Discovery, full of fortuitous promise and felicitous prophecies, a time of world-wide scope and universal activity and a fine example of purpose and a single will. We can still feel the full impact of its inquisitive spirit. Never, in fact, has human history appeared so readily changeable for the better. It has been denounced, nevertheless, by more progressive and, frankly, defeatist generations at odds about its scope for much the same reasons really that we deplore the irruption of the barbarians into the Roman Empire. But then, it has been the case throughout historiography that the Romans were taken out of the stream of life when they were infirm of will, replete with domesticity and, whether by deliberation or not, idle and dissolute shirkers with a death-wish upon them. The *Conquistadores*, by contrast, were a different class of men. Come to think of it, given the overall complexity of the Commonwealth of the Roman People in its truly multinational extent, they were probably more than marginally 'better' men than the late Romans with their vast corpus of emancipated slaves and admixed Oriental, Punic and Levantine populations that sprouted in close conjunction with the expansion of empire and maritime commerce into the over-crowded Mediterranean basin.

The world was wide, and if not every man fleeing beggary at home was born to rule, snatch a dominion, subdue whole empires, proclaim himself a conqueror, or make a name for himself with but a handful of determined men, the possibility at least was there. A gallant young man could always prove his worth. Only a spark of the imagination was needed, and a backing of troops, to reach for kingly opportunities. Taken by itself, this may sound unreasonable. But is it reasonable to ignore altogether that evolution progresses by conflict? To ignore that whole nations firmly believed in the virtue of conquest and that they did so without knowing, or seeing, a great deal of that part of their own humanity of which we at any rate are obliged to be conscious. Nor does it determine the vital question whether that humanitarianism should have been spread by the great rising Empire of England or of France. This question, in fact, cut right across the widespread commercial power-play and tempestuous nationalism which involved the two historically most important protagonists in the close and bitter struggle for supremacy and the leadership of the West. In fact, it is reasonably accurate to say that if the history of the previous two centuries had largely been a record of their struggle, it was only with the beginning of the nineteenth century and the now developing humanitarian phase that the question of whether the libertarian or the authoritarian view would prevail, had finally been resolved.

At this point the situation changed enormously. Now it seemed much more lucrative to be 'protectionist' rather than imperialist and, under a policy of avowed mercantilism and thrifty managerial principles, to give practical lessons in equality and human self-respect. That there followed a genuine tendency – which Britain carried to a point unsurpassed anywhere else in colonial history – to transform conquered dominions into allied protectorates rather than to keep them in subjection, is difficult to contest. Civilizing as it was, a combination of the stick and the carrot, or what Charles Napier, the Conqueror of Sind, once called 'a good thrashing first and great kindness afterwards', appears to have been the usual method favoured by the British in order to provide the necessary encouragement for immense new territories to enter more profitably into a common market economy. And unless we join those who consider that the British were fully engaged in naked theft, in a ruthless and aggressive drive to further their own influence on behalf of commercial and imperial prosperity, we must accept that, wealth and empire aside, there have been few greater moves towards political emancipation and the exercise of civil and individual rights than under the *pax britannica*.

Indeed, pacification of this type in its original form appears to have begun with the systematic imposition of *Graecia Magna* and the *Imperium Populi Romani* which, in its truly immense extent as a sovereign administrative and cohesive Empire of the Roman People, seems to have been the most notorious for this kind of colonial amelioration. It was usual enough for the Romans who came as often as not in association with bankers, traders, commercial travellers and other purveyors of merchandise, 'to wage war in order to bring the gift of liberty to other people' (Livy). At least that is what was supposed to happen, 'not merely that we might draw annual profit from them, but that we might diffuse among their inhabitants, long sunk in darkness, vice and misery, the light and benign influence of the truth . . .'[1]

Probably true enough, though hardly the whole truth. This last quotation, not perhaps entirely above suspicion, actually issued from the East India Company's Court of Directors, the real representatives of British sovereignty at the opposite extremity of the overseas Empire, who were fond of comparing themselves to the best of Greece and Rome. And on the face of it at least, the same spread of attributes characterized the pan-Britannic idea. A belief in Empire indicated a belief in vast idealistic issues. Today the meaning of empire and idealism are ranged on opposite sides. Indeed, the sharp contrasts which sometimes seemed to exist between vast idealistic issues such as creating a civilized world, and the ungenerous championing of mercenary and personal interests, are now much more readily recognized. But if one asks why, the short answer is not so much because the mercenary and the parochial corrupted a strong grasp of right and wrong, but because they seem to have absorbed most of the attention the imperial idea has subsequently received. Because, in all honesty, the resentment of posterity against the invading past has had a tendency to prevail over any real understanding of the vast expediency which motivated the imperial idea. Perhaps Cicero, very brief and to the point, should have the last word: 'Our empire', he said, and the gist of his argument is immediately apparent, 'was acquired in defending our allies'.[2]

Whether missionaries or merchants, the British whose thinking had always been much absorbed with the defence of their allies or, by a different interpretation, with 'gaining their consent' to annex suitable parts of 'allied territory', certainly had no intention of being left out of the eastern trade. Indeed, their initial failure to secure the Spice Islands, Ceylon, Malacca and Sumatra, of which the Dutch, or by extension, the Dutch East India Company whose power and prosperity was to grow enormously during the seventeenth century, now claimed sole ownership, was but a temporary setback to their imperial ambitions which were soon transferred to the Indian Main. Nor did they have to burn their boats, those ample and 'proud East Indiamen', in order here to secure the exclusive right to trade. It was the precise opposite of the conquest of Mexico and Peru. The discerning moguls and mahrattas actually welcomed the friendly approaches of the 'company of peaceable merchants' for their own developing purposes, and the first English 'factory' actually appeared in 1608 on the Coromandel Coast of Madras, to be followed, before long, by tiny coastal enclaves at Surat, Bombay and Calcutta. This was no time to quarrel. And the East India Company's 'peaceable' merchants and factors did not at first meddle in domestic politics. It is however impossible to argue that such trading stations, factories and fortresses serving as *entrepôts* in the spice trade, were merely so many openings for commerce. The economics of the struggle for immensely valuable trade monopolies cut both ways. And with the famous principle of *divide et impera* deliberately provoked and pursued, the stirring of neighbourly discord and the exploitation of domestic quarrels between the local princes and maharajas being a favourite instrument of British imperial policy, we may be sure that the Company's agents were soon manipulating local affairs with all the discrimination of Hindu pundits and Muslim divines.

Thus, at any rate, arose the famous East India Company which had first received the privilege to trade, that is, the sole right of commerce with the islands and ports of Asia, Africa, and America in the last year of the sixteenth century. And from 1600 onwards when it was incorporated by Charter of Elizabeth I, until after the Indian Mutiny when it was forced to cede power to the Crown, the Honourable Company was to exercise a unique influence over the political fortunes of the Indian sub-continent. Actually by this time already it is beginning to become apparent that the 'First Power' in the world was acquired, or very nearly so, on a private basis and by a system of syndicates which brought about a concentration of power into the hands of merchant-oligarchies, or of the said Merchant Adventurers, that far exceeded even that of a Roman provincial governor who, it is worth noting, could neither raise troops nor impose taxes on his own initiative. Nor was commerce at bottom the real issue. The chief aim was to build an empire and the thinking behind the famous 'three C's', one might as well say infamous, of Christianity, Commerce and Civilization was, first and fundamentally, that its geographical structure itself might be used to further the migration of British communities interested less urgently in trade than in establishing themselves abroad. This they very effectively succeeded in doing: 'We acquire territory for generations yet unborn, trusting thereby to find an outlet for surplus populations in the congested days to come. It is to the future benefit of the race that we look. We expect no immediate returns.'[3]

Immediate returns or not, the Hudson Bay Company which had done as much to secure the whole of the Canadian west from the American frontier to well beyond the Arctic Circle, did neither fail in this particular issue, nor did the great chartered corporations of Victoria's empire which, though eventually scheduled for abolition, could still effectively rise to the position of ruling powers. Of particular prominence, and in many ways considered to be marking the highest peak of British imperial power, was the British South Africa Company, whose charter, approved by the Colonial Office and issued from the Privy Council in 1889, secured Cecil Rhodes *carte blanche*, so to speak, for the establishment and foundation of his own private empire in south-central Africa and thus put Rhodesia on the map.

These, then, were the heydays of British commercial imperialism before the political privileges and trading monopolies of the Companies were gradually whittled away and, their essential task completed, they ceased to be the great ruling corporations of the Imperial Commonwealth. But once again, the 'anachronistic' context notwithstanding, the idea of synicalism as a method of imperial advancement continued to persist. Even after it was well-nigh all over, there was, nevertheless, a resumption of conquest and expansion, now extending to central Africa. Rival companies, notably the German East Africa Company, and, from the centres of imperial rule, the latest European interests, were beginning to make themselves felt. Particularly towards the last quarter of the nineteenth century and 'the vilest scramble for loot that ever disfigured the history of human conscience and geographical exploration';[4] or, with somewhat less biting perspicacy, the openly acquisitive partition of Africa by Britain, the French, King Leopold of the Belgians, Italy, and the Imperial German Government.

From the beginning, however, when it received its Charter on behalf of the Crown, there was much that was unique about the Honourable East India Company. Once happily described as 'the most formidable commercial republic known in the world since the demolition of Carthage', it was indeed capable of putting over a quarter of a million men into uniform. The Imperial Roman army itself, it should be remembered, as a standing professional force, only amounted to somewhat over a quarter of a million fighting troops. And when coupled with the right to collect public revenues, to maintain its own foreign policy and to make war or conclude peace with independent potentates, it is not difficult to believe, that the East India Company's imperial writ virtually had the force of law. In truth, it is hard to form a more accurate impression of the kind of commercial magnates with the power – the term itself not being without moral significance – to determine the very nature and definition of Empire:

'But scarcely any man, however sagacious, would have thought it possible that a trading company, separated from India by fifteen thousand miles of sea, and possessing in India only a few acres for purposes of commerce, would, in less than a hundred years, spread its empire from Cape Comorin to the eternal snows of the Himalayas; would compel Mahratta and Mahommedan to forget their mutual feuds in common subjection; would tame down even those wild races which had resisted the most powerful Moguls; and having united under its laws a hundred million subjects, would carry its victorious arms far to the east of Burrampooter, and far to the west of the Hydaspes, dictate terms of peace at the gates of Ava, and seat its vassals on the throne of Candahar'.[5]

Since it well retains the sense of opportunism, that is, the historical pedigree and principal demonstration of the East India Company's mighty *raison d'être*, I am going to assume that Lord Macaulay's accomplished epitaph is worth an enlarged quotation. As the Company's territories extended towards the Northwest frontier, the Court of Directors no longer even considered it necessary, in their own words, 'to borrow from the king of Delhi any portion of authority which we are competent to exercise in our own name', nor would they concede that their position in India was anything less than that of 'absolute sovereigns of this splendid empire'.[6] And if the objectives for which they strove seemed as much mercantile as political, financial as imperial – and dear to all good Englishmen – it is obvious that in its effect on

Indian society and India's social and mental attitudes, civilizing experience and collective assimilation of that experience could not be kept separate from the personality of the Englishman himself. Nor, in demonstrable achievement, can it be kept apart from his powerful grasp of right and wrong in respect of precisely those social or humanitarian intentions which posterity's verdict now so strongly endorses.

Hence, to comprehend the dual nature of what was not simply the joint interest of the individual and the collective but a purposeful historical movement articulating certain economic or mercantile priorities which, at any rate, no one doubted to be conducive to an humanitarian policy that was manifestly working, the picture drawn by Macaulay must be held against the evolution of the human race itself. Nor is it enough merely to unmask the ambiguous humanity of the ruling race, such as the concurrence of political idealism with mercantile hard-headedness, or the connection of the visionary with strongly protectionist manufacturing interests; or – with all possible effect – to maximize an alleged disparity of principle – such as 'waging war in order to bring the gift of liberty' – and thus to transform a need to civilize the world that grew out of history's necessity into nothing better than a jingoistic commitment to expansionist aims. A commitment, it may be protested, that runs much deeper than any such shallow moralism in which the inhumanities of Western civilization are seen as ratified and endorsed by the aggressive imprint of an expansionist imperial power.

Empire-building, in any case, was never going to be easy. It is important, therefore, to be on guard against confusing form and substance. And this, too, we must remember: if the tendency of the new 'consciousness-raising' anti-imperialist school – like so much else that has passed for progress – it is to emphasize the mercenary character that Anglo-Saxonism developed in conjunction with a sometimes inordinate lack of political propriety, the general effect of what seem to be propositions that various artful thinkers and social commentators now appear to be sharing with the new mythos of historicity, is to abdicate evolution altogether and to reduce to nonsense its dynamic origins and profoundly underlying causes. None of this is to belittle an adjustment of critical perspective. But it *would* be absurd as well as monstrous to try and picture the struggle for Empire simply as a dispute between opposite anthropological types in various regions of the world oversaturated with arms and demographic power. It is much more accurately described as a struggle between the historically progressive forces of the world (I believe I have indicated that), and those forces often directed congenitally at resisting what is as demonstrably a part of the evolutionary order of things as the fact that the universe is infinite and will expand forever.

Not everybody may agree, but, as every student of physics knows, to reverse that process is going backwards in time. It introduced new values, seen in retrospect as crucial; new civic statutes of equal advantages to all, new levels of trust, hope and indeed, human expectation and has led both to the institution of a democratic authority under the protection of its various national constitutions and the considered elimination, in a civilized society, of naked violence as a means of settling its differences. Humanly fallible an imperial society may often have been in the interpretation of its historical franchise. Needless to say. But its historical capacity, in the long context of political development, for enhancing the values inherent in human nature and demanded of humanitarian principles, is indeed hardly contestable.

Of course, no one can suppose that a nation or imperial power expands beyond its own boundaries unsupported by a strong backing of elitist value distinction, by 'belief', in Nietzsche's words, or 'pride in oneself'. One should, however, try to separate the substance of this pride from its more unfortunate totalitarian forms, for when considered in its proper context it becomes clear at once that Britain was already then attempting to formulate the high ideals under which the greatest possible good for the greatest possible number was ultimately going to be realized. The results, as pioneered by Britain, are in any case accomplished facts of our present time. As set out in the United Nations Charter: '*To achieve international co-operation in solving international problems of an economic, social, cultural, or humanitarian character, and in promoting and encouraging respect for human rights and for fundamental freedoms for all without distinctions as to race, sex, language, or religion.*'

This, essentially, is the challenge which the Anglo-Saxon had taken up. A challenge, in fact, which is infinitely capable of illustration. So far from being selfish, this, as I see it, is precisely what Nietzsche had in mind when, on his favourite subject of a master morality, and in contempt of all 'slavish' or subjugated values, he

declared that 'The noble type of man feels *himself* to be the deter-
miner of values, he does not need to be approved of, he judges
'what harms me is harmful in itself', he knows himself to be that
which in general first accords honour to things, he creates
values'.[7] *He*, in any case, though much more truculently British,
had too strong and steadfast a sense of his own humanity to need
appreciation of his motive nor, least of all, the sight of trembling
hands untying Gordian knots, to raise the sword that cut them.

5

CIVIS BRITANNICUS

> But he has discovered himself who says: This is
> *my* good and evil: he has silenced thereby the
> mole and dwarf who says: 'Good for all, evil for
> all.'

Nietzsche, *Zarathustra*

Whether we do or do not accept the theory to which Cecil Rhodes so fondly inclined, namely that the Anglo-Saxons 'are the finest race in the world and that the more of the world [they] inhabit the better it is for the human race'* (and we are at liberty, of course, to substitute his with quite another assertion), the fact is nevertheless that Cecil Rhodes' suggestion, though now simply out of date, does convey to us something of the force of the motives which determined the extravagant opinion many a nineteenth century Englishman appears to have had of himself. And even though the recognition – or the frivolity of it – may have exited no great cordiality from those peoples and races which appear to have registered a very different impression, almost certainly, most of us would probably say that nothing is so characteristic of our time than an increasingly identifiable Anglo-Saxon way of life. Particularly so when expressed in terms of an increasingly predominant Anglo-American entrepreneurial society, with its emphases on political internationalism, commercial pragmatism and the material pressures to succeed. In fact, it is impossible, in

* Confession of Faith, 1877.

my view, to do justice to the Anglo-Saxons without reaching the conclusion that they fill a larger part in the mental horizon of our time than that occupied at any other time by any other race, nation, or people to whom the term 'civilized' has with justice been applied.

There is, on the other hand, little resemblance now between what was once very unequivocally indicated by Anglo-Saxon imperialism as an assertion of cultural supremacy and, at a much more subdued level, the peculiar, some would say conspicuous, reticence which appears to define the current state of the art of Englishness. Reading them, one is haunted by the words of a self-confessed 'British Race Patriot' who once expressed the view that his patriotism knew no geographical but only racial limits.[1] One is intrigued, at the same time, by such conspicuous effusions of racial cordiality as testify to the contemporary, almost apologetic, self-effacement which, today, make even an Englishman seem strangely un-English. And if it is hard today to think of a political situation in which racial tension is not either present or involved, racial supremacy was a subject to which Victorian England had consecrated the chauvinistic fervour of an entire way of life. It was also a way of thinking in which men like Cecil Rhodes or Sir Alfred Milner, in spite of a fine classical education, were completely at ease. Creating conditions for much of the distrust, resentment and suspicion that now splits Europe from Africa like some geographical fault, imperialists of Lord Milner's ilk accepted the Empire as a machinery for promulgating their racial excellence to peoples and nations for whom the distinction meant very little. 'I believe in the British race', therefore was the Secretary of State for the Colonies, Joseph Chamberlain's enunciation on the subject, while Charley Gordon – General and Pasha – never doubting that one Englishman was worth five foreigners, cautioned another 'to thank God that he was born an Englishman', and it seems permissible, perhaps, to suppose that the latter, with the wryness peculiar to his race, may have congratulated himself with an affirmative 'God knows best'.

Be that as it may, what seems to me certain is that such differences as exist, or did exist – and it is not merely a matter of a difference of outlook or attitude – between the English and other peoples were never, in fact, between opposite races of men. Nor, in actual fact, did such differences have anything to do with those aspects of nationalist thought which stress the idea of racial supremacy as an instrument of their own glorification. At the same time, of course, it is not impossible to believe that a 'British Race Patriot', culturally resistant to oriental proclivities and aghast at the ethnic, social and economic corruption produced by plutocratic oligarchies, would aim for the rule of power or even strive to appropriate it himself. It all seems a long time ago now at any rate, but even though we, for our own part, may no longer agree with him, we can hardly forget that such a rule could not be constructed except upon a foundation of effective authority – and I am thinking about an authority that speaks for itself and can be found only in moral strength and integrity.

His moral objective, then, the objective to promote a unifying humanitarian ideology, can scarcely be held in doubt. A more extensive and candid examination of the English as one of the most seminal of historic races, moreover, will inevitably lead to the realization that those peoples, nations, races, communities, or indeed, individuals who, rightly or wrongly expatiate on the necessity of reaction and, as they were bound to sooner or later, militate against the great historical legacy of what, for them, has ceased to be the Empire, do so commonly enough – and ever word-perfect – in the idiomatic accents and vernacular renderings of what by now has indisputably become the *lingua franca* of the age. Nor is it part of my admiration that there should be anything gratuitous in this appreciation of the language of modern science and technology, or indeed, of commerce, sport and recreation. There is no need to offer an inflated appreciation of its linguistic accomplishments. The enormous capacity of the English tongue is as plain as it is useful. It has readily allowed itself to be adapted to every single purpose to which language and literacy can lend themselves. Personal attitudes are a different matter. Nor does it follow that the student of modern English is certain to reach a higher level of culture or intelligence, let alone appreciate the literary English of Shakespeare or Johnson. But as the language which, today, is understood by perhaps the greatest number of people, it nevertheless seems to have satisfied everybody. Willingly or not, on this point I side with the literary critic Cyril Connolly who, already in 1938, determined that 'the idiom of our time is journalistic and the secret of journalism is to write the way people talk'.[2] So if the language of the British Empire has been debased and even bastardised by its very response to the rapid pace of cultural change, of all the forces shaping the modern world it is nevertheless closer to us today than the language of Shakespeare and Johnson.

When the reaction against the Empire set in, as it did among intellectuals in the first and among the general public in the second half of this century, it put an end to what Winston Churchill once called 'the triumph of civility over barbarity'. Indeed, it remains one of the supreme ironies of modern imperial history that the nation which, as Arthur Bryant so justly remarked, 'has led the world in every branch of humanitarianism', has chiefly been charged with snobbery, rapacity, hypocrisy, and condescending jingoism. Which does not mean that the world was entirely misled. But it is unlikely at the same time that any other nation ever bequeathed so significant and so lasting a proportion of its genius upon the rest of the world, to say nothing of the freedom of Englishmen as a powerful inspirational force. Nor has there been a subsequent inspirational force to parallel such unmistakably Anglo-Saxon activities as kicking a goal, hitting a century, scoring a try, serving an ace, or playing a birdie. The true symbols which to this day commemorate its genius, not to mention the Englishman's customary self-complacent conception of the rest of the world which, whenever returned, makes each of us just as bad a bore as the original John Bull, whose world is thus in truth our own.

It will have been gathered by now that I am not an Englishman. Nor do I claim to be detached. On the contrary, without necessarily wishing to impose my own upon the reader's judgement, I shall nevertheless permit myself the freedom of being as discretionary as a philosopher of history who means precisely what he says. This, perhaps, does not allow much room for arbitration. But then, we must not suppose this to be a vindication of the Englishman at the expense of the rest of the world. Far from attributing to Englishness any sort of intrinsic merit, I am merely bearing witness to the theory freely credited by pundits of all kinds, that 'the English *are* a race apart'. Which observation, incidentally, has also been made by Napoleon Bonaparte, Emperor of what was, and reputedly still is, the most intelligent nation on earth, though on this particular occasion as one of the *dramatis personae* in Bernard Shaw's *Man of Destiny*, and one well worth quoting at some length:

'No Englishman is too low to have scruples: no Englishman is high enough to be free from tyranny. But every Englishman is born with a certain miraculous power that makes him master of the world. When he wants a thing, he never tells himself that he wants it. He waits patiently until there comes into his mind, no one knows how, a burning conviction that it is his moral and religious duty to conquer those who have got the thing he wants. Then he becomes irresistible . . . He does what pleases him and grabs what he covets . . . he pursues his purpose with the industry and steadfastness that come from strong religious conviction and a deep sense of moral responsibility. He is never at a loss for an effective moral attitude. As the great champion of freedom and national independence, he conquers and annexes half the world, and calls it Colonization'.[3]

All this is true enough, or rendered, at any rate, with the convincing ring of truth. But even though the famous Irishman is seldom short of sense, to anyone holding a more balanced opinion it is difficult to credit attacks of this kind. But then, I suppose, one must make allowances for the natural chasm fixed between the imperial English and those who thoroughly detested them. Nor is it easy to judge, given the circumstances of his day, if Shaw's words convey more morally earnest contemptuousness, or admiration mixed with envy. For if the latter is the case, a somewhat similar sentiment is readily apparent in the first speech Thucydides assigned to the Corinthians whose notion of the Athenians, as he has represented it, corresponds in almost identical terms to Bonaparte's perception of the English as rendered by Bernard Shaw:

'If they aim at something and do not get it, they think that they have been deprived of what belonged to them already; whereas if their enterprise is successful, they regard that success as nothing compared with what they will do next. Suppose they fail in some undertaking; they make good the loss immediately by setting their hopes in some other direction'.[4]

So much for Greek democracy. The resemblance of these arguments to those developed in *The Man of Destiny* is altogether apparent. But in spite of the alleged shortcomings of both English and Athenians, progress and prosperity do not always proceed from the spirit of democracy alone. Besides, if British imperialism within the context of, on the one hand, its humanitarian ethic, and on the other, its wonderful and much maligned rascality, has rarely failed in its application, neither has it exactly been a break with Classical convention, for the world would look very differently today had it never deviated from the nobler aspects of the human condition. It was Sir Robert Peel, at any rate, who made the interesting admission that 'I am afraid there is some great principle at work wherever civilization comes into contact with barbarism which makes it impossible to apply the rules observed among more advanced nations'.[5] Which, 'in principle', is one aspect of the matter while it would be an ungracious oversight not to mention that Shaw has plenty more to say on the same subject without once erring on the side of magnanimity.

It was, in any case, a condition of his derisive genius that he was at least as unfavourably impressed by the imperial English as was the young law-student Heinrich Heine by the Romans, or more precisely, by the Roman *corpus juris*, 'this Bible of selfishness', as he referred to it in an extremely venomous passage. 'I've always found the Roman code as detestable as the Romans themselves. These robbers want to safeguard their swag, and they seek to protect by law what they have plundered with the sword; hence the robber became a combination of the most odious kind, soldier and lawyer in one. Truly we owe the theory of property, which was formerly a fact only, to the Roman thieves; and the much vaunted Roman Law on which all our present-day legislation and state-institutions are based is nothing but the development of this theory in all its pernicious implications, in spite of the fact that this Law is diametrically opposed to religion, morals, common humanity and reason.'[6]

Having been raised in a country which showed all the evidence of an oppressive judicature but which at the same time widely admired classical learning and Roman virtues, it is obvious that the first impact of Saint-Simonianism and the spread of radical opinion was already strong on the indignant Heine. Nor can one honestly say that his views are an altogether inaccurate reflection of the facts. Nevertheless, the evidence is contentious in both cases. Since it is obvious that both plaintiffs, the Irish Fabian and the francophile Heine, are wholly failing to respond to the larger context, they are wholly misled, it seems to me, by their perhaps understandable failure to appreciate its changing circumstances. For one hardly needs to be reminded that the past and the present can be linked together in an inherently co-operative way. The result, in any case, is the exclusion of all reasonable evidence in favour of a vastly complex and involved ethical, socio-political and historical ideal. And one is glad to know it. For the point, at

92

all events, is not their high-principled passion for the rights of man, but the fact that the rights of man form a fundamental part of the principal humanitarian ethics of the civilized community called the West.

It is not here necessary to discuss the merits of such ethics. But it may be worthwhile to note that they have their roots in a tradition which it is not difficult to trace back to almost three-thousand years of progressive cultural assimilation linking the present with the past in a spiritual unity of history on whose fate also depended the fate of the West. Indeed, the association is suggested quite unmistakably by the words of a freedman in the *Satyricon* of Petronius: 'Thank heaven for slavery', he exclaims, 'it made me what you see me now.' Unlike Shaw and Heine he had no objection to admitting to the roots of his humanity as a triumph of 'civility over barbarity'. From it, at any rate, derives that system of states, society, law, life and letters which, as a triumph of moral principles over political expediency, is the real intellectual inheritance of a once great imperial civilization. And thus – to hand on the torch – we find in them, almost against their will, the highest realization of the 'converted native' and the nearest approximation indeed to the ethos and ethics of which, as much by expediency as by principle, they were so inalienably the product.

When the Marquis of Salisbury, Leader of the Conservatives and, intermittently from 1886 onwards, Victoria's Prime Minister, made the contentious point that his first duty was to his country and only his second to humanity he probably did not expect his audience to see anything amiss in this order of priorities, though he might have been chastened, had he been informed of it, that 'the progress of the human race', as Queen Victoria has observed more generously, 'ought to be the final object of the exertions of each individual'. For my own part, too, I can never persuade myself, either as an individual or as a converted native, of anything more fundamental and all-embracing than the idea, as far as it is feasible and within reach, that the permanent progress of the human race must be secured at once. This is an idea which is no doubt obvious enough. But since, in endeavouring to formulate a moral justification for what may appear to be an admission that principles matter less than destiny, such destiny cannot be considered in national isolation, the logical conclusion is not that the great law of historical evolution outweighs the need for its humanity, but that the rights of humanity come before the rights of men.

Only a democratic purist, I am sure, would object to such a line of reasoning. And if it were not for the fact that too many wrong leaders have been followed, too many *fides* or principles betrayed, it might indeed have been thought that the pivot of history does not turn upon public processes of majority decision-making but upon the effective exercise of responsible authority and independent judgement of action. Nor would one shed tears for the abolition – if necessary by making unpopular decisions – of slavery, or of such gratuitous customs as human sacrifice, suicide by fire, ritual strangulation, infanticide and domestic mutilation, or regret other long-term benefits that have accrued to all – and to the relief of all. Or is it to be supposed that such frequently forgotten aspects of British imperial tradition did not in fact assert greater wisdom or magnanimity but demonstrated yet again the fundamental despotism of the invaders, fundamentally charitable despotism perhaps, but despotism nevertheless?

Though, in the long struggle against Empire, one half recognizes the incongruity of being an indigenous vassal in a land of alien occupation, as far as empires go, the British prototype has been far truer to its humanitarian ideals than either of its French, Spanish, Dutch or Portuguese counterparts. Not being English, some of us are of course incapable of fully appreciating those finer – and 'very advantageous, useful and humane'* – shades of rascality that characterized the true historic manner of the Anglo-Saxon rulers, lords, barons, kings, soldiers, generals and statesmen who have been present at the making of the world's history – so dismaying to progressive posterity – during a thousand years from Alfred to Victoria. But so it has always been. From the first full- bearded rulers of the Iron Age, untiring contenders for power whose law was the command of their chieftain, to Portuguese explorers and Spanish conquistadors who began the real scramble for the world. The limits of their imperial progression were the limits of civilization. There is nothing nostalgic about this. It is as true of the first Elizabethan seafarers whose preoccupation with maritime trade inevitably involved them in territorial expansion as it is true of convinced imperialists like Cecil John Rhodes who firmly believed that he owed his first loyalty to the Empire and whose extraordinary 'racial patriotism' was

* 'We have no right to seize Sind, but we shall do so and a very advantageous, useful and humane piece of rascality it will be.' Sir Charles Napier; Commander of the British forces in India, 1841.

perhaps the most conspicuous part of a pattern which had indeed become self-perpetuating until reason and progress would reach the world's subject populations and strive to justify its presence.

Cecil Rhodes was a thoroughly ambitious man. Perhaps the most complete embodiment of British political mercantilism, nothing was too much for his gargantuan appetite. Alternatively extolled and execrated as the type of unifying champion who was looking towards the ultimate federation of all territories in Southern Africa under the British Crown or very remarkably, for a native policy which was as forbearing and benevolent as its later South African equivalent was not, much has been written both to his discredit and to his undying fame. But nowhere has Rhodes' grandiose dream and personal doctrine of Race and Empire been so clearly and unambiguously revealed as in his 'Confession of Faith' of 1877, which reasserted the historical supremacy of Anglo-Saxons in all matters of British policy, culture and tradition. If nonetheless he declared for a policy of uniting British and Dutch interests as the only enduring basis on which the ideal of a South African Federation could be built, there is ample confirmation that he took more seriously than any British statesman before or since, the necessity of consolidating British civilization and of extending – though under what legal pretexts may have been questionable – the traditions of Anglo-Saxon customs and behaviour, in the contemporary phrase, 'from the Cape to Cairo'.

The white man's invasion of Africa, now advancing to inevitable conflict, was a movement unique in history both for the rascality and, in the culmination of a long process of political development, the political and human benefit of its wider achievements. More immediately, of course, the annexation of as yet unclaimed territories in the interior could not be achieved without necessarily committing the Westminster Government to actually granting a charter for the British South Africa Company, the instrument of Rhodes' great drive across the Limpopo into Mashonaland and through the domain of the Matabele. And this in turn called for a special treaty with their paramount chief Lobengula, still a king to his own subjects but effectively a vassal of the English queen and thus in no position to contest the occupation of the lush Ndebele-Shona country which was not only fertile and promising for European settlement but undeniably a natural and lucrative objective for all entrepreneurial undertakings in pursuit of land and monopoly concessions.

It was not just every combination of craftiness and cunning, more euphemistically termed diplomacy, nor even bribery, threats or the use of brute force which made the notorious Rudd concession, so named after the emissary who concluded the agreement with Lobengula on which the BSA Company Charter was based, so odious. Rather it was the fact that the 'final amalgamation' of all of Lobengula's dominions under the auspices of the new chartered company was something of a put-up job. A sort of Sting one would say in the American phrase – it is hard to refrain from the use of a rakish vocabulary – by which Lobengula had been tricked into a fraudulent concession. It is true, the exclusion of all rival concession-hunters from Matabeleland which Lobengula had stipulated, was provided for by forestalling and precluding any subsequent foreign penetration. But formal acceptance of the treaty also rendered it inevitable that the Matabele kingdom would be absorbed into the British sphere of influence, giving it the character of a political alliance. Obviously, this would give the utmost latitude to British and South-African concessionaires and thereby render the agreement, which was ostensibly intended to relieve the pressures of modern civilization, something of a dead letter.

Never had hospitality in Lobengula's *kraal* been so basely returned. And never again was he to acquire the smallest liking for the British who had treated him like a half-grown boy and whom he had liked well enough until he stumbled on the ways of 'the fathers of liars' who said one thing when they meant quite another. Cheated by a spate of embassies, baffled by swaggering agents, denied justice in his own territory and outmanoeuvred by every refinement of diplomatic cunning, Lobengula was bitterly aware that this development went hand in hand with a fundamental change in the whole social and moral order of African absolutist chieftainship and that the end of his sovereignty, having already been reduced to the level of a local vassalage, was only a matter of time. So much he had reluctantly come to understand.

But that was hardly the end of the matter. While British interests had been eminently served by the Bulawayo connection and the pioneer Boers lived well enough on the labour of the natives, the Matabele themselves were scarcely a reciprocally faithful tribe of fraternally-hearted brothers. The white man no doubt had been guilty of almost every possible form of cruelty and deceit – so for that matter had the African – but to a people inured to mastery, mastery was the accustomed prerogative of the strong-est. One of the major African tribes south of the Zambezi, the great Matabele people, themselves credited with many misdeeds, were no descendants of a submissive race, no chattering riff-raff of uncertain extraction. As a branch of the famous Zulu they were naturally of a rather special kind. Tall, strong, impressive, and brave in the true romantic manner they were powerful masters in their own territory, having been tough and formidable enough to rise to the top in a cut-throat environment. Migrating, some years earlier, from Natal in the south there was no serious opposition to their predatory advance northward beyond the Limpopo and across what was to become Matabeleland proper, to the Zambezi. They subdued the Mashona, Makalaka and Banyai and all the lesser tribes in years of ruthless conquest, thus establishing a military despotism over an empire of slaves who chose vassalage not because of the anthropological tradition associated with it, but because they naturally preferred a manner of submission to com-plete extermination. Accordingly they were subjected to the authority of the tribe, economic exploitation of tribal vassals and retainers being an important part of Ndebele custom.

Here, then, we have the urge to power in its purest form. Nothing can disguise the fact that the men who courted it courted it not for its heroic attributes alone, nor because they were the kind of people who cannot bear to live in peace, but because their concern with war was the instrument of a profoundly solemn interest in the continuation of life itself, in virility and vitality. Their chief occupation centred, naturally enough therefore, on hunting and the neverending skirmishes for which the eligible men were distributed in regimental kraals reminiscent, one might say, of Dorian Greece and Sparta. This, in fact was the legacy of the fearful military system of the Zulus who had evolved the compact and enormously effective semi-circular *umkhumbi* for-mation, the primary striking force which could all but match the strength and cohesion of a Theban phalanx. But even though the Ndebele distinguished themselves by their bravery and as warriors who boldly faced death, that the finest military reputa-tion could be no match for machine-gun fire was demonstrated to appalling effect during the slaughter which we now call the Matabele War and which was out of all proportion to the military objectives at issue.

But Lobengula was not only a king, he was also a statesman

cast in the mould of a warrior whose word was never broken and whose misfortune it was to be matched against two men so intelligent, calculating, powerful and, perhaps, disreputable as Cecil John Rhodes and Leander Starr Jameson who behaved so unbecomingly towards their fatuous host by practising forms of deception which he could not understand. There was no opposition now to the advance of the men who had succeeded by bribery as much as by conquest and whose authority was to run as far north as the earliest tributaries of the Congo River. 'The stronger takes the land', are the words of an African chieftain, and the historical record tends to support him. Though it has in justice to be remembered that Rhodes' first concern was for the ideal of a Federation of Southern Africa as envisaged by Lord Carnarvon* and a great many other kindred spirits, and that there is a redemptive significance in the fact that as one of the leading advocates of Disraeli's federation policy his thoughts and anxieties were primarily for freedom of transit and the establishment of a customs union throughout Southern Africa. And if, on both counts, it was the beginning of a larger political design that provided for the extension of Britain's South African empire northwards to the Zambezi and, a feat never in fact accomplished, for the construction of the Cape to Cairo railroad down the eastern spine of Africa, it was also an issue of sufficient importance to justify his infringement of the sovereignty of a king whose good graces it had been his objective to secure and whose good faith in the event so contrasted his own duplicity.

It was an astonishing performance from the son of an obscure English vicar who had come to Natal at the age of seventeen (on account of ill health), and to whom fate had indeed been kind by offering him the huge financial resources that were to become his hallmark. To be sure, he had not much to show for when he arrived in Kimberley on the back of an ox-cart. The gold was the key to it all. Nor could it have been anything else but Kimberley and the Rand, a source of almost incalculable wealth, which confirmed him in a fate that, prima facie at any rate, could be said to be complete when Lobengula left the stage and the Matabele Kingdom became Rhodesia by proclamation. The fact that Britain, over half a hundred years later, found herself obliged in some embarrassment to dissociate herself from a self-governing

* Colonial Secretary

colony with which she could no longer see eye to eye, does not stand in the way of Cecil Rhodes' reputation as one of the greatest Empire-Builders of his century, and one of the shrewdest politicians to boot.

Such sentiments might well seem indefensible to men of good will who aver and will no doubt continue to aver that he was also one of the most unashamedly opportunistic. That his opprobrious genius was but the catalyst for the disasters that would lead the following century into a remorseless contempt for the patriotic sentiments of empire-builders and imperialists. But if one cannot advocate political change and social renewal without at the same time continuing to defend centuries of cultural and historical 'Hellenization', then I cannot see what, as concerns these changing circumstances, we have gained by all our civilizing. 'All who have taken it upon themselves to rule over others', as Pericles was to bear witness, 'have incurred hatred and unpopularity for a time; but if one has a great aim', he went on to say in a memorable speech,' this burden of envy must be accepted'.[7] Rightly or wrongly, Pericles appears to have understood, as did few of *his* contemporaries, that viewing the future against a millennial background must, in the long run, be the wisest policy. And if Cecil Rhodes' notorious failures, in the short term, to desist from personal ambition and all-out assaults on political propriety, did not suggest Periclean statesmanship, there is, nevertheless, a measure of agreement between a peculiarly upright man of destiny who viewed the extension of empire as Britain's historical duty, a 'new Elizabethan' in the words of a contemporary, and the remarkable Athenian who, however great or humble, has caught the imagination of almost every historian from Thucydides to a latter day.

But one should spare a thought for Lobengula. If he needed proof of the white man's untrustworthiness, it was abundantly given. Having surrendered the freedom of royal autonomy for the enforced liability of being a puppet king, he was but an unwilling tool in the hands of a foreign government. And yet, there remain compensations. I dare say, in retrospect it is almost possible to assume that he might have felt less aggrieved had he been able, as we can see them, to see some of the long-term results of his acquiescence to the concessions, the seed in fact from which with the aid of modern civilization the future nations of Zambia and Zimbabwe have sprung – and poor post-colonial management is no argument against that imperial inheritance. An extremely powerful, black, absolutist ruler, Lobengula was nothing if not a patent tyrant. A tribal wielder of power, he subdued his own as he was subdued by others, tribal despotism having been ousted by the much more cunning despotism of the imperial forces. Stated otherwise, Rhodes' political strategy would have caused him little uneasiness were it not for the fact that the actual course of events irretrievably wrecked his own imperial dreams. The simple truth of the matter is that in the potentially neverending sequence of skirmishes and campaigns that had marked his imperial progress, it would have been astonishing if in such uncompromising circumstances requiring heroic deeds and drastic solutions, Lobengula could have achieved anything worthwhile without some slaying on the way. And instead of rejoicing in the barbaric splendour of his formidable reputation, the only form of immortality known to a *man*, he would have remained a minor chieftain in search of pride and renown. Surely an affliction to cloud the memory of his existence and a calamity as unendurable as it was rare for a king who prided himself on being a warrior.

But now, to crown the affliction of this potentially immortal man, there follows a sequel worthy of our consideration. The sort of afterthought which is in no sense history but rather an irony of fate to be hauled upon the stage and to be gaped at. Or, at any rate, far removed in history from what we have come to expect of our classical heroes: the sort of parallel namely which seems like a return to the Roman provinces of Africa and Asia Minor and, now more of a myth than a memory, to 'the greed of their Proconsuls, the extortion of their tax-collectors and the injustices of their magistrates ...'[8]

Whether or not the moral is valid in precisely those terms of cultural subjection and fiscal exploitation that Rome prescribed for some of her provinces is perhaps debatable. But if Lobengula had contrived to live a little longer he would have caught a glimpse of his old royal kraal at Bulawayo, or *Gubulawayo* – 'the place of the killing' – with Cecil Rhodes, a 'new man', or *homo novus* in the Roman phrase – who had come a long way since his boyhood in Hertfordshire, in odd, if royal usurpation of an imperial province stretching from Bechuanaland to Mozambique and the Zambezi. Undisputed master of his world, Imperial *Proconsul* (real or imagined, a distinction he would have prized), prime minister of the Cape Colony, head of the British South Africa Company, of De Beers and of Consolidated Goldfields,

100

and the most powerful man on the Continent, Cecil Rhodes' natural self-esteem was in no way diminished by the knowledge that he had deposed an insubordinate king, boasted of his killing and, with a fine regard for classical tradition, compelled the sons of his defunct vassal to live with him in honourable captivity at the Cape.

Here, then, compounded with resoluteness, ruthlessness, even a certain nobility and bogus majesty, is the essential, irresistible and incomparable empire-builder of whom such a great deal has come to be written. One might have expected me to produce some sterling Englishman, true bearer of the white man's burden, the pride of a conquering race. I never was fool enough to look for that phenomenon. Since it may mean so many different and conflicting things it is scarcely credible, in appraising a national character, that the virtues which spring from a sense of national destiny should ever found to be absolute. Though it may lack moral perspective, judged by a more overriding interpretation of ethics, there can be no possibility of mistaking the fact that among architects of empire Cecil Rhodes must be acknowledged as one of the greatest, if guilty sometimes of an extraordinary lack of any sense of political probity (as for instance in what could probably be described as 'the swelling act of the imperial theme' [*Macbeth*]: the Jameson Raid and its unfortunate aftermath).

It is sometimes debated whether the Empire-Builder was an immoralist. But this debate gets us nowhere. Nor do I care, quite frankly, to contest the point. Plotter, conniver and taker of other peoples' property he may have been, but he was never mercenary and never a knave. Though it does not necessarily lend strength to his case, in history the parallel is as old as Athens, Rome, or a great many kindred empires whose splendid deference to evolutionary principles rather than the avenging furies of posterity was, in truth, a deference to mankind. And there is consequently a sense in which we may ask ourselves whether the mettle that has always distinguished the strong from the weak, the powerful from the impotent, the great from the small, the lion from the lamb, did not, in bringing law and order to a turbulent majority, also represent reason and progress such as is derived from the assumption of the authority necessary – if not always by right or even with discretion – to harness the immense collective power of humanity as the only truly permanent and cohesive element of its historical life.

I can merely suggest. But whatever may have been said to the

101

contrary, in the context of his time I would recommend the reader to consider whether anyone who ever trespassed on the rights of men has in fact done so with more regard for the rights of humanity than Cecil John Rhodes; for therein, I confess it seems to me, lies the ultimate gist and essential significance of the grand imperial maxim *Civis Britannicus sum.*

PART TWO
THE DECLINE OF THE WEST

In these times, something enormous is dying: a good part of the Western tradition and environment. And something enormous is being born. And there is, paradoxically, in the depths of the various despairs of these times the glimpse of our highest hope.

Micheal Harrington, *The Accidental Century*

The highest must arise to its heights from the deepest.

Nietzsche, *Zarathustra*

6

AGE OF REASON

> We live in the age of the atom, of the atomistic chaos.
>
> Nietzsche, *Thoughts out of Season*

> You will become smaller and smaller, you small people!
> You will crumble away, you comfortable people! You will yet perish – through your many small virtues, through your many small omissions, through your many small submissions!
>
> Nietzsche, *Zarathustra*

It is true, we owe much to the *philosophes,* those social idealists, and predominantly French, scholars and controversialists, whom historians of the Enlightenment have generally agreed to regard as having been singularly influential in shaping the judgement of posterity. Inevitably it seems, and sometimes against their own conscience, for them nothing was harder to accept than the monopoly of the church as the repository of divine revelation; as a powerful dynastic and socio-political institution which made its chief merit consist in seeking to discredit secular scientific instruction and the means for obtaining it. But, living in a revolutionary age, they were as much concerned with questioning established constitutional principles as using to the full whatever influence they possessed to challenge an altogether higher form of creation: the divine nature of kingship; an institution to heed but scarcely to love, and soon to be rendered out of date.

I believe they meant well. Though it must be said, and this may seem a reactionary point of view, that it is precisely because they were highly successful instigators of the Age of Reason and its new intellectual consciousness that one senses that the rationalism of which they conceived, its critical, enlightened, psychologically liberating elements, and the scepticism about the spiritual, the soul, and religion which they generated, were hostile to human nature and, hence, that the conventionally canvassed view that religious obscurantism lost the battle of purpose to rational enlightenment is in open conflict with frequent statements of our own about an increasing dearth of spiritual ideals and a growing plethora of intellectual monotony. Certainly, there is a curious absence today of any expression of faithfulness where faith should be expected and where intellectualism and reason merely disguise a good deal of uncertainty. It is true, moreover, and the point may or may not be significant, that with the decline of apostolic power over the course of the past two centuries or so, a number of new and remarkable passions have surfaced to take the place of the old. In the case of the Romantic movement this was a reaction against reason and the part played by material utilitarianism in early industrial civilization. Today it is an extension of that very general reaction against a profoundly factual and essentially material imagination. Cloaking itself in an ever-increasing number of arcanely derived or esoterically constituted creeds and persuasions it is apprehended with an intensity certainly not secondary to that of the most piercing religious inspiration if implicit, none the less, of prevailing deprivation.

We are at liberty, of course, to see in this only further evidence of the irrationality of the human mind. The truth is, however, that spiritual disillusionment with revealed religion has always and everywhere required such vents. Their exact definition, moreover, is an extremely complex point. Though Carl Gustav Jung could say for example in 1928 that he was not 'thinking merely of the interest taken in psychology as a science, or of the still narrower interest in the psychoanalysis of Freud, but of the widespread and ever-growing interest in all sorts of psychic phenomena, including spiritualism, astrology, Theosophy, parapsychology, and so forth. The world has seen nothing like it since the end of the seventeenth century. We can compare it only to the flowering of Gnostic thought in the first and second centuries after Christ. The spiritual currents of our time have, in fact, a deep affinity with Gnosticism'.[1]

Here then, in an extraordinary responsiveness to the psychic life, we can detect the underlying cause for an essentially irrational religious revival. An increasing number of people, in Jung's own day and since, have attempted to achieve it through the visionary and utopian aspects implicit in a mass of quasireligious movements rather as I have said, than by means of ritual and ceremony or systems of revealed religion. Then again it is well to bear in mind that some of the former simply cannot avoid assimilating some of the ideas of the latter, that fundamental to all of them is an idealized conception of the human soul, a pathetic craving for otherworldly hope. As one contemporary writer, debunking the UFO obsession, has remarked: 'The highly ritualized religions mediated by highly organized priesthoods now seem to be giving way to much more individualistic, idiosyncratic modes of religious life – in which gurus, mystics, prophets, mediums, channellers dowsers, healers, fortune-tellers, self-help psychoanalysts, and similar shamanic figures again play a central role'.[2] But whether, according to this view, they are centred on mysticism, astrology, the paranormal, or the esoteric and occult practices which are themselves a peculiar amalgam of philosophical speculation, transcendental meditation and popular superstition, the fact remains nevertheless that interest in the subject has developed to such an extent that, rightly or wrongly, it has all but compromised the authority and prestige of metaphysics in systems of 'revealed' religion.

Humans have always believed and always will. The mistake to make, therefore, is to suppose that a condition of reasoned and sceptical intellectualism can be anything like an effective substitute for the uncritical and superstitious treatment of intuitively apprehended or spiritually revealed truths. Indeed, to Jean Jacques Rousseau, in many ways the most controversial figure of the Enlightenment, such a state of things left a lot to be desired. He called attention to the fact that reason was opposed to emotion, sensation, feeling and intuition and that the academic climate of the age, in terms of its clericalism and urbanization, of the sciences and the fine arts, in a number of aspects, had made the world a worse rather than a better place to live in.

The importance of such and similar statements first put out in his famous *Discour sur les arts et sciences* was soon to become apparent. It was not so much an argument he felt to be palpably and painfully true as a brilliant outburst against the effect of the progress of civilization on morals and its interference with a natural and inalienable human purpose that supposedly centred elsewhere. And whatever praise the intellectual exchange of the sciences and the progress of scholastic discussion and theological debate may have won, the admirable simplicity with which Rousseau clinches the matter when he brought to the attention of his contemporaries the sum of his convictions can in fact be expressed in no more than six words: 'Almighty God . . . give us back ignorance!'

Though untypical of the Enlightenment, it was a *cri de coeur* that did not lack force. As might be expected, however, Jean Jacques was in the event much more explicit in his vociferous condemnation of modern culture as a disreputable symptom of moral disease which, be it said *tres affectueusement,* sounded at times like the outpourings of a madman. With such unorthodox convictions it was hardly surprising that, in an age of extreme sensitivity to anything that could be considered inimical to it, he should have contrived to give offence and earn himself lasting notoriety throughout the whole of Europe. But, as a man of original views he cared nothing for a reputation that did not bear the mark of unconventionality; and indeed, there was a credit side to it. His ideas did not go unrewarded.

Scarcely influential enough by themselves to be considered in isolation, they yet made a profound impression in educated circles. And not least because they were taken up all at once as part of that cult of the primitive on which they came to depend for their effect on the feelings, emotions and personalities of those inspired by the changing tenor of the times, they stand out as a most poignant example of the art of social innovation, an astounding, totally effective success in philosophical irreverence. Indeed, it is perhaps the greatest part of Rousseau's achievement that he inspirited his fellow men with a new sort of social and political contract, or a new and explicit need to dedicate their 'natural right' to some manner of General Will, for from an historical point of view his revolt against the existing social order unquestionably established the philosophical basis of the Enlightenment as a revolutionary one.

The main thrust of Rousseau's popularity, however, was essentially based upon his championship of the 'natural man'.

Hypothetical and speculative though it was, he had struck a blow against the widely accepted notion, cherished by most representatives of the Enlightenment, that man was essentially a rational being and that his merit consisted in being able to act independently and entirely as his own good sense might see fit. Nor would it have been lost upon the age just how much of an outsider Jean Jacques really was. The *philosophes* and other makers of public opinion, besides being great rivals among themselves, took strong exception to reverting to a primitivism that seemed all his own but little suited to the sustained application of comprehensive scholarship and intellectual principles along progressive lines. They would raise a different cry. And indeed, it is hard to see how the cause of ignorance as something concerning the soul and not the intellect of man, could possibly have aspired to being an issue in the march of knowledge and progressive enlightenment, except perhaps in the sense that it would have contradicted its own most cherished assumptions of the infinite perfectibility of men.

There were, however, other and equally seminal ways in which this era showed its limitations. For in carrying out its initial promise and by openly challenging ingrained constitutional principles and traditionally orthodox methods of religious and political thinking, it would not only prove once and for all that the common people were competent to take part in the wider political processes that forever linked the history of their country with the triumphs and disasters of the French Revolution but, under the extravagant delusion that the worship of reason as an existential ethos can lay claim to its own absolutist values, the Age of Enlightenment grossly overestimated the extent to which men are immune to their own irrational cravings or the ease with which they can repudiate things that matter to the human soul.

Even though it was only towards the close of the nineteenth and with the beginning of the twentieth century that the Enlightenment achieved its real apotheosis in the foundation of analytical psychology and the great deliverance from metaphysical contribution, for an open-minded and systematic inquirer like John Locke, father of the Age of Reason and philosopher *par excellence* of empiricism, it was already beginning to play an important role in the intellectual emancipation from subliminal superstitions. Absurdly, though it seems that the idea of the supernatural cannot be reduced to a mere elucidation of the psychological mechanisms which characterize its psychic life, it may fairly be said that for the great men of epistemological genius, as typified by the rationalistic scepticism of David Hume or the German metaphysician Immanuel Kant, it had all but lost its primacy. Denied by empiricists, devoid of any sense of awe, and operating, henceforth, on fixed measurable principles or synthetic *a priori* judgements, it inevitably declined into a state of analytical petrification.

Thus began almost imperceptively and all but inadvertently, a revocation of its transcendent *pneuma*. The killing of God, as distinct from the degree of emphasis which could be found in the excessive revolutionary changes of the Enlightenment, did not, when one looks back on such an enormous event, evoke any comparable resonance in the secular temper of the age. But other than that it was far less forgiving – in a purely subliminal context – than any of the moral intentions with which men were wont to improve themselves. So far as religion went, it left them with no beliefs. Today religion and psychology are virtually identical. What is more, the entire modern concept of the human psyche both as a theory of the personality and as a phenomenology of the (un)conscious life, can be traced to a theory of knowledge which maintains that metaphysical perplexities can be clarified by the epistemological science of the mind. In short, reason itself has become unreasonable. For the triumphs pure reason brought us are recognizable today in the language of analytical psychology where the remedy may give rise to greater injury than the disease itself, ending in the agony of an anxiety more desperate than the condition it set out to cure. Or, as one may prefer to term it, where the remedy and the disease display the same pathology. An equivalent choice of two evils, strangely enough. Not identical perhaps, but indistinguishable nevertheless and consistent with the complete mutual reciprocity of action and reaction.

Here, then, is a study in Nemesis, the apotheosis of the irrational. Although his case was conceived in a spirit of profoundly scientific inquiry, Freud affords perhaps the most poignant example of what I mean by irrational. If he thought of himself as a 'fisher of men',[3] his teaching, except in a strictly psychoanalytic context, was closer indeed to the great ayatolla's than to the man of science as we ordinarily imagine him. In fact, whereas some years ago it was supposed that in the world of his science the prohibition of the taboo had no application, there was a price to be paid for its transgressions. To be specific: *He has tamed monsters, he has solved riddles; but he should also redeem his monsters and riddles . . .* * Freud failed, as he was bound to fail, because the new ideas had all the defects of the old principles. Indeed, their power has increased because our knowledge of the unconscious has increased. Rationalized and no longer acknowledgeable incubuses have become nightmares. New riddles or neuroses, in other words, are only as real or unreal as the old monsters they have gone on to replace.

It will quickly be realized how closely the psychological effects of this ambivalence bear upon the social structure of the West once it has been understood how completely indeed the ancient contest between the *ego* and the *id* has impinged upon twentieth century intellectual life. Objectivity is the tyranny of facts. It has an unmistakably pathological outlook when confronted with the psychological evidence of its own enlightened transgressions. It is this objectivity, as we shall shortly see, side by side with the forces of reason and enlightenment, which devours its custodians, which is responsible for a clinically unrecognizable syndrome known as sociopathology and the part it plays in modern society. Far from being a vast therapeutic exercise, the worship of reason has indeed contributed to the decisive establishment in the culture of the West of a very close connection between the idea of decadence in the history of the human spirit and the historical decline of an intellectual and cultural elite which is best perhaps defined in the appropriate words of the great German economist Max Weber who once described this class of men as 'Specialists without spirits, (and) sensualists without heart'. And the great irony of what is quite true, and indeed obvious, is that – to formulate it for all concerned – 'this nullity imagines it has reached a level of civilization never before attained'.[4]

This, then, is the problem of the West. It may not be simple, but it is unambiguous: 'Man is on the brink of catastrophe because our age has denied him the capacity for belief in the magical and the wonderful'.[5] This is an obvious enough point. I will emphasize it by saying that the magical and the wonderful are elementary to every true therapy of the soul. By which I do not mean that they belong to an essentially illusory province. On the contrary, I am quoting this – and here I will anticipate – as evidence of the spiritual and philosophical enrichment yet to be attained from it.

*Zarathustra: Of the Sublime Men.

Walter Sullivan, however, makes the definitive comment on this type of attainment: 'The world desperately needs a global adventure to rekindle the flame that burned so intensely during the Renaissance, when new worlds were being discovered on our own planet and in the realms of science'.[6] In short, when Columbus sailed westward across the Atlantic and proved that the world was round; when Vasco da Gama led a Portuguese expedition round the Cape of Good Hope; when Magellan rounded the South American continent through the strait which now justly bears his name. It was highly magical and wonderful stuff. Indeed, one cannot imagine this time without the men most closely associated with the repudiation of the ancient Ptolemaic cosmology, Nicolaus Copernicus and Galileo Galilei – founding fathers, maintained as it usually is, of modern science and astronomy – nor, in its inevitable consequences, forget that renewal and renascence peculiarly expressed themselves in a new age of adventure and the enjoyment of discovery, science and learning.

The past, needless to say, is beyond recall. Yet, all the world, East *and* West, is in need of renewal: politically, socially, economically, in the case of the East; spiritually, above all spiritually, in that of the West. Future progress in theoretical physics, as a distinct branch of philosophy, might well adumbrate the sheer extent of its investigative spirit. The business of the physicist, after all, is to divine the Creator's intention and to interpret that intention, not merely as a means of giving coherent expression to his physical experience, but as a stimulus to his own scientific imagination. He is a maker and solver of riddles. The point has often been made that many people reject scientific values 'because they regard materialism as a sterile and bleak philosophy'. Not everyone may agree with me, then, that the physicist's labour has an accessible metaphysical meaning. But it is curious to note nevertheless that the sudden introduction of a Faustian aspect into the science of physics has impressed itself upon modern man with a far stronger purpose than the type of spiritual life that finds expression in forms of religion essentially concerned with ritual and the careless intonation of prayers. Whatever guesses are made about the nature of the universe or, which is after all the same thing, the universe of nature, the physicist has a lot to explain. But while we may feel that the modern physicist has not given the public the inspiration they need, for him the real problem is to find a language and symbol sufficiently powerful and inspiriting to replace the function of myth in theology.

It has been claimed accurately enough, that we can no more invent a new religion than we can build a tree. And in a sense, of course, it is fortunate that 'religious' proselytizers are unfamiliar figures in the world of the physical sciences. Scientists, it has been said, are distinct from ordinary people by what they do *not* believe in. Instead there is a deliberate matter-of-factness, the disciplined, concise ingenuity which constitutes what is called 'the scientific mind'. But with a hint or two of genius and basing his beliefs not upon faith, but reason and physical fact, the modern physicist nevertheless carries a strong and potent suggestion of what our future spiritual and intellectual development is going to be like: He believes in physical uncertainty but not in immortality. In a universal science that includes all and promises hope for the solution of all, but not in God's own communication. In the thermodynamic arrow of time and the Immutability of the Law – in the words of the Gospel: $E = mc^2$ – but also in a new super-sensibility and its elementary duality of wave and particle theory as two different aspects of the same complementarity. He is pious, touched perhaps even with a deeper motive, but extremely rational and intellectually circumspect. He is thoroughly intro-spective and almost prophetic in spirit, but he leaves nothing to chance. In him the real and the ideal exist side by side.

Before I am through, however, there is at least as much to be said – and it is something well worth saying – for the great Apostolic Age of science which began with the genius of Copernicus, Kepler and Galileo, and culminated in that of Boyle and Newton. Since reckoned legendary and variously represented as intellectual giants or, as in the case of Newton, as a 'demi-god', each was a founding father in his role if not in actual achievement. Their greatness was a product of enormous cognitive powers, not the result of complicated mathematical reasoning, and unless we do call them 'demi-gods' we have no word properly to describe them. But then, ancient religion, too, rested on idols, altars and priests. In fact, it was unthinkable without them. Nor must it be assumed that a great spirit was not also at the centre of such a personality as Nicolaus Copernicus, or that Galilei's genius was not 'in some way or other part of a single, all-embracing psyche, a single "great man", the *homo maximus*,' as the late Professor Jung has suggested, quoting Emanuel Swedenborg. Insight and intuition, finally were the outstanding characteristics of Albert

Einstein, whose theory of relativity marked another important change in the scientific practice of physical introspection, for it was in his period that an altogether new kind of rationalism was born.

Here, at any rate, was the real apostolic spirit in its new genius-begetting dispensation. On the whole, however, comparative proofs of the *homo maximus* have ceased to be conspicuous. A hundred and fifty years ago Thomas Carlyle could still conceive of the genius as a hero who provided visionary inspiration rather than advice or simply information. By contrast, the contemporary type of genius comes down unambiguously for the direct expression of material facts rather than speculative knowledge. That a century or two ago it was still conceivable for an educated individual to have a comprehensive grasp of almost the whole of human knowledge does not bear on the point of the comparison. Over the past few generations, it is clear, a considerable enlargement of the educated public has made it much more difficult for a comparatively great or deserving individual to present such an outstanding profile. In fact, by the early 1920s already it seems to have been apparent that, in Lord Haldane's rendering of the same idea, 'there is an absence of conspicuously outstanding prophets'. The facts rather tended to confirm, as he said, that 'the taught are not separated from their teachers by the wide intervals of the days that once were'. (*The Reign of Relativity.*) The Cambridge physicist Stephen Hawking, in 1988, said much the same thing: 'Seventy years ago few people understood the general theory of relativity, nowadays tens of thousands of university graduates do, and many millions of people are at least familiar with the idea'.

Few thinkers today are prepared to gainsay the necessity for adapting to the intellectual requirements of our time, and if there were a would-be apostle, it is all he could do to keep up with the rapid advance of scientific knowledge. Already 'in the nineteenth and twentieth centuries,' as Professor Hawking remarks, 'science became too technical and mathematical for the philosopher, or anyone else except a few specialists. Philosophers reduced the scope of their enquiries so much that Wittgenstein, the most famous philosopher of this century, said, "The sole remaining task for philosophy is the analysis of language." Linguistic philosophy, of course, is no guide to greatness. 'What a comedown,' Hawking exclaims, 'from the great tradition of philosophy from Aristotle to Kant!'[7]

Wittgenstein's metaphysical concept of the world as portrayed in *Tractatus*, which first appeared in English in 1922, consisted of elementary or 'atomic facts'. Here the logical outlook on positivist philosophy, besides being very perplexing, received its most crippling representation. Few would wish to read it a second time. Indeed, it is hardly necessary to do more than glance at his 'logical atomism' in order to realize that contemporary society is not kept in movement by the visionary mentors or moral supermen of old but, as the astute Max Weber has already reminded us, by 'Specialists without spirit, and sensualists without heart'. By the men of the moment, to be perfectly accurate, rather than by so-called men of destiny or, indeed, the great guiding spirits of the old idealist philosophy which had produced such momentous achievements.

Today these spirits have departed, banished by objectivity and the primacy of material facts. In a number of ways the victory of reason and enlightenment is evidently complete. Nor does it speak well for the twentieth century that the soul and spirit of the age itself lacks the very elements that make for greatness, that the discourse proceeds as an antithetical conflict between atomic facts and spiritual values, or that the atomistic age is kept small by the levelling process of a limitless dialecticism and alive by a widespread mood of perennial scepticism. 'We live in the age of the atom', Nietzsche said scornfully, 'only in that, in the small thing, is integrity still possible'. And this is obvious to anyone who looks at it in isolation. The range of vision is very much smaller. But it is also of considerably greater penetration, disclosing, at its farthest recession, a universe constituted not of massive proportions and vast dimensions but of negative magnitudes, of diversity and complexity. A universe which is functional rather than real, the world of minute scales, of the micro-cosmos in which everything is balanced by its opposite, is held together by tension rather than harmony.

More than a century ago. Nietzsche already distinguished 'complete realists' as men 'without belief or superstition', or 'walking refutations of belief itself', as he called them when he was not dismissing them as *'Unworthy of belief'*. Add to this the burden of initiating the truth according to exactly predictable causes, and in order perhaps to fathom the nature of the universe, no one proclaims the dignity of the intellect more skilfully than they do, even though as an aspect of modern philosophy and the duties it prescribes, it has the wrong sort of stimulating effect upon a society sold on the view that matters of metaphysical supposition demand supernatural causes and bound, therefore, to distrust the type of genius the arid intellectual represents.

Needless to say, true genius is in no need of trained experts with a prescriptive right to split the difference between the world of faith and physical facts. Nor, where the imagination is concerned, is there room for a categorical authority engaged in imposing a certain discipline of rationalization upon those who seek satisfaction in elementary needs rather than in the physical language of symbol and number. They do not like science to be exacting and difficult, and to deny them a more inspiring and convincing experience is to deny them a part of their humanity. For whatever form the inspired genius of indeterminism will take, it will be a form of the supernatural. It is, for this reason, all the more essential for anyone involved with the philosophical consequences of the natural sciences to exercise a measure of forbearance toward the extra-academic public and to give them the vision they need. For the outstanding individual, too, or stated in Nietzschean terms, the *superior man,* like the cock on top of the belfry, most benefits the people among whom he has risen – rather like Carlyle's hero as king, prophet, poet, priest, or man of letters – because he embodies a moment of vision.

As delivered here this may sound flamboyant. But there is nothing flamboyant, in the context of the narrowness and aridity of the modern mind, about an assertion of something deeper and more universal than academic intellectualism, even if it is contained in allegory. As Hemingway so succinctly said, 'the dignity of movement of an iceberg is due to only one-eighth of it being above water'. To assert human greatness in this way is enterprising perhaps, but if it is proper to speak of moral power as being endorsed by personal composure or dignity of tone and movement, the slide into vociferousness certainly speaks of the loss of profundity and detachment. On a more prosaic note we may perhaps conclude that it is because Thomas Carlyle himself appears to us as one of those isolated, larger-than-life figures, that not only his heroes seem as though they were hewn out of a mountain but that their closest epigones and other arbiters of Western spirituality, appear as figures of lesser stature, uninspired by the same heroic omniscience.

Somehow they give the impression of men out of their depth in the translucent geometry of today's intelligible infinite. In the most stupefying juxtaposition of ideological, social, political, economical, ethical, moral, psychological and theological angles of all time. In the pursuit of more objectives, the application of more theorems, the elucidation of more laws, the expansion of more frontiers and the expression of more criticisms than ever before. Indeed of criticisms as the dominant source of new ideas, especially the political, radical and polemical ideas since poured out by each upon the other as part of this disintegrating dialecticism that, in view of so much disaffection – with every intelligent man a prodigy in every subject save his own – it is almost possible to believe that some of these agents of our deliverance might have mistaken a state of intellectual confusion and philosophical decline for the ideal society of the future. Might have, I am tempted to say, led us from a noble conception of the infinite perfectibility of men to the disturbing presence of an exasperating universal antagonism between them.

'Everything cackles', according to Nietzsche's caustic elucidation of a similar thought, 'but who still wants to sit quietly upon the nest and hatch eggs?' Very few nowadays! 'Neither is a writer improved by sitting on committees and cultivating the chairmanities', as Cyril Connolly was quick to point out.[8] It is possible that this is indeed the age of the atomistic chaos, of Einstein's 'puny demigods on stilts', politically correct little creeps and irate commissions of inquiry. But even when looking at things in a matter of fact way, it is not difficult to see that without a new and enlarged vision of the world, a new and unifying purpose to give the world something to believe in – and a *transvalued* view of the future seems to have been on Nietzsche's mind – today's intellectual prodigy, rising to no great heights on fluttering wings, is more of a cockerel in a farmyard than a cock on top of the belfry. In a farmyard, I should add, skipping through a more or less reliable paraphrase, rent with the cackling of geese, the bleating of sheep, the braying of asses, and trampled on by herds of swine.

7

GREEKS AND TROJANS

> You should spare yourselves, O my friends, for a
> worthier enemy: Therefore you must pass many
> things by.
>
> Nietzsche, *Zarathustra*
>
> O my Will! My essential, *my* necessity, dispeller
> of need! Preserve me from all petty victories!
>
> Nietzsche, *Zarathustra*

'The animal', in Nietzsche's own emphasis, 'lives unhistorically;
. . . it does not know how to dissimulate, it can therefore never be
anything but honest'.* From which we are at liberty to understand
that the dividing line we draw between the highest and lower
types of animals is one of intellectual distinction as well as of
moral constraint. The animal, as Nietzsche sees it, is honest, or
essentially so, not because it is morally superior but because it is
an animal. Man, being a fundamentally rational creature is prefer-
ably honest without being essentially so. He differs from all the
other animals in that he can compromise. Which is to say, he can
consciously draw inferences not only from rational, but even from
irrational or emotional premises, whether moral, spiritual, doctrinal or otherwise. And that, in essence, has been the genesis of dissimulation. Dissimulation requires evidence and argumentation.

---

* *On the Uses and Disadvantages of History for Life.*

118

A peculiarly human concept, it bears no sign of a struggle even though it is clear enough that the behaviour of the human animal, when examined in its entirety, is determined as much by strongly personal attitudes as by the clear and rigorous logic of rational or permanent principles.

We may see the manifestation of dissimulation for instance in the care we take for the promotion of a public persona. Public careers, above all, show the extent to which dissimulation plays a part in the promotion of a personal reputation. It is in any case a fact, and in many ways an obvious fact, that it operates in the fields of political diplomacy, religious worship, ideological doctrines, social ethics, human morals, and other such spheres of potential deception. For in distinguishing between what historians are wont to call 'primary' and 'proximate', it has been, I rather incline to think, one of the most widely diffused or proximate causes of human conflict.

'Glory is my object and that alone,' Nelson wrote to his wife Fanny, and according to this philosophy warfare is a normal and inevitable consequence of the pursuit of honour and glory, of a thirst for fame, the desire for rich spoils, for military distinction and, above all, for an honourable place in history. On the surface, to be sure, so much at least is arguable. Indeed, for those who love the eventful in history it may seem difficult to imagine that the pursuit of honour and glory does not also and inevitably attend every single moment of high historical drama. But though Nelson and Fanny might talk of fame, surely there is a lot of furious hate and merciless brutality in the history of human belligerence. First of all, it is plain enough that nowadays warfare has become a science, in everything but fundamentals a sophisticated and tactical game. Then, one could make a very tolerable case for saying that among the proximate causes of war, above all, the mutual dislike of one man, race, nation, people, creed, or ideology for another, is incomparably the most predisposing, and hence, that the origins of enmity are to be sought less perhaps in any traditional consideration of human belligerency than in the considered study of human psychology and opposite psychological types. Types – and I am not necessarily thinking of either Stalin, Hitler or Mussolini, to mention some obvious names – who know how to dissemble history by dissimulating the real nature and principles of political power.

The object here is not, of course, a learned critique of the uses and misuses of history; but in distinguishing what is relevant to history and what to psychology, historical enquiry is often relevant only insofar as it contributes to a better understanding of the historical problems posed by the nature and psychology of men. And since history is not an exact science, susceptible of clear and objective categorization but, as someone else has said, 'a more or less fallible means', it may perhaps be questioned whether historical detail is capable of encompassing, much less mastering its own representation of events without applying psychology to its uses as well as presenting a picture of the actual historical events. Above all, it must be said that historiographical detail is not a mere factual reference; it has its own intuitive life, insights, standards and values, and it is more than likely that it is from these that we get our chief evidence and enjoyment of historiographical genius.

Be that as it may. Sir Laurens van der Post once made a thoughtful point of this particular matter by dividing all men, with the exception perhaps of the unclassifiable few, as he put it, into 'Greeks' and 'Trojans', or opposite psychological types and, by extension, into the differences of character and personality which distinguish them. In fact, we are not too far off if we couple this with a reference to the myth of Troy as a symbol of their mutual alienation. For by splitting their differences into the two main headings of Greeks and Trojans we may, for one thing, infer that it corresponds to the deeper distinction between different psychological attitudes, and for another, perhaps even offer a credible explanation for the universal irrational dichotomy of the instinctual historical life. We can recognize it in the case of the Greeks as some sort of inner urge towards destruction and, if we think about it, in the case of the Trojans as a longing to preserve, to safeguard, or more especially to defend. Perhaps, since it is Sir Laurens' own expression, the latter term is preferable; nor does it invalidate the Homeric example.

From what has come down to us about the Trojan War in Homer's *Iliad*, we can readily sense the intensely personal nature of Mycenean politics in the Heroic Age which carried the force of this argument to the destruction of Ilium, the city which had been raised by the Greeks. The mythical conflict between Trojans and the mainland Greek coalition with its hero mythology and its allegorical features is an instructive episode and remains a classic representation of the perennial antagonisms in which human personalities rather than political conflicts play determining parts. And if it has a large psychological element and sometimes seems to resemble the epic conflict between such old absolutes as the eternal revolutionary and the defender of tradition, between progressives and unprogressives in short, the issue has remained essentially as it has been for the past three thousand years.

To be perfectly honest, if more *casi belli* were needed, there have been as many such clashes of different psychological attitudes as there have been different eras or epochs in the history which followed upon the Heroic Age and helped to sharpen the polemical differences between such arbiters of good and evil as Hellenes and Orientals, Romans and Carthaginians, *optimates* and *populares*, patricians and plebeians, Cavaliers and Round-heads, Anglicans and Puritans, *Girondins* and *Montagnards*, Tories and Whigs, Republicans and Democrats, hawks and doves, reactionaries and radicals, and so on and so forth, who have never ceased for one moment to excommunicate one another as ardently as they might the Original Sin. One of the first effects this had on the *status quo ante,* it may be remembered, was that Adam agreed to its preservation and Eve to its violation. Together they agreed in the matter of dissimulation and, having succeeded in deceiving each other, the world was condemned on moral grounds.

Still, one must not lose faith. This crisis of virtues had a significance which has also been expressing itself in the protracted spiritual transition by which the great sedentary world of classical civilization transfigured itself into that of our Christian era and, in consequence, came to a most important parting of the ways. Whether one can distinguish what is in reality of course only another aspect of the perennial conflict between different types of civilization, as another instance of the struggle between Greeks and Trojans, is perhaps reading too much into the hypothetical case above. Of one thing we can be certain though, that there is no denying whether we divide men psychologically or ethically, racially or politically, into vehicles of ambition or repositories of benevolence, into male or female, black or white, vertically, horizontally or diagonally they still show the same dichotomy: the everlasting struggle between the immovable object and the irresistible force, which is as old as the world itself and as inevitable as the rivalry between East and West, however trivially motivated or carried on for whatever purpose.

Why? That is unanswerable! What is certain is that ultimately the half-mythical half historical conflict of Greek versus Trojan may be summed up in the everlasting struggle between conflicting ideals of good and evil which, in their many circumscribed and contradictory forms, may be justifiably, and historically, described as 'dialectical opposites', thus further demonstrating that they are not two fundamentally different things but two distinct and mutually antagonistic conceptions of the very same thinking. Nor indeed is this a characteristic confined to post-Socratic Greece or, indeed, to Socrates. This controversial gentleman, for example, has had an enormous and, as a number of critics have noted, not always beneficial influence upon the history of the dialogue between individuals, indicating perhaps most of all the limited conclusions one may draw from a method of dialectical enquiry which can easily lead to logical absurdities.

When first the Sage appeared on the Attic stage he was not, we may assume, a man much given to consorting with Xanthippe. But his curiosity was inexhaustible. He not only discussed the mysteries of the Delphic Oracle and the wonders of antiquity, but also devoted considerable efforts to devising a method of scrutiny which would determine and explain the basis of reality and truth. A complex and somewhat factious man he seems to have found it difficult to contemplate truths which conflicted with his own petulant inclinations, for Socrates never gave a straight answer in his life. Electing instead to profess either complete ignorance or to answer a question by indirect argumentation, a learned and close encounter with him could always lead to painful humiliation. He developed an affinity, a liking for polemics, albeit, as readers of Plato will remember, that apart from incurring official displeasure, Socrates on the whole got along famously with all those with whom he conferred, which is rather more than can be said for today's political dialecticians who are rarely on the same excellent speaking terms and never, to be sure, with such scholarly erudition.

If Socrates, then, was a far better dialectician it should not be inferred that a liking for polemics is a very certain measure of a person's intellect. Nor, in other respects, should it be the chief purpose of those who speak and vote on matters of public policy, to develop a facility for the *reductio ad absurdum* as a method for political controversy. It is agreed, moreover, that Socrates' purpose, having for its aim not victory but the discovery of truth (and some ambiguity about his obstinate spirit is no doubt explained by the protean quality of truth), was not simply dialectical. Alas, however objective and sincere he tried to be, the method he employed could be used to prove or disprove almost anything. And in spite of his enlightened intellectual purpose, his capacity for lucid distinction, his determination to remain a rationalist, and his desire to improve men's moral outlook, few will deny the fact that he had wit, but neither discretion nor delicacy. He was, to do him justice, one of the most contentious men who ever lived.

Argumentation has never changed human nature, nor its irrational needs. Men have continued to retain their essential characteristics, on the surface and in their depths, in their strengths as in their weaknesses, and in politics as in social life. The conclusion therefore is obvious. Human perfectibility is a claim which cannot be compounded for facts. It is a fairly modern, artificially contrived and somewhat hopeful creation of educated nineteenth-century minds. Perhaps one might even go further and, precisely for the reasons just given, say that no truly wise and virtuous man (to say nothing of educated men in positions of responsibility and political power) whose sympathies are truly on the side of humanity and decency would ever wish to achieve such wisdom and virtue at the expense of his own humility.

In the case of the British House, some call it the Mother, of Parliaments, what we do know is that according to a certain parliamentary patter all insults are titulary directed towards the Speaker and, down to the final affront, meticulously submitted to the considered judgement of the House. Everything is open and above board. Having mastered the method of the Greek dialecticians, Right Honourable and Honourable Members appear to be perfectly at ease as they bully one another in the name of the one debating society in Britain whose *dissimulations* can be heard and seen by all. An attitude which is as well expressed in the paraphrased words of George Eliot that 'persecution may become sweet to a man when he has christened it opposition'. Nor is it difficult to guess at the prospect of parliamentary deliberation as a constitutional convenience while vulgarity of this kind prevails. For it can hardly be an accident that a morally earnest concern should take the form of abuse. But the really significant fact, if my Learned Friends will permit me to say so, about these ill-tempered parliamentary wrangles – and inasmuch as this is the substance of my argument – is that they are the starting point for a much more complex political debate.

123

The first thing to realize is that with the intellectualization of its historical sense, Western statesmanship has lost much of its idealism, vision and purpose. Indeed, the more one reflects upon this vision as a culminating triumph of the evolutionary spirit, the more demeaning appears its forfeiture. Nor is it difficult to believe that with the triumphs, the stirs and carousals of Western imperial expansion long having passed on their way, with the colonial idea proscribed in every continent and social exploitation all but extinct, with a uniform record of economic success in most parts of the Western world, with more practical wisdom, political sense and intellectual perspicacity than ever before, and ever higher degrees of statesmanship the earnest concern of diplomacy, men's treatment of history differs fundamentally from that of generations nourished on tougher and more heroic values.

The conviction that some final unknown purpose is inherent in men might be difficult to prove at the strictly sociological level, but it presents no obstacle for the individual who is disposed to plead for its philosophical extension and who may well deplore the uniformity of history, the intellectual confusion of man and the monotony of his institutions; the false idols of automation and material progress which give no indication of the depth of an earlier approach to history but which help to maintain the illusion that modern civilization is superior to the vast historical arenas where it once achieved greatness. Under such circumstances all heroic perspective is lost. Perhaps we might even find that the political, social, psychological, military, constitutional and diplomatic evolution of the modern nation state has altogether been dissociating itself from the grasp of heroic causation to which it owes so much and that the purest form of heroism – according to the wars of the market-place – now consists in the determined pursuit of wealth, in a desire to compete, in being able to equate a persistent and ruthless lust for enterprise (a bastard form no less of the pursuit of honour and glory) in terms of mere profit or loss.

Embodying all that which is most mercenary and the least idealistic we find that the increase of personal wealth and the accumulation of private property – the economic motives, nevertheless, for three generations of (Greek, Roman and Anglo-Saxon) colonization – is of the greatest psychological significance today in replacing a truly active and 'historically dynamic' existence based upon the concept of power. Material influence and financial might is the manifesto of a new 'heroic age', the surrogate to the unconscious day-dreams of the original power drive. But next to those qualified for the extremes of fortune, the heroes, warriors and merchant-adventurers of the modern world, are those who are not. Starting at the lowest level there is the vast amorphous mass of the people for whom it is easier to lose than to win. For side by side with the tough commercial operator capable of great entrepreneurial deeds, lives the labourer, unskilled and bearing the stigma of his class; the worker, or employee as he should be called, possessing neither genius nor valour; and, indeed, the chronically unemployed for whom the state is the only paymaster, wasting his substance on days passed in sleep. In truth, the latter activity brings out the achievements of an ideal society as well as the difficulty of coming to grips with the realities of its social institutions, millennial as they may be. For if, in the name of humanity, it is to mark the end of all prospective utopias, final purposes, and higher values, in the name of the future it is but a danger to its possessors.

Obviously, one can always make some sort of distinction between personal corruption and collective degeneration but – because it conveys to us not a sense of social decline but of social anxiety – only in the West does one find an enlarged urban class powerless to make use of their higher civilization. Often leading futile and ineffectual lives they all have the misfortune of living in a millennium which can be defined neither as historical nor heroic but as 'post-historical' or 'post-modern' at best, and therefore as evolutionary meaningless and ultimately barren. The price of social perfection is the emasculation of the individual by the state. In no other system has communal interest trespassed so forcibly on the personal rights of the individual and nowhere, before or since, has conformity of individual expression been taken so far. Nor, thus compromised, could it be more stultifying for those inclined to independent views, for the young and the hopeful with a need to project themselves. Rocking the boat thus becomes a compulsion. And here in fact is a formula according to which a youthful sense of mischief soon resolves itself into disruptive social behaviour and, even more appropriate, criminal delinquency. Appropriate, because in part such a development is the outcome of the informal evolution of the heroic as a sub-cultural force and – this is immensely important – less and less as a professed or openly aspired to ideal.

No doubt there are individual exceptions, but there is no heroic idea with a universal appeal to the hearts and minds of millions which can offer hope of new life to a cataleptic society. To be perfectly frank, there are ample indications that, though standing highest among all the theories of human government ever devised and attaining to standards of democratic freedom, political wisdom and social security previously unattainable, the twentieth-century socio-democratic welfare-state yet plumbs new depths in its debilitating sense of social futility. In no sense creative, it has lost its vision as a result and therefore knows nothing of destiny. It is a dangerous loss, moreover, but it is by no means exclusive to our own time. It is endemic to the history of civilization and just another example of 'death following life, rigidity following expansion, intellectual age and stone-built, petrifying world-city following mother-earth and the spiritual childhood'.[1]

Oswald Spengler's morphological annotations concerning the inevitable destiny of Roman culture and civilization which did not, in his own italics, '*precede* but *closed* a great development', were prophetic rather than retrospective. Of course, it is easy enough to say that there are exceptions to all those rules and guidelines concerning history's cycle, that a new genius finds purpose as a new destiny develops. But even with that tacit reservation there is no reason to suspect the precedent given. Nor does it lack point. The acute sense of moral disorientation, the lost sense of direction, the enjoyment of leisure or even vice are re-interpreted and speak in the deliberately cultivated images of our own time. In the Roman context, as matters turned out, maturity, decline and fall, inevitably followed the first vigorous resumption of the Hellenic legacy. For it was not just their peers, if indeed such ever existed, not just the Gauls, the Carthaginians or the Parthians who showed no inclination to come to heel, but the waves of barbarians from beyond the Danube and the Rhine which carried all before them; the vast host of Vandals, Suebi, and the Alans who fell foul, like the Germans and the Visigoths, of Roman imperial rule. Intolerant of any constraint they refused to subscribe to the *pax romana* which had rarely been free from their attentions, preferring instead the ravages and spoils of war as they delivered the *coup de grace* to Roman imperial greatness. It did not, in the event, significantly detain them.

Rome itself, to judge from Tacitus' comments on the greatness of the old Republic and from the deterioration under the post-Augustan empire, was by no means unaware of the dangers

126

constituted by the debasement of old Roman virtues and the loss of its former heroic qualities. The plebs had degenerated into riff-raff with a craving for mass-amusement. And the nobility of the patriciate? Once so unmistakably portrayed in triumphal statues, arches, fountains and the great *thermae* of imperial times, in the splendour of fora, temples and porticoes, in the solemn monumentality of the colossal mansions and in the magnificent settings of the great terraced and sun-swept gardens of the aristocracy, now it no longer seems to have been reflected in the conduct of those who dwelt in them. It had given way to the more corrupting tastes for prodigality and debauch, to a hankering after lascivious spectacles and ostentatious banquets. And if the moral decline under the Julio-Claudian emperors, the dissolution under Rome's principal dynasty is, literally, a classical study in deterioration, Tacitus, sensing the causes before the effects, gave it as his opinion that the plainer virtues – the regard for religious sanctity, for heroism and austerity, for the sacredness of chastity – peculiar to the barbarian tribes contrasted but favourably with the vitiating urbanity of Roman civilization since the end of the Republic.

Writing history introspectively, and reading it partly with a view to parallel cyclical situations, Edward Gibbon, himself one of the last great Augustans and, stylistically no less than didactively, a writer much like Tacitus in respect to the eloquence and substance of his monumental bequest, once expressed the point of view that, in so many words, 'The savage nations of the globe are the common enemies of civilized society'. Then, in the context of a highly interesting addendum to Chapter 38 of his *Decline and Fall of the Roman Empire*, he went on to enquire more specifically or, as he put it, 'with anxious curiosity, whether Europe is still threatened with a repetition of those calamities which formerly oppressed the arms and institutions of Rome'.[2]

To discuss the latter point first, the matter Gibbon raises in the tract entitled 'General Observations on the Fall of the Roman Empire in the West', can be summarily translated into modern demographic terms. In fact, it is difficult not to endorse his 'anxious' anticipation, because the great tide of alien immigration from Africa, the Middle East and the formerly Communist East may well held to be the symbol *par excellence,* when used in that potential sense, of 'those calamities which formerly oppressed the arms and institutions of Rome' – and in the case of Rome – purely as an ethnological consequence of Roman imperial over-expansion. The former assertion, however, that the savage nations are the common enemies of civilized society, is no longer addressing the educated public when under the rubric of 'enemies of society' one would expect to be told of the corrupting processes of large-scale social demoralization, such as high criminal delinquency, endemic structural unemployment and the ongoing collapse of traditional moral values, rather than of barbarian invasions or post-colonial military incursions. None the less, it is here that certain distinctions should be made and demographic conditions brought into the discussion. For whatever the issue of a potential cultural collapse as one of the fundamental symptoms of the decline and fall of the Roman Empire, as an issue of current controversy one may easily ascertain that its 'decline', in the particular case of the modern West, is not so much cultural as it is in the nature of a significant and inescapable demographic development.

The first fruit of this has been a story of alienation of identities. The rise, particularly in countries like England and France, of the most intransigent of ethnic minorities as organized centres of disaffection; as the most assertive of political pressure-groups, extraordinarily overwrought and constantly at odds with Western European cultural, constitutional and educational practices. Of course, matters are not improved by the fact that overwhelmingly the greatest single motivational drive behind a flood of refugees who exploit asylum as a means of immigration, is that towards economic sanitation or, for one good reason or another, towards public assistance of various kinds. Nor, in considering the relation of one culture to another, can one avoid value judgements, relative though they are. Standards are formed in comparison, and if sometimes we speak of one culture assimilating the values of another, strictly speaking this should mean that new ethical values and associations are able to emerge. That, it seems to me, is the sum and substance of social integration. Yet, no sooner is this said than elements of what seems to be, and often is, an outright refusal to take the final step in the process of social amalgamation, are being alienated into the objects of a fundamentalist doctrine which instead professes isolationism and a total rejection of Western indigenous values.

These observations, incidentally, are equally applicable to most parts of the Western world. But although Germany, which long boasted some of the most liberal and generous asylum laws in the whole of Europe, has received more than half of the total number of migrants who have entered the EC in the 1990s, no part of the entire migration to the West, to the European West at all events, has been so symptomatic of the general ethnographic diversity than that across 'England's green and pleasant Land' – the first such country to be flooded – with its new blend of Indian, African, Afro-Caribbean, Muslim and European cultures, necessarily vitiating much of its oldness and conventionalism and constituting a threat not only to its traditions, customs and manners but, paradoxically, to its very spirit of freedom and toleration and, hence, to the essential Englishness of the British Nation herself.

We may compare this if we wish with those calamities which had behind them the history of the foreign invasion of Rome, but perspectives are still in a flux and not conducive perhaps as yet to a clear enough recognition of the necessary cause and effect relationship that extends from the British Empire down to some of the most recent events which now occur in the Western world. But the relationship is doubly significant nevertheless. For rarely in the history of conquests can a surreptitious invasion have been more potentially threatening than that which was able to reach Anglo-Saxon genius and, we can scarcely doubt, part of the essential repertoire of Western cultural thinking, at its base in the sheltered English countryside. And it is with this in mind that we can the better understand the peculiar social significance of Juvenal's vitriolic protestations that 'the rivers of Asia had flowed into the Tiber.'[3] He understood well enough that the massive influx of foreign races and alien customs into Rome, and the confluence of immense numbers of eastern slaves with the unemployed Italian proletariat was bound to be in conflict with the needs of what may best perhaps be described as a predominantly mercantile and agricultural society. And on what hindsight there is it seems that we are in an even better position than the Roman satirist to understand how the discomfited and defeated were able to reconquer the empire and discomfit and defeat it in their turn without the whole mighty system of Roman fortifications being once fairly brought to the test.

The most extreme comment on this type of development is by Johann Gottfried von Herder. 'Thus Rome was punished by Rome: the oppressor of the World became the most abject servant of the most infamous slaves'.[4] In quoting this it is worth remembering, however, that Herder was formulating what was the essence of an historical theory, a point of view which had long since become common historic convention. The conquered, said Horace, led captive the conquerors. On the one level it was the contemporary analogy of the historical problem which Gibbon defined in the chapter on the collapse of Roman authority in the West, on the other it is something that cannot have been foreseen by a writer who was striving to understand and express his own eighteenth-century racial and demographic prejudices. But assuming for a moment that the eighteenth-century historian were to put his fundamental political beliefs into a twentieth century formula it would not be very surprising if it went something like this:

The West has sustained a steep decline from the heroic age of discovery. Its genius has departed. The decline has been the decline into egalitarianism, into everything that can be epitomized in the term *democratic equity*, its one distinctive quality. Nor is it possible to give guidance on the renaissance that one might expect, except perhaps that such a renaissance would be most likely to follow a period of universal confrontation. For understandably, though one does not stress the point, decline and rebirth involves the entire history of anthropology; the demographic balance of power as an activating cause for the racial conflicts of ideology and political wars of aggression which go back to Thucydides, Herodotus and the beginning of history. It may take many forms. Today it is determined by an ideological conflict of personalities between statesmen, diplomats, administrators, intellectuals, poets, priests and mullahs as much as by national differences and anthropologically recriminative characteristics, both ethnic and racial, and vicariously adapted to a fundamentalistically sanctioned confrontation. It is the confrontation between North and South.

Within that confrontation, whether of ancient origin or of comparatively recent development, the real crisis is not only demographic, brought on so to speak by the human creature's own progenitive excess, but one of the 'cosmopolitan' versus the 'fundamentalist' tradition and, whether ethnic, racial or ideological, of the conflicting elements of both. The most telling development that is relevant here is the newly concordant superpower relationship which almost seems to have shifted the world's axis of potential discord from a division of the world between East and West on geographical lines to poles whose opposite boundaries

130

cannot be determined any more geographically than some primitive distinction between North and South marking customs and patterns of racial or ethnological behaviour. Ideology has consequently ceased to be analysable in terms of political geography and the diplomatic and military relationship between constitutional nation states and become much more uncertain of identification.

If all this seems speculative to the sceptic and recriminative to the 'alien', as some readers may well object, the fundamental argument that is here being made is that the process of amalgamation and syncretization of alien cultures or, if one wishes to be unkind, the invasion of the 'barbarians' as agents of renewal – that combination of racial, social and cultural alienation namely, by which modern civilization appears to have been split ethnologically down the middle – has given a new face to Western civilization. This would seem to be an extreme statement of the gravity of the problem of alien immigration as an instrument of Western cultural penetration and in profound contradiction, moreover, to the fundamental doctrine of a moral and humanitarian obligation which lies at the root of the highest and truest function of Western democracy today. Yet, one may reasonably be permitted to ask whether the encounter with the 'savage nations' or – on more recent evidence – an increasingly self-assertive and (at its most extreme) rebellious sense of ethnic hubris, in coming to grips with its alienation from almost every vital aspect of the indigenous cultural life, can altogether be kept separate from the varied and violent effects which the new, tumultuous forces of nationalism have had upon the letter and the spirit of such a moral and humanitarian obligation?

In the event, then, this obligation seems to have led to an intense refurbishment of fascist movements in countries such as Germany, France, and Italy etc.; to a newly renascent nationalism which, in both tone and content, has retained its former fanaticism as well as its grievances and objectives. And so it is that, approaching the problem, as it were, from opposite poles, there seem to be two alternatives here. It is possible, in other words, to look at the matter in either of two ways: *in extremis*, as a descent towards a new barbarism whose search for fundamentalist values, it must be confessed, has become more explicitly political and doctrinaire, indeed more rigidly dogmatic, fanatical and persecuting than at any time before or since Barbarian culture and

Christian doctrine were set upon the great edifice of Rome's classical civilization or, troublesome as it may be, as representing continuity, as another instance of history *regenerating* itself.

It is of course perfectly possible to accept this loss of an autonomous Western evolution without being wholehearted about it. But it can hardly be denied that it was the Barbarian Revolution which transformed pagan antiquity into Christendom and, hence, into a civilization higher than its own. That consideration, indeed, was put forward by an English man of letters, Hilaire Belloc, who wrote that 'Those who are hostile to the Conversion of the Empire and who regret it as a prime disaster (a common academic attitude) . . . are fond of describing the Church and all its culture as a product of the lower classes swamping the upper: barbarians and common soldiers imposing disastrously their superstitions upon the fine order of the Greek and Roman World.' It is in the same reference that Mr Belloc points out that 'There are those of course who come to an exactly contrary judgement and tell us that the Conversion of the Empire saved all that could be saved of pagan civilization sinking in sterility to its death'.[5]

Or was R. H. Barrow nearer the mark when he suggested that 'Rome never fell, she turned into something else. Rome, superseded as the source of political power, passed into even greater supremacy as an idea'.[6] And surely, if we take this last into account, there is no good reason why one order of civilization should not be allowed to impinge upon another even if, as seems inevitable, we must pass through some terrible catharsis to reach the hoped for renaissance. There is, moreover, no reason at all why what Gibbon described as 'the triumph of barbarism and religion', should not, far more than any momentum ancient civilization might have had on its own, have changed the face of the Roman West and given a new purpose and new motives to what was then considered the world of high culture and true civilization. In estimating the extent of its influence, we must bear in mind of course that Rome, so far from being the Empire of the Roman people was a melting-point of many races, a nation of migrants, an amalgam of Greeks and Romans, Iberians, Illyrians and Gauls, Saxons and Celts, Phoenicians, Goths, Jews, Arabs and Orientals, and that – and here comes the crucial aspect of the whole matter – the irreversible demise of great civilizations that possessed sophisticated administrative systems and comprehensive indigenous cultural traditions, has generally been their failure to evolve.

8

GOD'S ENGLISHMEN

> Let the shopkeepers rule where everything that
> still glitters is – shopkeeper's gold! The age of
> kings is past: what today calls itself the people
> deserves no king.
>
> Just see how these people themselves now
> behave like shopkeepers: they glean the smallest
> advantage from sweepings of every kind.
>
> Nietzsche, *Zarathustra*

In his altogether exceptional study of the progressive decline of classical civilization, Santo Mazzarino introduces the modern reader to an immensely erudite vista of history, examining the causes of the fall of Rome and illustrating the various ways in which the problem of the 'decadence of Empire' was defined, from that time onwards to the present day, as a recurring theme in the history of ideas rather than as a historiography which deals with concrete discussions of actual historical facts. Few things, in any case, have been written about more exhaustively than the Roman Empire's unique greatness, and for those who follow the main points in the general conclusions of *The End of the Ancient World*, it becomes at once apparent that the question of the decline of classical civilization has essentially been a problem of interpretation. We can follow its progress throughout the history of successive ages. As each new age or epoch begins, a different retrospective explanation seems to have been placed upon the main events of the momentous decline of a proud empire which has agitated thinkers and historians ever since it began, purportedly, with the foundation of the Roman imperium by Caesar and Augustus.

There is no point in referring to specific instances of a whole series of analogous truths, or differing doctrines of decadence, since they may be found in Mazzarino's own book.[1] But, as formulated on the eve of Empire by Cicero, whose *virtus*, as Brutus once said, 'could be compared with any of the ancients', the problem of the decadence of Rome may conveniently be viewed against the background of 'the decay of manners and the lack of really great men (*virorum penuria*)'. As Cicero saw it: 'Before our times the customs of our people produced outstanding individuals and ancient customs and traditional institutions. In our age, however, the state has come to be like a painting which is remarkable but already fading because of old age, and people neglect not only to restore the original colours in it, but even to preserve its shape and outlines'.[2]

Discount such a judgement as we may, if one of the ablest and most brilliant men that Rome ever produced expressed such a point of view, it is important to understand clearly the criteria which we apply. Old tradition required that the great type of manhood, the type – as suggested by a conservative historian – that served mankind from Aeneas to Augustus, was a Spartan model of austerity and moral discipline albeit that such a model may well have lacked some of the fascination and charm of a Cicero who, according to the same historian, 'introduced Western minds to Greek thought (and) gave the West a philosophic language in which to think'.[3] Or, as St Augustine has noted before him, ' . . . by whom philosophy in the Latin tongue was begun and was brought to perfection.' Greatness, of course, does not necessarily imply conquest, nor mere military purpose, but character, intellectual and spiritual, on the part of those men who had contributed to the expansion of Empire, or, like the great Scipios, to its firm and decisive establishment. Nor, if that distinction is maintained, does it necessarily mean the acquisition of supreme military power such as was held by the major Roman commanders during the last century of the Republic, by Marius, Sulla, Pompey, Caesar and Augustus or, to give him his adopted name, Gaius Julius Caesar Octavianus.

The Gracchi were great men for almost opposite reasons.

'Great' is a vain term for Marius who was a *man* nevertheless, a 'new man', and a popular general and politician to boot. Sulla acquired his own, imperfect form of greatness. His tyranny was both a symptom and a precedent for what, at a later stage in history, would be another aspect of the problem of the decline of Rome: the use of military force against the State. Of Pompey it has been truly said that he was one of Rome's most capable generals, irresolute though he was. Conqueror of half the world, of Spain and Asia, he had the capacity but not the vision for either true greatness or supreme statesmanship. That distinction belongs to Caesar whose supreme genius as a soldier and statesman was uniquely and archetypally Roman. Augustus gave the world peace. *The unmeasured majesty of the Roman peace . . .*, as summarized by Pliny the Elder in one immortal phrase. Heir to the most distinguished title in Roman history, and no doubt deservedly so, he was destined, against the background of these suggestive names, to be the guardian of tradition and the restorer of an order in the Roman universe as awesome as the contrast and comprehensiveness which marked the end and final dissolution of Roman authority in the West.

After the end of the Republic or, as we have said, with the Ciceronian view of the absence of 'really great men', a quite different type of classification may be undertaken of the great figures, and above all, the personalities which were reshaping late Roman civilization. Indeed, it is well to bear in mind that throughout his study of the end of the ancient world, Santo Mazzarino always had a higher type in view. Nor, in attempting to explain that 'States do not fall because of the elimination of hypothetical descendants of men who were superior', does he neglect the opportunity of representing 'late-Roman civilization as rich in very great and indeed gigantic personalities, from Septimus Severus to Diocletian, Constantine and Julian the Apostate, from Tertullian and Origen to Ammianus Marcellinus and St Augustine'.[4]

Here, then, we have a point of view that is defensible enough if we bear in mind the context. Its significance, in other words, lies in the enormous psychological transformation it wrought upon an empire which was congenitally unstable and as deeply demoralized as the society it accommodated. Nor was it only the force of 'very great and indeed gigantic personalities' that produced these transformations. Clearly, for all the personal colouring that the greatest rulers of the late Roman Empire imparted to the deep-seated changes which had been gathering momentum for the best part of three centuries, once removed from this purview, it was at bottom but a reflection of the tremendous social flux in which they lived. Diocletian, Constantine and Julian, to illustrate the point, were very different figures from Pompey and Caesar, either of whom had the genius of a Marlborough or a Napoleon. Augustus, so decidedly one of the very great, is something else again. First of all it is as well to remember that his philosophy of Empire was static rather than evolutionary. Also, of course, he was succeeded by many men far inferior in genius. In actual fact, if the Christian spiritual revolution could absorb the central power of the state, the problem of decline was coming close to the attrition of something that ultimately existed in the inner constitution of unresolved national divisions. In this respect the late Roman empire was clearly unrepresentative of the spirit of martial vitality and masculine virility such as the rise of the Roman Republic exhibited in the course of its irresistible progression.

To this period belongs Herder's assertion that 'It was the Roman art of war to attack rather than defend, to fight rather than besiege, and to take the shortest, straightest way to victory and to fame'.[5] Few words, but straight and very pithy. Truth to tell, it is here that lies the secret of the whole system of Roman honour, courage, discipline and resolution. Plainly, one only has to compare the triumphant Roman pride that had been the concomitant of republican growth and imperial progression, with the Julio-Claudian excesses that marked the transition from dynamic rise and vigorous expansion to the eventual cessation of the great wars of conquest. For the result of such a cessation was national pessimism, defeatism and the kind of apathy which (apart from civil wars and barbarian invasions) dominated civilized thinking in the Roman world – with the notable exception of the second century – until the final collapse some three hundred and fifty years later. In actual fact, even the wars of the second-century emperors such as Trajan and Marcus Aurelius had primarily been frontier campaigns and defensive actions. Which is precisely why one must be careful to avoid the impression that the unremitting martial impulse of early republican rise could be substituted by a combination of relative tranquillity and contingent prosperity such as marked the age of Trajan, Hadrian and the Antonines.

There is, however, an alternative explanation, indeed, an

instructive contrast here, with the *res publica* as a strong central-ized state that had not yet found a stable social form and, hence, was still in a process towards an enormous historical evolution which gradually enabled different leaders and levels of social organization to come into play. As a matter of fact, nothing is more characteristic of the fundamental difference between the great heroes of the republican past and 'the individuals of great stature which the age of the death of Rome threw up' than that the former was a succession of quintessentially younger, and in many ways almost objectionable, men, if of great distinction and character, who subjugated and ravaged the world on a truly aggressive scale. Whereas the momentous issue foremost among the latter was the struggle for personal authority in a destabilized and monolithic state characterized chiefly by its defensive qualities.

When the problem is set out in this way, it is impossible not to conclude that it was war and a martial policy which conditioned the growth of the Roman Republic. So long as this pattern remained unchanged and wars were waged aggressively, there was no reason to doubt the continuity of Roman arms and of the great military geniuses they never ceased to produce. When, at length this was no longer the case, there was nothing so obviously unpatriotic, within the context of the type of all-encompassing supra-national state that was gradually developing, than the unsatisfied inner constitution and economic requirements of in-completely romanised provinces. In short, the whole aspect of the Roman world had changed. It is said that Pompey once boasted that he need only stamp with his foot and armed men would spring from the soil of Italy. Now men found themselves in an empire that no longer retained a strong historical sense. On the one hand there was administrative corruption and monetary infla-tion, and on the other the apathy of moral values aggravated by famines, plagues and diminishing military effectiveness.

Thus there is truth in the observation that 'great nations give way and break down more often from internal than external causes'. Causes, it might be argued, that were directly connected with the profound economic and social effects the enormous unloading of foreign slaves onto the Italian market had on Roman society. First of all a growing geographical adulteration took place in the Roman sense of identity. Then there was economic stagnation. Still more fatal for the social fabric of Roman unity, its traditions and its institutions, was an immense and wretched mass of plebs, slaves and freedmen and an impoverished nobility and declining equestrian order while a small class of territorial magnates held tremendous latifundia. Hence, there was a corresponding loss of cohesion and the almost total disappearance of its homogeneous national character towards the end of an empire whose highest, or indeed archetypal, characteristics had been formed and furnaced in the crucible of a pre-eminently military or soldier-state. Other reasons may have added their weight, but almost certainly, its breakdown became inevitable once these characteristics ceased to be predominant.

In the case of Britain, particularly when measured by Roman standards, we are not, of course, talking about a military society. Though the British Empire laid claim to a global objective its martial attitude and aspirations were far more restricted. Its purpose was, in fact, essentially entrepreneurial and economical. But whether we speak of Greek, Roman or Anglo-Saxon civilization, or of an intermingling of Teutonic, Latin and Anglo-Saxon economic cultures, it is enough to say that if the abandonment of the highest or patriotic elements in a supra-national classical culture strikes us as inauspicious, we had better look to our own. Certainly, its 'disintegrating' tendencies are operating on a lesser scale and with lesser severity. But more important, because fundamental to it, is a new conception of confederate identity, peculiarly deficient as it is in any patriotic motives for nationhood. As a matter of fact, coupled with the corresponding surcease of national interests, such a tendency certainly sanctions, if it does not make inevitable, the demise of that particular species of patriotic virtue which more traditionally tended to make a nation, which inspired the Greek and Roman character, and which has always been a proximate cause of the British Empire or Anglo-Saxon civilization.

The bearing of these remarks, I should mention perhaps, is a mere summing up, and not as might wrongly be supposed, in any spirit of support for an imperial philosophy of state. Nor, in the name of an idea, would it be presumptuous to assert that England is a very different nation today, or that even in her case one might consider the really decisive loss to have been virtues, as I said, which are proximate, not primary ones. Which are, in a quote, 'something that is inborn, and subtle, and everlasting . . . something like a solid principle, and masterful like an instinct – a

138

disclosure of something secret – of that hidden something, that gift of good or evil that makes racial difference, that shapes the fate of nations'. (*Youth.*)

Joseph Conrad, who thus endeavoured to formulate the condition, was peculiarly perceptive on this point. Unfashionable though they may sound to us today, his words nevertheless make it clear, if only for rhetorical purposes, how completely the genius of those who once took pride in the thought that they were God's own Englishmen has become diluted by egalitarian ideologies implying that because social compositions have become homogeneous, racial characteristics, too, are no longer distinct. For even with this reservation in mind it is still possible to exhibit certain attributes that are representative. Indeed, there is a symbolism in Conrad's words which depicts racial or national qualities that stand out in the English character as in perhaps no other. Nor may the point seem of much importance now, but the significance of it is that since it is undeniable that national, not to say racial, characteristics must of necessity preponderate in the shaping of historical events, one is forced to resort to the special qualities of a people in any statement of the causes that would explain its rise. Above all, we must bear in mind the unique assimilating power of Anglo-Saxon culture. Nor is it impertinent to remark that the British united in a single society well over a quarter of the world's people. Some 500,000,000 Hindus, Moslems and Christians, I repeat, whose many conflicting cultures would hardly have been blessed with one basic article of political faith – albeit often flavoured with their excessive sensibilities – nor with an equally pervasive preoccupation with the common ideals that rule the evolution of all free and democratic societies everywhere.

'. . . that thou mightest bring under one law the customs and the ways of different nations, their tongues, their genius, and their faiths.' So the Christian poet Prudentius, entreating, with an almost Victorian flamboyance 'that the whole world should serve the Roman toga and yield to Roman arms'. One can see how this may have been done. For in any examination of the causes which brought so many 'tongues, their genius, and their faiths' under the suzerainty of the British Empire one recognizes the authentic designates of a national identity – if it matters, the legitimate province of *race* – in its pragmatic purpose, its resolute commitment to extremes of either bravery or folly, in an altogether altruistic kind of arrogance rather than jingoistic pride, and, as

139

evidenced by a great number of triumphs in disaster, its capacity to survive.

Thinking of the latter or, *mutatis mutandis,* of the Anglo-French struggle for Empire, it is of course difficult to be specific about what Napoleon might actually have said regarding assertions of this kind. But some idea of his potential attitude can perhaps be derived from Shaw's *The Man of Destiny*, from which I have already quoted. Here G.B., for reasons perhaps which had nothing to do with his own views, gives it as Napoleon's opinion that the English are a very stupid people, '. . . too stupid sometimes to know when they are beaten'. No more a recent than an isolated imputation – Heine referred to Wellington's reduction of Napoleon at Waterloo as the victory of 'stupidity over genius' – it is worthwhile to realize that it is here indeed where lay the uniqueness of that rare and remarkable phenomenon which became the peculiar possession of the English people, at all levels of society, to an extent perhaps beyond any other race: they refused to be beaten. Chiefly, as one commentator observed of the Englishman, because 'He is a man who possessed such natural pride of birth that, through sheer contempt for others, he refused to learn or be defeated.'[6] A fact, if it is a fact, which explains many otherwise inexplicable things about a race whose contempt was essentially pragmatic and whose historical ascent, whether in terms of international trade and conquest or throughout 'an unbroken national tradition of decency and institutionalized freedom',[7] was all of a piece with its Protestant or Puritan religious beliefs and the conception of personal superiority they tended to impart. All in all, perhaps the clearest insight into this character is to be found in Queen Victoria's words when she retaliated with the memorable line: 'We are not interested in the possibility of defeat'.

If Victoria's rejoinder is a masterpiece of royal contempt, Tacitus was rather less categorical. 'Defeat in battle', he tells us, 'begins with what you see'. And if one examines the basis of the doctrine of British invincibility in history, to give an even more precise meaning to what one writer has described as 'one of the great traditions of the British army: courage matched only by stupidity',[8] it is in fact questionable that anyone in these isles, in the summer of 1940, when it was becoming increasingly clear that Britain must stand alone against the power of the Reich, may have been such a dupe as not to see that German military might had reached the point of absolute supremacy. In every sense the reduction of Europe could be said to be complete. Czechoslovakia, Poland, Denmark and Norway had ceased to exist as a fighting force. The astonishing defeat of France was virtually an accomplished fact. The Low Countries had been reduced. Italy had returned to the Eagles. The Channel Islands themselves had fallen under Nazi rule. In effect, given the abundant evidence of the power of the Wehrmacht in the aftermath of its triumph at Dunkirk, Nazi Germany seemed invincible, if not on the high seas, at least on land, and not only on land, few would deny, but even in the air. For the all-powerful Nazi warlord England had already lost the war; as he said in March 1941: 'it is only a matter of having the intelligence to admit it.'[9]

Yet, looking at the British Empire about to face the new barbarians, it is extremely difficult to believe that Churchill was without insight, that he did not have the intelligence to know he was faced with tremendous odds, or that he had no consciousness of what defeat would ultimately have meant. It would have been so easy to lend an attentive ear to ideological appeasers and potential collaborators at home. But this Churchill utterly refused. He had an acute enough sense of the nature of the British people to realize that without making a stand, they should have ceased to be British, ceased to be the defeaters of invincible Armadas, the 'pugnacious and unconquerable bulldog race'. Of course, he was equally conscious of the fact, as had been Burghley and Cecil, or William Pitt, that Hitler, like Philip and the Duke of Medina Sidonia, or Napoleon on the same occasion some two hundred years later, could not defeat Britain without first having invaded her, and if the defence of the liberties of Europe had been the British case throughout history, she would never make peace from a position of weakness. 'England', said Pitt, 'has saved herself by her exertions, and will, as I trust, save Europe by her example'.[10] This notwithstanding, it has often been asked why Great Britain should have fought on 'alone against helpless odds? Especially', William Shirer remarked, 'when it could get a peace that would leave it, unlike France, Poland and all the other defeated lands, unscathed, intact and free?' Significantly, as he also informs us, 'this was a question asked everywhere except in Downing Street, where, as Churchill later revealed, it was never even discussed, because the answer was taken for granted.'[11]

But there was another reason why. The point has been well made that history is made by the ideals of great men, and the idea of greatness has no better representative among modern statesmen than the person of Winston Churchill as a man obsessed by a conviction of unusual severity. Churchill, it must be remembered, gave perhaps the ultimate speech, one of the greatest ever delivered, upon the British resolve to continue the war; for it was then, and not until then, that the patriotic imagination of Englishmen was fated to take on the heroic dimensions that Churchill had already carved out for them:

'Let us therefore brace ourselves to our duties, and so bear ourselves that, if the British Empire and its Commonwealth last for a thousand years, men will say: '*This was their finest hour!*' (Radio Broadcast, 18 June 1940.)

Here at last, in the pride and defiance of one of the world's masterpieces of political oratory, was encapsulated 'that ardent Spirit of Liberty and that undaunted Courage in the Defence of it, which', as Benjamin Franklin had once felt it necessary to record, 'has in every age so gloriously distinguished Britons and Englishmen from all the Rest of Mankind'.[12] Stupidity, at all events, was not involved. Very far from it. As the Western Allies combined in that half-decade of supreme war effort, without which there would have been no freedom as we know it, they not only liberated Europe, but rendered the extirpation of Nazism in 1945 quite as complete as had been the reduction of Carthage in 146 BC.

Thus, within the confines of these ideas, all that can be said is that if it had not been for the alleged English 'stupidity', the world would have been very different from what it is today. Of course, it is always possible to interpret 'stupidity' somewhat too narrowly. For it is certainly worth pointing out that however little they may have realized it, the English have perforce remained unconscious of that one share of the common human experience (and of the moral lessons that might have accrued from it) which it is impossible to acquire by any other means than defeat. 'A people needs defeat', Alexander Solzhenitsyn once remarked knowingly, 'just as an individual needs suffering and misfortune: they compel the deepening of the inner life and generate a spiritual upsurge'.[13] And certainly his words express an important aspect of the peculiar significance of the fact that 'sorrow is knowledge' or that 'grief should be the instructor of the wise'. No tribute is more apposite than Byron's which includes these words, and both men make it perfectly clear that any view which assumes otherwise does not implicate the truth that this, when put into the relevant ethical terms, means a fundamental difference in our conventional notions of humility or of freedom from pride and arrogance.

For once, then, we have parted company with the English, 'for maturity is the quality that the English dislike most'.[14] It is not, of course, intended for one moment to cold-shoulder the problems involved in leading an ethical life, for as an index or proof of Anglo-Saxon emotional immaturity, the idea of the absence of suffering and misfortune is of necessity relative. Every mature individual knows that misfortune before all else is a personal matter, a matter for the individual character. But if we admit, as I think we ought to, that too much pride and arrogance is destructive of the human character, the fact remains that too much humility is none the less so. There is an old biblical saying that God rejects the proud and gives his grace to the humble. Humility, therefore, is doubtless a praiseworthy thing. But – to the best of my belief – if the evolution of the civilized world depended to a considerable degree on English national or racial ingredients, it is nevertheless the case that their chief and foremost contribution to it has been the long and fortuitous history of a Charmed Life rather than the humility of those who can surrender themselves, for the sake of Christ, to pacific or passive influences. Somehow or other (no ones knows how), God would 'always reveal Himself . . . as His manner is, first to His Englishmen',* and take an incalculable and felicitous hand in British affairs, casually adding an element of chance or a capricious force that the Englishman would call British Luck (and others the Luck of the Devil). We may think of such luck what we like, but if it indicated the remarkable way in which historical genius asserted its congeniality with the English mind of that day, it is difficult to dispute that her astonishing fortuity also made Britain one of the greatest powers of all time, spelling damnation and defeat for whomsoever confronted her as a military aggressor.

This, as we have already noted, was surely the case with the great Spanish Armada which the Dons had fitted out against England in 1588. In a somewhat similar case d'Orvilliers' Franco-Spanish invasion force of 1779 was ravaged by small-pox, scurvy and typhus even before it could come to grips with Sir

* Milton, *Areopagitica.*

143

Charles Hardy's vastly inferior Channel Fleet. Trafalgar, to take another instance, once and for all destroyed the power of France on the seas. There are other, and equally obvious examples. But in any of these cases, and the Battle of Britain is surely the one we are the least likely to forget, the island-fortress Albion seems to have possessed to an almost supernatural degree the capacity to divine and fathom the impenetrable design of any historical moment or situation upon which history's *synchronicity* came to depend. Her very existence endangered, she was not only convinced, congenitally one might say, that destiny had provided against defeat but also, it almost seems, superhumanly receptive to the idea of her own constitutional invincibility, ... *the inherited belief that she could not be beaten* (Trevelyan).

Reflections such as these may seem like a mere diversion. But, however incongruous or imperfectly comprehended, there is a considerable inducement here to detect the mark of destiny in special forces of this kind. In '*a tradition of confidence* – an assurance that is essentially religious',[15] to borrow a phrase no more severe than the assurance of faith in reason and objective fact. Add to these facts the particular nature of their national identity which constitutes the real English uniqueness and one is left with the feeling that this is not an inapposite rendering of the nature of the prerogative which the British seem to have claimed. Oswald Spengler, in undertaking to state the case, thus took the significant view that the historical pre-eminence which the English have traditionally regarded as theirs was the privilege of their faith. Nor would the notion of such a privilege add or subtract from the moral bond upon which it was exercised. And if we bear in mind also that faith is an inherited rather than an acquired characteristic, a bequest rather than an attainment, it is perhaps appropriate that its effect upon a pugnacious and purposeful English destiny should have been incomprehensible or incongruous to the humble and faithless alone.

But before we leave this Englishman, let us remember that in doubting his we must not forget our own humility. For the point of the story is not our own humbleness which, indeed, is by no means admitted, nor the fact that he is too congenitally self-sufficient ever to enter into states of minds other than his own, but the fact that *he is beaten at last.* That his prerogative has been made redundant at length by the simple and final termination of a moral contract through the historical demise of a certain kind of global purpose. This is neither surprising nor proof of moral bankruptcy. It was certainly inevitable and it may even be desirable, but it is a moment of truth for us all. Time was when few thoroughbred Englishmen would have relished the thought of aspiring to the heaven of others for as long as they could find their own. Now, it is somehow affecting to read, 'she barely has the strength to perfidy. Poor Albion!'. Struggling to survive the loss of her past and increasingly troubled by the problem of her own relationship to the outside world, by the need for retrenchment and the necessity to clarify her attitude towards a factious world in which England will never be England again, it seems that she has succumbed to it, or I am much mistaken.

There are further considerations, of course, which point in the direction of developments which a country the size of Britain is not perhaps at liberty to desist, but essentially it is England and the English spirit for which we mourn. 'A nation behaves like itself', it has been succinctly said. And accordingly, in a contribution to the 1939 edition of *The English Genius*, its central doctrine could still be expressed as follows: 'What pleases us we take from Europe, what displeases us we leave to Europeans; for only accidentally do we consider ourselves as such'.[16] Few, even a short while ago, would have liked to read this differently. But we live in the age of 'Confederalism' and its mastering doctrine abdicated, the new policy of this country and its discontinuity with her old traditions has become quite unmistakable. No, it was definitely not for the love of Britain that the Iron Lady, Margaret Thatcher, who understood better than any statesman since Churchill, perhaps since Palmerston or the Younger Pitt, the fundamental Anglo-Saxon verities, was bundled out of office by a Party of *Little* Englanders and followers of opinion who understood the lessons of humility and of their own limitations before they understood anything else.

'So, not understanding or no better than half understanding, I indulge myself in the dream that the world, my own world, has come to meet me and will still be there when I depart. Delusion it may be, but let me keep my delusion that the British people, somehow or other, will not be parted from their right to govern themselves . . .'[17] In making this remark, J. Enoch Powell, of considerable patriotic attainment himself, has the final word. It is the word of a man who has prophesied plenty and deplored it all. Let's face it, the removal of Margaret Thatcher, by the party

145

directly concerned, from the management of the government was more than a mere change of leadership. It was a watershed in the destiny of Great Britain. As significant a change of direction perhaps as was the departure of the Iron Chancellor, Prince Otto von Bismarck, from the national destiny of Germany. Nor did it come about as the result of a royal dismissal. Almost certainly, it proceeded from the action of a persistent and comprehensive propaganda and publicity machine, representing and articulating the opinion of certain 'progressive' elements, and undoubtedly conducted over an extended number of years.

In the words of a political columnist: 'The failure of the Thatcher phenomenon was that she gave the country leadership but no new role'. And to the extent this is an issue, not of national polity but of the logic of events in which Britain's position has become relativised, it must clearly lead to results that are in profound contradiction with the age-old assumption that its own inherent genius is the soul and body of a nation. Whether we admire it or not, and regardless of whether or not it is to be subsumed under a confederate ethos or made to partake of an ethical re-interpretation of the world, this, at all events, is the very genius which conquered the world, 'Hellenized' it and formulated the conditions under which the greatest possible happiness for the greatest possible number was actually going to be achieved. *'Essentially religious'* or not, one might as well admit that it has brought into existence laws and rules of behaviour that we now recognize as universal; liberties not so much of Englishmen as of all men; rights that are constituent elements of our very own time. And that, in fact, is why we are compelled to say, when brought face to face with the enduring quality of certain unalterable codes of British conduct, with a spirited and courageous historical conscience, with 'that perfection', finally, 'of moral, intellectual, and professional qualities' which Trevelyan called 'the Nelson touch': *This was their finest hour!*

9

DEATHWISH I

I War and Peace

> You will soon convince yourself that war is part
> of my programme.
>
> Bismarck, 1865

> You should love peace as a means to new wars.
> And the short peace the more than the long.
>
> Nietzsche, *Zarathustra*

> Now we suffer the evils of long peace.
>
> Juvenal

*'That war should ever be banished from the world is a hope not
only absurd, but profoundly immoral. It would involve the atrophy
of many of the essential and sublime forces of the human soul . . .
A people which becomes attached to the chimerical hope of
perpetual peace finishes irremediably by decaying in its proud
isolation . . .'*[1] This unequivocal outburst, so in line with the philosophical thought of the nineteenth century German mind, has
come down to us as something like the definitive statement of the
period. In truth, there is no more extraordinary illustration of, in a
quote, the 'weird mixture of the irresponsible, megalomanical
ideas which erupted from German thinkers during the nineteenth
century',[2] than this extravagant deposition by the German
historian and political publicist Heinrich von Treitschke.

147

Author of the *History of Germany in the Nineteenth Century* and of a passionately and ruthlessly advocated Pan-Germanic pre-eminence, von Treitschke was a patriot of the most uncompromising tradition. More than anyone else he preached the Prussianisation of Germany and the cause of a triumphant Teutonic culture. Far too long had it lacked resolution! Now it was to be noted for its utter resoluteness! Nor was the Prussianisation of Germany going to be impeded by lack of leadership. When the time for national unity was ripe it would come through the House of Hohenzollern. On that point he was adamant. Nor was it surprising that von Treitschke owed his views on these subjects in part to nationalist thinkers like Fichte and Hegel and in part to soldier-philosophers of war such as Karl von Clausewitz. 'More Prussian than the Prussians', as William Shirer says, 'his influence on German thought in the last quarter of this century was enormous and it continued through Willhelm II's day and indeed Hitler's'.[3]

Probing the intellectual roots of the Third Reich, William Shirer's evidence and investigation is not, of course, confined to this one example, but inasmuch as von Treitschke's exposition of Prussian nationalism as an instrument of Germanic salvation became something like the foundation and epitomizing force which separated the cause of Nazi Germany from the rest of the world, it is referred to in a particularly significant chapter.[4] Absorbing a tendency that had been gathering strength ever since the beginning of the nineteenth century, many of von Treitschke's contemporaries were already convinced that the moment had come for the rising power of Germany to establish herself as the universal conqueror, and nowhere are the antecedents of the Prussian doctrine of 'might against right' more obviously apparent than in his uncompromising emphasis on the function of war as a business, in the words of his disciple Bernhardi, 'divine in itself and as needful and necessary to the world as eating and drinking'. Needless to say, the whole point of his uncompromising exposition of this philosophy of war was, in fact, to constitute a counter to the atrophying experience 'of many of the essential and sublime forces of the national soul', even if it had to take place on the firm foundation of potential aggression and the German ideal of a *Weltmacht*.

What was accepted without question was that only Germany could act as a regenerating historical force. That was the conclusion, at any rate, of patriotic German philosophers like Johann Gottlieb Fichte and, at a later stage, Georg Wilhelm Friedrich Hegel. The first produced the stirring and reverberating *Addresses to the German Nation*, which more than anything at a time of struggle for national independence carried with it and moulded the minds of the rising German generation. Hegel decried the power of the solitary human being with a sense of the futility of individual action and exalted in its stead the fundamentally absolute power of the autocratic state, not unnaturally expressing some of the most persistent and characteristic aspirations of the Germanic world, then, as ever, in the full flower of great national developments.

This, in a nutshell, was the spirit that launched the national fundamentalism of the Third Reich with its Aryan messianism, its deification of the Machiavellian superman, its exaltation of the authoritarian state, and its invocation of the master-doctrine *ein Reich, ein Volk, ein Führer*.The meaning, sense and significance of catharsis however, remained firmly rooted in the rationale of an age which was prone to view everything in terms of an unadorned power-struggle. It prefigured all the elements of the tragic drama that lay ahead and, for reasons which were both ideological and socio-political, would engulf the great tide of humanity in a military conflict whose actual scale and dimension would simply have been unimaginable and – paradoxical as it may seem – probably utterly abhorrent even to nineteenth-century military theorists and national-social idealists.

It is half a century now since 7 May 1945, or Victory-in-Europe Day. And what do we find? In one respect alone has the holocaust tended to have a positive result: the demand for peace has become an international movement, politically and administratively tied to every national constitution and more popular and better organized internationally than at any other time in human history. Few things arouse more public indignation than any kind of aggressive behaviour. Whether communal or international, it is liable to provoke the most furiously hostile publicity. The quest for peace rules everything. It has become an exercise in public melodrama as necessary, inevitable and salutary as was the remarkable transformation in the international diplomatic position which seems to have engendered it.

So in what did this transformation consist? Apart from all other reasons, the way in which it is usually demonstrated is by pointing to the deterrent effect that nuclear power has had quite generally upon any pursuant of an aggressive foreign policy that would come under its supervision. It is in fact a tribute to the nuclear doctrine of *mutual assured destruction* that, as far as can now be judged, it has proved itself time and again in the course of modern history. But what, then, of its adverse implications? Extensive claims have also been made that it was in the Third World, in Asia, central Africa or the Middle and Far East 'and not in Europe, that the major conflicts between the Soviet and the US systems since 1945 have in fact occurred'[5] Nor can there be a more overwhelming admission of the failure of nuclear deterrence than an estimated one hundred and twenty new wars in Third World countries since, or, to put it even more bluntly, the tragedy of no fewer than thirty million dead. That was the body-count of 1986. Since then, of course, this number has enormously increased. In 1993 alone there were 43 full-scale wars, or 60 'armed conflicts' worldwide,[6] and there is every indication that what the world might in fact be experiencing is a runaway surge of military conflagration.

At all events, if we understand the principle of nuclear deterrence correctly, and without minimizing its unique contribution to the spirit of a long-lasting peace, the original terms of reference do in fact confine it to an examination of the conditions existing in *cold-war* Europe and America, rather than today. But again it should be stressed that the principle of nuclear deterrence alone cannot provide a unique prescription for the way peace is preserved other than by its restraining effect. For even as a primarily cold-war affair, the emphasis is laid on the wrong factor. The truth is that in practical domestic terms nuclear deterrence has achieved very little. In fact, if there is anything at all to be said for the proposition that aggression justifies itself on its own increasing scale, it is that disruptive social behaviour has been the onerous result. Indeed, perhaps the most distinctive aspect of the deception on which rests the case for peace has been the substitution of the struggle against war with the struggle against an increasingly violent society. The result, so far as the West is concerned, has been a revolution in the very nature and meaning of peace. It involves not merely the substitution of one form of violence for another but the very institution, in order to make the one conform to the other, of our modern forensic state. Even in political life the emergence of radical concepts, of clandestine

150

underground organizations and secret conspirational groups increasingly testifies to the persistence of a desperate and violent mentality. What is more, since it is a complex peace and not all of its manifestations appear in the context of political or social tensions, it is not always a simple matter to distinguish between one form of violence and another. Yet, so far as one can generalize it would seem that its enormous increase marks a profound transformation in the very patterns of human conduct, affecting all norms of social behaviour and every institution in society from the family to the State.

The difficulty one sees here for the idealist who believes in large ideas about human nature and the natural goodness of human reason is obvious. Obviously, too, it would be very pleasant to be able to say that the men who deplore or condemn violence were also seeking to restrain its excess. One can see, however, that although our social aspirations are absolutely unequivocal and unambiguous on this subject of peace, the reaction against it has been aggressively pacific in a very destructive way. It would be unfair to urge that violence is fomented solely and specifically by means of this contradiction, but it forms a worthwhile introduction to the subject nevertheless and even illustrates how social tensions seem to determine themselves without an act of ill will. Indeed, it is one of the most striking features of modern social flexibility that it should have adapted itself so readily to this new form of hostility. And this being so, the extent of *that* hostility could scarcely be more considerable than in the United States – to take the most notorious example – where the increasing violence of the struggle between the forces on both sides of the law effectively appears to have acquired the state and character of a disguised or latent civil war. Here law and order is not a manifestation of the widely shared notion of good will to all men, but the very profanation of it. Such at any rate is the most probable explanation for a grand total of 240,000 persons having been murdered in the USA during the decade of the eighties, even if we are not told in what way. Alongside this, and serving as its true correlative, a 'mere' 58,000 Americans lost their lives during twelve years of warfare in Vietnam.*

*From a study released in August 1990 by the Senate Judiciary Committee in Washington.

As elsewhere in the world, violence in America is on the increase, so that we now hear of a staggering 25,000 annual deaths by handgun alone. It is equally true that this excessive emphasis on purely violent factors is intrinsically part of America's inherently villainous social structure, and not caused by a temporary social breakdown or due to special political conditions. So what does it all mean? There are various suggestions, but first and fundamentally it means that the alternatives between war and peace are not nearly as clear-cut as the doctrine of nuclear deterrence once appeared to make out. It is true, no one can say that the world has not tried; but we must now ask why it has failed? 'Peace', as Plato's Cleinias conceived of it in the opening passage of the first book of *Laws,* 'is merely an appearance'. He avowed that 'in reality all cities are by nature in a permanent state of undeclared war against all other cities', and elsewhere even anticipates Hobbes' *homo lupus homini,* in contending that everyone is at war with everyone else and that each man is at war with himself. Admittedly an extreme belief. But we are not offered wit and foresight for our moral edification alone. On the contrary, what needs to be stressed is that although nobody likes the disproportionate stress the ancients sometimes placed on military matters, they saw and judged warfare in competitive and cathartic and not just in destructive or immoral terms.

In the case of the Greeks and the Romans, the possibility of a moral problem was in fact never raised. Nor, on the rare occasions when they actually acceded to a state of peace, did they renounce what one feels even at this moment to be a precise and execrable truth: that warfare, by its peculiar hold on the human mind, makes a very direct appeal to those elements in human nature which the sterile, sophisticated age in which we live is entirely failing to satisfy. That none of the interminable wars of antiquity ever seems to have constituted a moral conflict of values is perhaps most clearly revealed in the heroic pride, martial prowess, and gladiatorial ideals of the ancients which only somewhat belatedly experienced Nemesis in the form of the spiritual problems of modern man. But if I am right about one of the most recondite and abysmal problems confronting humankind today, there is something decidedly incongruous about a Nemesis which is not so much for the cause of law and order as for the actual replacement of a natural sense of aggression by a debased love of peace as an activist force which has produced many great waves of hostility among many extremely virtuous and peace-loving people.

Whether this assumption is or is not correct, there can be little doubt that when a natural impulse has its validity denied, much as it may be done in the name of peace or for purposes of moral purification, it is as successful in discharging the same function in aggressive patterns of substitution as it is in sublimating itself into the superior philosophical values of the social theorist and the political idealist which transcend the sectarian situation. Indeed, the principal revulsion we feel is not against the instinctive sense of the original will to power as a symbol of potential evil, but against the brutalizing effect of the sectarian causes in which so much evil finds itself embodied. I use this argument to suggest that any of those fast, furious and full-scale assaults on the very institution of civilization itself are the result of a profound and deeply felt alienation of which the absence of catharsis through the experience of a much greater cause is by no means the least.

Men need causes, no matter what the merits of their case. And no matter how sceptical we are of the validity of their motives, whether they specialize in the protection of some anthropological group, assert the rights of animals, or take care of some desperate environmental mission, we cannot question their devotion, the personal sincerity with which the majority of them believe in their own sense of vocation. Causes certainly have their uses. And if it is difficult to treat with becoming seriousness, or to take a reasonable view of secret societies dedicated to organizing bombing campaigns, of nameless desperadoes without the courage to function in the open, of the casualties of a constant and inconclusive war on drugs, vice and crime, of the most ill-used and abused of misfits and failures who are thwarted by their own ineptitude, of disillusioned men who revert to the life of outlaws, their cabalistic meetings, their hugging of secrets, their bandying about of explosives, of the tragic, the banal, and the ridiculous, as something which a great many people would find very difficult to explain, the need for a cause is nevertheless deeply felt and experienced by all.

On a more practical note, and perhaps more obviously, it can be agreed then without much further debate why, under the opulent auspices of the capitalist West we should have succeeded in substituting a latent, and sometimes acute, spiritual need with one of material principle and, together with the requisite distinctions between crime and decline, turned an anthology of human conflict into an analogy of our own psychic distress. It is difficult otherwise to explain the protracted and perplexing failure to curb a steady stream of homicides, robbery and rape, and cut short a flourishing crime rate which, on the face of it, is what one would have expected from a determined and obviously humane system of criminal reform that seeks to rehabilitate rather than recriminate. But whether it is actually true that Britain, according to the current figures, imprisons more people than any other European country, the figures also show that the problem of crime in the United States still dwarfs that in Britain, to say nothing of Europe or the rest of the West.

The mention of the American Republic may remind us that the failure of the Roman Republic was claimed largely to have been the result of Roman reluctance to change their method of government. Of the failure of the American Republic – which no one, admittedly, would predict with any certainty – it may likewise be said that much of it could depend on its blind adherence to the wrong constitutional development. In other words, it suffers from a lamentable proneness among the plainer sort of patriots to continue to subscribe to the original and constitutionally prescribed *American* rights of its founders; the first and perhaps most obvious of which is the right – which no longer distinguishes between the aggressor and the aggrieved – to buy, and bear, firearms. For whatever may have been true of the Roman Republic, if, from its opening years, the Republic of the United States has seen fit to retain those very liberties which were justifiably introduced into the constitution of its founders, it is certainly true to say that they cannot justifiably be retained as a matter of course without prejudicing the rest of the constitution. For closely connected as they are, by every possible association, with warfare, crime, and violence, the simple unvarnished truth is that men who may or may not be criminals and delinquents are in possession of an arsenal of weapons utterly adequate to start a major civil war. So whatever else it may accomplish, it needs no great forensic perspicacity to recognize that this can only be calculated to place many, perhaps the majority of those who would as soon abandon Christ as forfeit the right to firearms, potentially on the side of the evildoers.

These fears are far from imaginary. Conflicting more violently than ever before – and acting with equal inhumanity – the forces on both sides of the law (and both equally unreasonably) seem to conspire to demonstrate that fact. For instance, in July 1990, when former President George Bush opened the first post Cold War economic summit with an ostentatious challenge for the West to 'set the stage for a new millennium', at least one political commentator found it difficult to take him seriously. What actually happened is that he was speaking from 'an *air-conditioned* podium, surrounded by *bullet-proof* glass, after a *military* march-past'(italics added),[7] a poignancy which struck an ironic contrast to his blithe and sanguine announcement that 'A new world of freedom lies before us'. But whether or not *he* was, as he said, 'hopeful' and 'confident', one can plainly see that elsewhere a strange disillusionment appears to have taken charge when even civilian governments have had to conclude that there are domestic issues for which military solutions are far better suited than traditionally forensic ones.

So far from acknowledging that the contemplated rout of the conventional evildoer has in fact materialized, western political officials and military and naval chiefs have delivered themselves of some curiously ambivalent opinions concerning the role of the Armed Forces in the 1990s. One notices, for instance, that Germany has been debating a constitutional amendment to provide for the army's deployment against non-military or internal threats. Internationally it has been resolved to set up permanent national agencies to combat organized crime. In addition, a blanket policy resolution anticipated an era of increasing criminal activity and recommended the adaptation of essentially military methods to come to terms with such activity. Good reasons certainly exist for the deployment of a naval force, including the use of aircraft-carriers, submarines and Awac surveillance equipment, to deal with the threat of some of the world's most powerful criminal gangs, such as the notorious cocaine cartels, in their war on civilization. But, given these declared aims – and German intelligence services have already warned of a trade in nuclear material that has expanded to dangerous proportions – it is neither perverse nor malicious to suggest that the truth has been proved of the declaration by Heinrich von Treitschke, 'that war should ever be banished from the world is a hope not only absurd, but profoundly immoral'.

There is an old Platonic saying that only the dead have seen the end of war. And it is easy enough to be cynical. But it is a sobering thought nevertheless that the problem of war and peace is the

155

problem of choosing the lesser of two evils, with nothing in between. There are exceptions of course, but if wars are waged for the sake of peace, it seems a reasonable assumption to make that their violent functions, too, are being assimilated to those of peace or transformed into socially destructive emulation. Until quite recently, it may be said with some exaggeration, crime was considered a professional calling, paid for largely by insurance premiums. Crime today, as it turns out – to say nothing of the means employed in the prevention of crime, a desperate and violent means by any stretch of the imagination – has become a firmly established and irreducible part of Western forensic civilization.

'We are moving in a descending spiral of iniquity!' Thus the incomparable Margaret Rutherford in the 1950 motion picture *The Happiest Days of Your Life* . Nor, at this extreme moment of machoism, is this descent a question of the integrity of our youth. The corresponding exaltation of their role model, the antithetical hero as kind of admirable outlaw, is the product of a specific cultural situation which has produced no true hero if its own. In our own day, as we are constantly able to witness for ourselves, it has fallen to this mythmaker with his stylish machoism to mould a whole generation to his conception of a life force which is open to the worst kind of abuse and profoundly antipathetic to a civilized community. A splendidly confident figure, he is a man for whom society is the natural enemy, an individually licensed and apocalyptic genius, both extremely proud and exceedingly wilful. Incapable of not asserting himself, he seems to epitomize the worst of this irresistible macho-cult whose gallantry may always be appealed to but whose swagger must never be affronted.

Coarsely made and immensely strong he embodies at least one heroic truth, for whatever the motives behind his exploits, it is not to be supposed that his personal integrity is, on that account, corrupt. He may not be right on binding points of law but he is justified. And justifiably, therefore, he projects himself as the defier of the world; indeed, by virtue of his own laws, as a tribune of the people. 'My conscience is mine, my justice is mine, and my freedom is mine!' So Joseph Pierre Proudhon. In actual fact, there is no aspect of his twentieth century behaviour that does not express salutation of this nineteenth century anarchist adage. Instantly converted into acts of virtue, his vices become the manners and customs of his audience and exist for the pleasure of

156

any one of us. In fact, it is difficult sometimes not to share in the sheer majesty of his great machismo or not to be swept along by its defiance and audacity. By any measure, his contempt is supreme. The means he uses matter nothing to him; and if he remains an outsider, dead or alive, he is almost certainly one who expects to be judged by the end he achieves.

Some, like the French *Nouvel Observateur*, have seen this as the beginning of 'an outlaw movement that, for the first time for thirty years, is drawing its references and its mythology from that which is totally taboo'.[8] Others, like the Italian soccer magazine *Hooligans*, or that of the new racist right, *Blood* and *Honour*, are simply impersonating it. Hooligans are, indeed, soldiers before they are delinquents. They are supreme in the domain of violence and their objective will be to fight a great war. Prescribing and obeying their own laws and looking like heroes, their struggle, too – to keep it free from the terminology of crime – incorporates resistance, rebellion, combat, campaigning and either victory or defeat. Violence may become an end in itself, valued for its own sake, but one thing they must clearly do, they must give unconditional expression to their utter contempt for the falsified moral idealism worked out for them by a pre-eminently unheroic age. And it is hardly necessary to add that if opposite moral principles can be served by the same heroic strategy it is only for want of alternatives that dynamic and charismatic young men without a war to fight are turning towards moral defiance and social destructiveness.

'Oh, I lived in and loved darkness, and hated the light. I was the chief, the chief of sinners . . .' Thus Oliver Cromwell, once a hooligan to his boot-straps now the Lord Protector and commenting on his remarkable conversion from a sense of personal stagnation whilst praising the riches of the Lord's mercy in finally redeeming him. If truly it was a conversion it was certainly remarkable in its results. And one reason at least why the Good Lord took recourse to this step might well have been the misgivings He may have had about the Divine tendencies Charles Stuart's government was beginning to exhibit. But what, then, of the tendencies of history? This is said to be the age of the atom. And to few gallant young men today is it given to share the distinguished opportunities for high-handed deeds that can be said to have existed in an earlier age – nor is there much room for 'protection'. Perhaps the truth simply is that History, with a fine impartiality for the distinction between right and wrong, merely discriminates between men with a mission and men not so favoured, for as a personal manifestation of this distinction, as a formative code of law, an ideal towards which men and society must strive, such a mission is a need of almost spiritual necessity.

As I have indicated already, perhaps the highest vocation in their own estimation, of the Greeks and the Romans, and in the first order of priorities, was the appeal to arms with the allied art of individual combat. But whether we consider it on its own particular merits or as one of the eternally revivifying influences on the history of the world, its ideal character is plainest in its artistic aspects, clearest when caught in the imagination of painters, poets and sculptors. So, invigorating as it is and impressive as would be the enumeration of examples from which most varieties of martial heroism drew their highest inspiration, it is best not to emphasize this without emphasizing that, as we have come to view it, warfare is indivisible from our rendering of it as a destructive and contemptible force. No contrast could be more distinct. This comes out clearly in the classical admiration for the more individualistic aspects of martial combat. But there is a more obviously significant distinction. For it seems to me as certain as such things can be that, today, the contradictory trend of extreme individualism and extreme collective constraint is carried to its frightful conclusion in the kind of personal mutation which is as well illustrated in the Cromwellian sentence quoted above, and which is exemplified with a passion and emotional extremity rare in preceding social history.

There are, to return to Europe and the perennial question of war and peace, still many differences of emphasis, and probably also of principle, between East and West. But after a momentous decade which saw the resumption of active relations, both economic and cultural, with the formerly Communist East, most of its leading figures now clearly inhabit the same ideological world. We should therefore expect an era of harmony, accord and conciliation far beyond any that has previously been thought politically possible. But this is not so at all. Nor am I thinking about the appalling economic and social insecurity of that part of the world which first introduced violent ethnic persecution as an acknowledged political doctrine. The fact is, on the contrary, that I am thinking of forms of violence which are identifiably Western and characteristically destructive in every phase of their development. Nor are they of a kind more commonly associated with economic necessity.

To point out that fascist organizations are firmly rooted once again in such countries as Germany, Italy, France, Sweden and even Great Britain does not, perhaps, seem such a novel revelation. There is, however, a more sinister side to this. Whether simply bored by surfeit, goaded by rising unemployment or stung by waves of foreign immigration, mainstream hooligans from all levels of society and of unconditioned and therefore unpredictable power, are combining, and indeed conspiring, to produce the kind of social tensions which twice already this century have challenged the established moral and political order of the world. The implications are chilling. Not because an international fascist community devoted to violence by word and deed remains a terrifying spectre, but precisely because it is merely a part of a cumulative process of attrition through personal aggression. It is the vision of World War Three in the image of a new barbarism, the apocalyptic conception of a universal war which is sporadic and individual rather than being collectively organized and militarily conducted. Hobbes' *war of all against all* will not be fought with weapons of mass-destruction.

Clausewitz endorses this argument: *That which remains peculiar to war relates only to the peculiar nature of its means.* The test for this is simple: nowhere else today does the violent strain in human nature reach quite the same proportions as in its effect on social, cultural and domestic life. And in its effect on social, cultural and domestic life it is compatible already, albeit on an incipient scale, with all the values that challenge a civilized society's most fundamental postulates. So the question before us now – to give a just appreciation of the restraining part which cold-war political rivalry played in the life of the global community – is not whether or not, but for how long it is possible for modern civilization to maintain the status quo midway between war and peace without the forfeiture of destiny and historicity itself?

Those prepared to take a more optimistic view of the kind of consequences that lend themselves to correlate the presence or absence of crime and decline with certain discrepancies between men with a mission and rebels without a cause, may also prefer to take a more positive attitude towards what appears to be the absence of a higher vocation. I lack the capacity to view such a dearth with quite the same complacency. To be sure, no lucid individual would, or even could, maintain a complete contradiction, least of all that the resort to arms should constitute an advance on the many disturbing aspects of the present cult of violence. Nor, it may be objected, is violence the same as war. But it is nevertheless unlikely that a civilization which lays no stress on either destiny or the heroic in history can maintain confidence in itself even for another century. I fear, on the contrary, that it will only be possible to maintain a morally high standard of human civilization if that civilization receives its impetus from a correspondingly high standard of moral or historic activity. The nature of such activity I hope to have shown. Nor is it convenient to refer to it again here. But insofar as mankind's future might yet turn out to be the self-fulfilling cosmic destiny that evolutionists have been prophesying for centuries, it seems, if I may say so, preferable to concentrate upon the more elevating aspects of that destiny than to inspire militancy in the hearts and minds of those who might yet provide us with an object lesson in Heinrich von Treitschke's very own philosophy of history.

II Crime and Punishment

> I am in favour of war, hanging and Church Establishment!
>
> Macaulay

> The broad effects which can be obtained by punishment in man and beast are the increase of fear, the sharpening of the sense of cunning, the mastery of the desires; so it is that punishment tames man but does not make him 'better'.
>
> Nietzsche, *Genealogy of Morals*

> We are waking up to the fact that although our social problems are less than they were 40 years ago and our society is much wealthier, we are facing rising crime because of loss of values and loss of a sense of purpose.
>
> Kenneth Clarke, Home Secretary. 1993

Some two hundred years ago, at the time when William Blackstone's celebrated *Commentaries on the Laws of England* (1765–69) were about to become a classic in the library of English criminal and civil procedure, those accused of common crimes were barely treated with the civility intended by this enormously fair-minded compendium of jurisprudential principles and legal methodology. There was, in actual fact, no necessary connection between what is now conceived of as supplying a moral element in Equity and abstract declarations of legal principle. Nor did it seem odd that the proclamation of equity was as much dominated by constitutional traditions and civil conventions as it was at the mercy of the King's conscience and due, therefore, to the practical application of the principle that the Crown was the true repository of justice. In fact, anyone who knows anything at all about the statutory and constitutional life of eighteenth-century England will realize at once that order and stability were not achieved by a system of justice reposing on the virtues of equity. From the outset, it is clear that virtue and equity tended to be peculiarly embodied in punitive or even vindictive legislation rather than in the spirit of the law. The whole notion of inculcating spontaneous obedience to the virtue of justice rather than enforcing compliance through fear of the penalty, is something new. In the full sense of the word 'justice' is the characteristic creation only of the twentieth century, since the nineteenth century itself was slow enough to perceive the fundamental truth of the fact that the application of punishment is a very contingent function. Far more important is a sound basis for judicial compromise and the lucid and forbearing handling of the problem of rehabilitation itself.

Though it would be impossible to say that any system of law was entirely equal to its purpose, it is plain from the extraordinary severity of the eighteenth-century criminal code that the legislator then interpreted the problem of rehabilitation as one of applying punishment. His purpose was not to reinstate but to set an example. The evidence for this is the provision for over one hundred capital offences in the English criminal justice system of the time. But the most conspicuous aspect of a century of oppressive judicial legislation, and not only in England, was the very brutality with which the political and legal institutions performed the task of discriminating against the victims of the whole unequilibrated system of social equality. An important feature of this was class selfishness and the domination of the landed interests. There was, in fact, no end to the number of crimes which alone arose from circumstances of hopeless and depressing poverty and destitution. In plain terms, when, as between 1700 and 1800, nearly a quarter of the population of England were classified as paupers,[9] and the unfortunate victims of economic inequality vindicating their need to survive were a power too great to be bound by any law, the law failed utterly.

'I have been in some of the most oppressed provinces of Turkey, but never under the most despotic of infidel governments did I behold such squalid wretchedness as I have seen since my return in the very heart of a Christian country.' Thus Lord Byron in his maiden speech to the House of Lords. In truth, we only have to think of the brutality of the factory system, the high mortality

162

amongst child-workers, the exploitation of the labour of women, of overcrowded industrial towns, dark and poorly ventilated coalmines, unsanitary working conditions, low wages and long hours, to understand why, even when the penal aspects of crime prevention went much further than judicial necessity did in fact justify, it had no morally improving effect upon the potential victims of economic and judicial barbarity. In actual fact, the urban 'mob' acting on the not unreasonable assumption that 'it was as well to be hanged as starved', had already supplied the essential rationale. It was as well to appease them with free beer and the spectacle of public executions when even the pangs of conscience would do nothing to diminish the criminal proclivities of what one contemporary described, perhaps matter-of-fact enough, as 'the disinherited among men, the outcast masses of humanity, who exist but to suffer and to labour',[10] and who, when choosing a 'life of crime' merely chose what seemed to be the lesser of two evils.

The first necessity, then, was an astringent law-and-order policy, even if it was altogether irrelevant to the basic problem: inadequacy of labour legislation and the peculiarly debilitating effects of the social conditions which, with few exceptions, effectively excluded the urban poor and the rural labouring classes from any real hope of advancement. Let us look back therefore to some of the nineteenth-century quests for a more equilibrated humanitarian society and glance over such matters as the Great Reform Act and the various steps in the democratisation of the popular franchise which were not only an immense departure from eighteenth century legislative tradition but necessary preliminaries to any genuine movement of social rehabilitation. For one of the most conspicuous things about Lord John Russell's electoral Reform Bill of 1832 was not so much that it extended suffrage and human rights in England but that, together with the Poor Law Reform of 1834, the Ten Hour Act of 1847, the Mines Act, the Public Health Act, Lord Althorp's Factory Acts which brought statutory limitations to the working hours of women and children, or Forster's Education Act of 1870 which followed the extension of the vote to working men and rural labourers and provided compulsory primary education for all, it also marked the beginning of social humanism and anticipated the Welfare State in its very modern sense.

Although the nineteenth century is now remembered almost entirely as the century of the struggle for the vote, and its legacy to the modern Welfare State thus mainly by implication, the extension of the parliamentary franchise which culminated in the successive Reform or Representation of the People Acts of 1867, 1884, 1918 and 1928 etc., also did much in the way of the amelioration of the conditions of the life of the masses through the introduction of socially remedial legislation. As increasingly representative Governments became increasingly aware of the negative disparity in social achievement between rich and poor, or what Disraeli once referred to as 'the two nations', the development of public health, penal reforms, popular education and factory and child welfare legislation also assumed a new importance. In our own day, of course, one is inclined to take for granted that the establishment and maintenance of compulsory insurance and state pension systems, of social security legislation and nationwide welfare and relief schemes, does involve nothing less than the institution of a permanent social services infrastructure.

It has been well said, that a society is ultimately judged by its attitude towards its poor. And even though it is never possible to account by social analysis alone for specific causes operating within the social context and relating directly or indirectly to individual aspects of criminal behaviour, the argument of first accomplishing social rehabilitation collectively as one of the means whereby it may be accomplished individually, is one that is familiar to all social theorists and modern reformers. We are encouraged, therefore, to compare the obdurate socio-political and economic conditions of the eighteenth and nineteenth centuries with that extraordinary humanitarian implement which the social theorist and constitutional lawyers of the twentieth century have devised: the modern Welfare State.

The obvious conclusion to be drawn, then, would be that a society ensuring the welfare of its citizens through social services operated by the state is also an inherently lawful society and that the exception to this would be the rare and solitary case. At the very least, however, this is a misjudgement of substantial proportions. It might conceivably have worked for England in the eighteenth century, but it would certainly misrepresent the reality of a more sophisticated and more economically advanced society. Truth to tell, few changes in moral behaviour this century would surprise the social observer of a hundred years ago more than the increasing rise in violent crimes under circumstances of generally increasing affluence. Short work is made of the clement vision that human perfectibility is determined by social conditions and economic prosperity. It may be tempting, as a matter of social theory, to institute an exact relationship between the destitute and delinquent elements in modern society, but in spite of the theory, or – turned into its opposite – of charitably expanded social services, minimum wages, limited hours of work, extensive periods of paid vacation and the statutory right of every individual to the freedom enacted by Parliament, there is, upon closer scrutiny, no alternative to the use of law.

There are, of course, laws which are self-evidently necessary. And not only that. Unless human beings cease to be human beings, there are laws that are necessarily self-evident. But, to take the laws which have been ignored since the day they were passed, it is worth recalling that the Queen's pleasure, as reflected in a successfully prevailing Commons majority against hanging, is presently the exact opposite of the relevant criminal justice statutes enacted in the depressed circumstances of eighteenth and nineteenth-century British society. Whatever its remoter benefits, capital punishment has ceased to be the constitutional expedient of an oppressive law-and-order policy. On the contrary, there can be little doubt that its persistent refusal to bring back hanging has made the British House of Commons decidedly unrepresentative in this respect of a very substantial body of public opinion.

This is, in fact, the very ironical thing. At the same time as legal experts in criminal psychology and responsible social theorists are urbanely given leave to resort to judicial discretion rather than the retributive aspects of penal doctrines, the *vox populi* by a more ruthless examination of the arguments, clamours for a reopening of the debate. A debate, incidentally, which in any case is not over hanging as such but over the deterrent efficiency of statutorily enacted capital punishment. In this respect the public demands little proof. The issue is decided, as most emotive issues are, not in a morally responsible manner, but by strong passions stirred. And the interesting thing about an attitude which is almost entirely uncontested by a moral conscience or feelings of moral responsibility, is that it has a marked affinity with the moral brutality of the object upon which it is exercised.

Violence between civilized people, to make the point very obvious, deals with all manner of rigorous and uncompromising excess. And if nothing justifies the deliberate taking of a human life, then, in saying openly what I have already said implicitly enough, the judicial and administrative arrangements that legalize 'murder' do nothing one way or another to moderate the very degree of violence which they profess to reprehend. Nor is this any the less true when singularly brutal acts of homicide, violent rapes, physical assaults or brutal stabbings in full view of petrified onlookers do not reflect crime or criminality so much as they reflect an increasingly pathological, not to say pathologically compulsive enjoyment of criminal activities. Activities, according to which life is being more and more destructively lived. For it is this, its purposeless brutality and insensate depravity, rather than the high index of criminal activity which justifies the sinister reputation crime has acquired in our time.

It is true, as Lawrence Stone has said, 'Right up to the early nineteenth century our ancestors tolerated a level of casual personal violence, and a degree of public disorder, which would be completely unacceptable in a civilized society today'.[11] But never before in the history of the psychology of crime has the common delinquent expressed himself so *pathologically* and *compulsively.* Criminals are becoming ever more aggressively criminal. In fact, the full significance of this propensity emerges only when we assume that the necessity for violence is, and it certainly has so proved, a fundamentally inexpiable atavistic compulsion. A compulsion so primordial that it is all but impossible for any human being to completely overpower it. There are, of course, other and additional reasons, particularly with respect to some criminal aspects of *sexual* behaviour which are clearly anomalous, and of which more must be said here. For if this peculiarly atavistic 'reversion to type' of the contemporary delinquent depends upon the (assumed) psychological necessity or need for sexual violence and aggression, we must not even begin to think that it can be contained within a set of decrees or be abandoned as of right. And the next thing to remark is that despite the enormous psychological effect of such a deterrent stand-by, capital punishment, whatever form it assumes, will prove no more persuasive at the end of the day than were the gallows, flogging or penal deportation at a time when men lived in dread of being butchered by those maddened by hunger.

The resemblance between hunger and sex may not seem at all close enough to make a significant context, but the whole point for me lies in the continuity of the effect – and that would seem to be the case here – of a fundamentally erotomaniac age upon those maddened by sex. When we consider how desperate was the struggle for life, and how the procuring of victuals to keep the body and soul together was the foremost concern not only of individuals but of entire sections of society, it is indeed revealing to discover that sex has become the biggest cause of all. The gratuitous sex-and-drug consciousness of the fin-de-millennium, the unmitigated exploitation of sex for commercial gain, the use of crime as a means even to predatory pornographic violence, all prove the same point, and attempts to control patterns of intimate criminal behaviour through formal legislation enacted by parliaments and enforced by the courts must fail almost as surely as public executions failed to infuse moral purpose into men who stubbornly refused it as an alternative to starvation.

Desmond Morris certainly spoke the truth when he said 'that the advance of civilization has not so much moulded modern sexual behaviour, as that sexual behaviour has moulded the shape of civilization'. As an insight into the requirements of our time, certainly, there is every reason to believe that the customs and patterns of our most intimate transactions may influence social behaviour more powerfully than the statutory enforcement of existing legislation. Indeed, there is no aspect of human behaviour in which we are less well equipped to legislate any enforcement at all. Even the misguided codes of modern homosexual ethics do lay some claim to the equity and endowment of the modern legislature, notwithstanding the fact that this raises fundamental problems at quite another level. But for all its obsessive carnality, it is unnecessary to reason moral atavism from the glorification of sex alone when society's essential immorality, if not as perverted, is at least as widespread.

Sex is at the heart of everything. It has even become a tourist attraction. The great lover has been reduced to the level of an athlete. The whole act has become a circus, a gladiatorial contest, surpassed only by the Olympic Games. Though like most athletic competitions, it requires sacrifice: loveless marriages and a phenomenal rate of family dissolution. Whereas one might have supposed that the promiscuity in the physical relations between the sexes was due not so much to a strong solicitous purpose common to both as to moral barriers which have effectively been withdrawn, nothing much is left of the original language of love. Nor is sex the equivalent of love. A cold carnal lust and a ruthlessly marauding sensuality are the new points of reference, instead, for a conception of sex which, not just from a conventional point of view but from any point of view, is not by a very long way the type of passion it used to be before Freud released it from the genie's lamp to perform such functions in close and profligate association with crime.

Face to face with nineteenth-century propriety, Freud himself did not think of sex as a particularly immoral principle; though, significantly enough, there might have been no psychoanalysis but for the demon in the glass. Once the message was dispensed, however, and the principle of sexual gratification accepted as entirely natural, it became far stronger than its purpose, requiring a fully developed moral being to make a responsible choice and, as a substantially uncontested desire, even led to an exaltation of sex for sex's sake that was calamitous to society and utterly alien to the spirit in which it had been so thoughtfully introduced.

'It tempts people to do an evil action and then kills them for doing it'. Gerrard Winstanley, seventeenth-century pamphleteer put the point forcibly when he condemned the barbarity of the law and contended that delinquency arose from circumstances of economic inequality: 'For surely this particular property of mine and thine hath brought in all misery upon people. For first, it hath occasioned people to steal from one another. Secondly, it hath made laws to hang those that did steal. Let all judge if this not be a great evil'.[12]

Whether to kill or to cure, from the point of view of *that* logic our permissive society, too, tempts people to do an evil action and then punishes them for doing it. Indeed, when all possible allowances have been made, for today's sexual offender, with no more moral sense than a beast of prey, the problem is actually insoluble. He can no more help preying than a beast can. What is worse, the beast cannot help but prey. Nor is he a criminal in the strictest sense. For what would be a crime in law, may not be a crime in fact. He first has to find a way of separating the passions which obtrude themselves upon his instincts from his legal and moral responsibilities and then balance against each other the responsibilities he owes to society. That may be a judgement a morally mature individual can make, but it is scarcely the type of judgement to be expected of the sexual compulsive whose personal experience of an unashamedly libidinous dilemma, conceived of on the grand erotomaniac scale, seems to be oppressive rather than liberating.

Given the tensions and conflicts of having to strike a balance between law and libido, few, one imagines, would deny that today's beguiled defaulter, if left to himself, is ill-equipped, psychologically, to accommodate a libidinous compulsion which in one form or another retains a high degree of vitality at a very low level of moral or legal rationalization. To him the licentiousness of modern society, its incessantly operative promiscuity, is but an instrument of compulsion. An erotic conspiracy and an extra source of confusion which dissipates any real sense of fulfilment or gratification and substitutes physical contentment with commercial titillation without offering sexual compensation. At the very moment he finds his ardour irrepressible the law compels him to discontinue it. In the end he is as ready as any man to pass from curiosity to cupidity and to transmute a comparatively innocuous catalyst into his lusts out of season, no matter how, where, or when – and be damned for the fact. To make matters worse, the only redress the law has for a fraud for which it does not stipulate, is to impeach human nature. And if that is not delinquent, I should say it ought to be.

Still, no inference seems to be drawn or even considered by the incontestable fact that the crime is not his but that of others. That libido frustrated is libido perverted. 'In fact, many of the finest minds in every nation are entirely devoted to defending or condemning poor cretins to months and years of incarceration or even death,' as someone said in a related statement of the case. No verdict, on the other hand, seems to be delivered on a libertine society in which fulfilment not only falls far short of promise but in which every single day thousands of 'poor cretins' become the victim of situations which must inevitably put them at cross-purposes with the law. It is true, nothing may be more democratic than the freedom to view sex in circumstances of exceptional explicitness or even degeneracy, such as the modern cinematographic industry alone can provide. But it cannot possibly be natural, or even pretend to be. Take it from me, one might as well taunt the Devil. Whoever has looked into the abyss will know that the fruits of this absorption are reflected in the wholly gratuitous nature of the type of violence that often follows or accompanies it. The point moreover is rarely made, although it is fundamental to the whole sordid business, that the character of society itself is altered as its freedom is being delimited. For conjoined with this kind of freedom is the new type of sexual deviant which modern libidinous society has been producing, in the ranks of its highest representatives hardly less than in its lowest.

And so we come to child cruelty and childhood sexual abuse, or, as would be far truer to say, the rage against our children, since the substance of it is usually aggressive enough. Not that this type of offence is new. To suggest that is nonsense. As the problem is constituted, however, there is a clear implication that 'our society has gotten sicker, and the abuse of children more bizarre.'[13] It is certainly the case that the largely domestic nature of this particular type of transgression makes the actual incidency almost impossibly difficult to determine. But on the facts of the evidence alone, the reported number of children being shot,* battered, suffocated, stabbed, burned, drowned, tortured, starved, or simply beaten to death, is of all the aspects of the modern sociology of crime not only the most difficult to accept, but immensely to the point in a world in which 'Man's inhumanity to man', as the poet Robert Burns once wrote, 'makes countless thousands mourn.'**

So if the inhumaneness of humanity as exhibited at this moment in time seems to confirm that crime adapts itself to new conditions in every generation, what is especially notable – and this would certainly have staggered and alarmed eighteenth-century social theorists – is that for once it has no economic motivation. Hence it must either amount to the general claim that children 'are seen as a social problem and dealt with accordingly',[14] a waste product of the twentieth century so to speak, or to the more specific claim that infanticide is one of the most portentous, and therefore sinister, facts of modern sociology. And unless, as one hopes may be the case, human nature proves more powerful in the end than the nature of the beast, it will be left to the twenty-first century to determine whether cruelty to children can be met by more stringent laws or whether it can and will

* (1992) Sources suggest that Brazil's child-killers have 'executed' some 7000 children over the past four years.
** The absolute figures are of course obscure, but whereas 30,000 children were on abuse registers in England, Wales and Northern Ireland during 1987, an NSPCC spokesman commenting on the Cleveland child abuse inquiry of 1988, concluded that at least four children a week were dying of 'neglect'.
(1993) German statistics indicate that every fourth girl and every eighth boy are the potential victims of child sexual abuse. An estimated annual 150,000 children are subject to violence at home.
(1994) Murder today is the third biggest killer of children in the USA.

rehabilitate the society which allows such things.

Finally, there is the great complementary issue of 'man's inhumanity to women'. The expression is that of an Old Bailey judge and the theme of this particular subject, like paedophiliac abuse or parental violence, a major one. 'One woman in ten has been beaten last year', in the words of an editorial, 'It is a crime often hidden but committed throughout society'. That it extends to almost every class, race, extraction and cultural level of modern society, is certainly the case. But whether or not this has ever been formulated in precisely such terms, it is also a constant and atavistic reminder, if not indeed a symptom of the very low level of 'domestication' at the fundamental base of a reproductive anthropological society. However, it is not necessary for us to insist on this atavistic ingredient in order to point out that more than sociological forces are involved here, forces whose elementary powers are outside the scope of forensic control. The State, said Milton, can keep the peace but it can never make men good or wise. Hence, perhaps the real lesson is that a society which possesses cathedrals and episcopal palaces, parliaments and constitutions, criminal and civil jurisdiction, courts and juries, equity and benevolence, also sins and trespasses with greater sophistication, effort and skill, adding nothing but fatuous moral criticism to the substance of the jungle laws that have retained great vitality everywhere in the civilized world.

What has indeed remained archaic about it is that between constraining and being constrained it has caught men in the grip of an invisible rage and entangled them in some decidedly psychotic forces, unimpeded by any law. Forces which, like the grim ambivalence of lust and cruelty, are themselves the peculiar increment of paradoxical self-contradiction and which, almost like something alien, something not human, makes men strive compulsively and determinedly towards paranoid and deadly self-destruction. Nor are we perhaps sufficiently alert to the fact that the conventional sociology of crime is unlikely to settle the ambiguities surrounding what has meanwhile developed into the gravest forensic crisis the West has experienced, combining, as it does, carnal with homicidal impulses and taking the whole subject out of the strictly criminological frame of reference by placing it into a psychologically entirely different category, making it ominous, alien and universal: a most unpropitious preliminary for a homicidal process of Malthusian attrition.

171

What is not really disputable, in support of the last, scarcely exaggerated point, is that if unacceptable demographic densities are at the root of social tensions, almost certainly they are the sort of tensions which are at the root of the peculiarly anti-social aggressiveness which, in much the same way, has been found in laboratory experiments with different species of animals. This point has been handled rather well by Desmond Morris, author of *The Naked Ape*, who found that 'aggressiveness can be increased by raising the density of a group of children. Under crowded conditions the friendly social interactions between members of a group become reduced, and the destructive and aggressive patterns show a marked rise in frequency and intensity.' He also points out that 'this is significant when one remembers that in other animals fighting is used not only to sort out dominance disputes, but also to increase the spacing-out of the members of the species'.[15]

Another clue, no less certain, is that intense conflicts between group members is an inevitable social response among communities of rats in confined circumstances of uncontrolled overbreeding. The older ones destroy the younger, the stronger mutilate the weaker. Indeed, it passes as a fact that rats will mutilate themselves. The motive behind this savagery is no longer economic. Nor is the impulse predatory. The explanation seems to be – and this may be taken as proof of our own abnormality – that they are no longer capable of distinguishing between natural and unnatural impulses in what appears like an alienation of the instincts. Interestingly, and no doubt quite consistently, if demographic imbalance helps to account for the behavioural idiosyncrasies which, in this type of social organization, are merely another example of absolute growth imposing drastic measures of Malthusian redress, it is on this account by no means inappropriate to the peculiar circumstances of some of our own overcrowded communities.

Perhaps the point can be confirmed briefly by reference to a recent German kindergarten survey on rising levels of infant aggressiveness. Violence amongst the youngest, it states, is directed not only against others but increasingly also against themselves, i.e. *'gegen den eigenen Körper'*.[16] But what of the others? It was certainly quite different with the abduction and murder of two-year old Merseyside toddler James Bulger. Bludgeoned to death by two ten-year old boys, one of the significant things about the case which at the time gained widespread attention, was that the abduction took place in broad daylight and in the massive presence of people. Which is exactly what would be expected if highly unstable demographic conditions were at the basis of social tensions. In saying this, of course, I am alluding to the above analogy. But whatever forensic arguments may be advanced for or against it, rather than making improbable or ill-informed suggestions, as an analogy one can certainly say that far more significant and conclusive – to lay down the law on a very deadly subject – was the insane and senseless killing of a seven-year old girl who died, stabbed seventy times, as if under the teeth of an enormous rat.[17]

'If I am sane, everybody else out there must be insane!' Serial-killer Dennis Nilsen brilliantly put his finger on the natural balance between his own mental compulsion vis-à-vis society's mental constitution as a collective source of moral responsibility which had utterly failed him. Found criminally sane and accordingly convicted, the belief persisted with him that he had been misunderstood. Therefore, the tensions and contradictions of our time being what they are, perhaps we ought to pay less attention to the character testimony of criminal psychologists than to the anaesthetizing properties of the loss of civilized values which perverts the development of a moral conscience. In a sense, of course, all power of lust over reason is a kind of compulsion, if not insanity. No man, other than a fool or a saint, would try and redesign the nature of the beast. Nor in a world so mad that madness is the only lucid response to it could any compliance look less like an assertion of free will.

Insofar as we are the product of a system of thought control so constraining that our personal compliance appears to proceed, not from our own free choice but from this very era of 'freedom' with its inflationary consequences, the question of guilt is of course beside the point. But one is justifiably apprehensive about the subversive psychological effects of years of relentless and unceasing agitation for the freedom of a permissive moral idealism as a recognizable social creed. As a matter of fact, if freedom of any kind is anything to go by, society has a regrettable tendency to deceive itself about what is a personal indulgence and what a collective aberration. For when it is no longer possible to say that one line of development is negative and another positive, the line between personal indulgence and collective aberration, too, is no

173

longer clear nor identifiable. And that leaves only a choice of anomalies, a mixture of moral contradictions rather than a true choice of alternatives, and no sane man, caught in the confusion of the moment, can guarantee that he would choose the 'better'.

10

DEATHWISH II

I Abortive Females

My intellectual and emotional position is in every respect a completely independent one.

Fanny Pistor-Bogdanoff (Mistress of Leopold von Sacher-Masoch)

Are you visiting women? Do not forget your whip!

Nietzsche, Zarathustra

It says something for the firmness of her determination to compete on equal terms or, as she might prefer to say, to be mistress of her own destiny, that Venus has cast off her furs and instead – so runs a phrase which intimates the important thing to consider – 'keeps a pistol in her knickers'. Which is precisely where one should look for the cause of the conflicts which have arisen as a result of the struggle between the 'natural' rights of a patriarchically conditioned society, and a very strong instinct for certain incontrovertible feminist liberties now held to be self-evident. That is to say, between a very strongly male-oriented society and female militancy as the chief philosophical defender of fundamental feminist liberties.

Formerly it was the duty of the female to experience every sex-act passively, or, in the case where passivity was not granted, to know nothing of ardour save its name. More recently, the purpose of the feminist attack on male privileges has not merely been to carry the fight into the professional and financial spheres but, as part of a long tradition of social reform, it has also been a break with the predominant myth of a passive female sexuality. Indeed, if reform will serve to characterize the attitude of the emancipated woman towards sex, it is scarcely possible any longer to see the dominant feminist theme as developing solely in the direction of equal rates of pay or greater equality for women at places of business and work. But the comment is hardly necessary. We are not dealing with relative freedom. We are dealing with the end of domestic dependency contrived and upheld by men who view every domestic problem in terms compatible chiefly with their own proprietorial interests.

The issue of proprietorship is particularly significant. And it is not enough to reply that Eve was told she would bring forth her children in pain, that 'thy desire shall be to thy husband, and he shall rule over thee' (Gen.3:16). Reading that extract, especially the last part, one cannot help but note the fact that men have lost much of their sense of marital responsibility while women, with perhaps better reason, derive their inspiration in some considerable part from the emancipated ideals the age has set before them, their submissive and passive roles abandoned without regret. Having been subjected to the wilfulness of the male in such moments of passion when male and female face one another like adversaries, they are all the more prepared now to extend an enthusiastic welcome to the intellectual freedom, sexual autonomy, and personal self-assurance such liberating practices and institutions as free love and equal opportunities entitle them to.

Hence, feelings have hardened on both sides. And it is precisely for this reason, one gathers, that the male line of response to the changing values of the age has been to wield his penis like a dagger. The determining factor, so to speak, in a long male tradition of opposing the female franchise. Indeed, it seems a reasonable judgement to make that its double-edged presence, its steadily rising force, has proved a means of resolving at least some of the traumas and conflicts attending the emancipation of the opposite sex. For whatever the precise tenor of the emancipatory recriminations in the war between the sexes, behind the power of the partial, often highly personal arguments, can be sensed a more fundamental rivalry: the rivalry of archetypes diametrically opposed, each guided by its own peculiar *animus*.

The one, being wholly directed towards patriarchal consolidation and decried almost to the point of travesty, is inherently chauvinistic. The other, essentially directed towards a new kind of social orientation, derives in no small part from its utter contempt for whatever has been specific to women as the weaker sex. The point of departure can be found over a century earlier in the conception of 'abortive females' (*Ecce Homo, 5*), of which Nietzsche had so much to say. Today it is embodied in the radical wing of the feminist movement; not by any means a majority, but precisely the sort one meets so many of at present. Feminism and male chauvinism, to marshal the arguments, rest on the tension between the sexes, each operating in its own complementary fashion. And if his allusion, in its uncompromising brevity, is clearly contemptuous like so much that comes from Nietzsche, it would not do to insist too severely that such a statement and its implications are beyond the ken of the nineteenth-century philosopher. Nietzsche, in astonishingly modern terms, had a good deal more to add in rebuke of 'emancipated' women who, to repeat the basic point in his more unequivocal phrase, 'lack the stuff for children'.

Of course it is true, given the profound changes the West has undergone socially and culturally, such a brief and one-sided glimpse can be very misleading. But whilst on the subject of a development unique for its social significance, it is by no means obligatory to understand by the spirit of female emancipation only what, in its essential purity, is meant by the spirit of feminism. On the contrary, the mainstream of female dissent, in love as in business, is devoted to the extended argument for the equality of civilized values which can only become relevant when they have been reciprocally acknowledged. For all we know they may even specify an ideal unilaterally acknowledged by women experiencing the morally liberating effects of a new kind of feminine radicalism which adds the spice of sexual gratification to the more publicly inspired development of new social attitudes. Nor have they rendered inoperative or suppressed the provisions of mischief that lie at the root of feminine life. Something, indeed, it is very hard to live without.

On this level the argument is confined to the simple desire to intoxicate; to possess without being possessed and, whenever possible, to create sensual sublimations by assuming allegorical forms suggestive of nymphs, vixens, she-wolves or tigresses, by turn chaste and shockingly erotic, even of vampires devouring their victims in a sexual embrace, or of temptresses as in Paradise before the Fall, posing as the helpless victims, especially of those they first wish to please and then to deceive. These are myths chosen at random, but the symbols of the allegory in which the feminine mind has laboured so imaginatively, are familiar to all of us. Together they make up a spectrum that serves to illuminate the whole scope and significance of the indomitable will and dynamic urge of feminine life itself; an urge, it should be plain, compared with which the 'prostitution' of the female body is but a small and minor affair.

Women are animated by men, for even the most intellectual of them – and there are not a few – are at times allegorical animals. And even though it is usual to interpret the female of the species as having mythological incarnations to confound chauvinistic male despotism, in real fact the pervasive, if sometimes veiled, desire to intoxicate is deeply innate. It is the whole causality of sex, the spark that lights the fuse. In fact, it may actually be true to suggest that it is to these embodiments, under which she appears as ever a different type to give libidinous expression to the pervasive theme of feminine existence – or at least to its indulgent imagination – that belongs the real credit for 'men's inhumanity to women', already remarked upon. 'There is no evil between men and women', it has been said, 'that is not a common evil'. No one, in short, is blameless, but as someone observed of D. H. Lawrence, he 'was no doubt right in describing as vampires his women characters; the men, soon to join them as "undead", have by some defect of the moral will, made them so'.[1] Bound together by one predominant quality – the power of the opposite sex – he is as much her victim as she is his.

Though allegories are ambivalent by their very nature, this much is certain: the serpent has triumphed. In this incarnation she is timeless and archetypal. We are so accustomed today to the use of particular crusading ideals that we may in fact miscalculate the degree to which feminist emancipation actually serves as a cause to dignify the absence or removal of certain fundamental elements from the social relationship between men and women. Elements that might otherwise commit them to love and intimacy in what has come to be a world of perpetual compromise between increasingly discontinuous interests. Yet, for all the increasing discontinuities between them, it has never been my opinion that female militancy is so much a pervasive attitude towards men as it is the intimation of a pervasive socio-cultural ideal. Nor is anyone likely to object to the suggestion that it is 'inconsistent and unjust to subjugate women, even though you firmly believe that you are acting in the manner best calculated to promote their happiness'.* But what might, in the past, have begun as a power struggle between competing elements of the prevailing social order rather than as a challenge to the pre-existing patriarchal structure, may also have served to create a fundamental shift in the whole life and movement of subsequent anthropological habit and thought.

The most exact statement, then, of the feminist's view of the 'pre-existing' situation is that 'Women started to campaign for particular reforms in the nineteenth century not because they saw themselves as feminist but because circumstances in their own life forced them to protest'.[2] These things mattered more than the existence of women as a free-willed, independent personality. It was not specifically 'female oppression' so much as the harsh necessities of the struggle for existence, particularly in respect to women's condition at work and in industry, which gave birth to female militants inspired by the idea of complete equality for women both in the realm of personal experience as in the sphere of their legally independent interests. In this sense the restrictive patriarchy which, on any pretext whatever, identified the public good with its own exclusive interests, was gradually retreating before the advance of the new female militancy which insisted upon a strictly egalitarian approach to social and ethical questions.

One might say, that the result has exceeded expectations. The passionate intensity of these efforts, the very urge to convert, was bound almost inevitably to suggest the possibility of extending such militancy to matters which had formerly been considered sacrosanct. For instance, since the fear of unwanted children or the fact of inadequate contraception has ceased to be a real obstruction to the abolition of double sexual standards, it has also become more expedient to distinguish sexual gratification from procreational purposes or, though it is not always put into such implacable terms, to insist on 'the right of women to control their own reproductive capacity'. This is a far cry indeed from accepting appeals on behalf of women in 'civil and domestic slavery' as

* Mary Wollstonecraft, *Vindication of the Rights of Women*

179

a valid way of explaining the original purpose of the feminist or suffrage movement. And if, as has been alleged by some social theorists, 'the position of women is an important indicator of the level of civilization achieved by different societies', it is probably no coincidence that not only have children increasingly come to be regarded as supplementary to the whole concept of sexual relations, but that an ever-increasing number of children is receiving an ever-diminishing amount of maternal attention. Many mothers, in other words, are no longer even involved in the rearing of them. 'The nuclear family', it has been succinctly said, 'has been replaced by the nuclear child'.[3]

In itself all this is important enough. But there is another aspect that needs noting. For what makes the sexual liberation of women of extraordinary significance is that the resulting conjugal responses which launched the notorious syndrome that – in the case of Germany (which has one of the lowest birth-rates in the world) – has earned itself the epithet of *Kinderfeindlichkeit*, also marks a definite step towards the absolute decline of the Western indigenous fertility rate. 'Hostility to children' is a concept which explains much, and without necessarily implying that it is as applicable in a feminist sense as it is abortive in a demographic one, it is only natural to suppose that the problem is being compounded by the social and sexual position of women. In effect, as Rabbi William Wolff says, 'The balance sheet approach has now moved from property to life itself. Is a baby going to be inconvenient? Then of course it must be killed in the womb. With that, the untouchable sanctity of life yields to the nebulous "quality" of life'.[4] Nor does he suggest that the social liberation of women is neither desirable nor fundamentally important, but a spirit of procreational pessimism is clearly reflected in what has been called an impending demographic catastrophe for the Old Continent (of Europe) and what might indeed have been called the projected demise of the historically creative races. As in the case of the declining fertility rate, to many it would seem logical to suppose that this demise is itself but a reflection and consequence of the social barrenness and cultural sterility which is just as deeply rooted nowadays as the procreational one and which, to summarize the argument, looks in every respect like an anthropological death-wish.

Here, then, is the end of that era of social history which can be authoritatively defined as its patriarchal stage and the beginning of a new era, an era of syncretic cultural ambivalence which might even include the eventual dissolution of concrete sets of generic relations. To be sure, the attempt to provide anything like a definition of sexual synthesis as part of the feminist design for restructuring modern society involves certain futuristic assumptions that cannot even be envisaged at this point in time. But what I have in mind as a good example of this attempt is something like the development which prefigured the contemporary debate on Christianity under the influence of feminism, including such topics as the degenderisation of devotional language, feminist liturgies, and the idea of divine transsexuality under which the adaptation of God the *Father* to the conditions of a syncretic androgynous society has led to an intermingling of theological archetypes that seems bizarre in the extreme.

Feminism, needless to say, can also be ambivalent in no small number of other causes, but no topic arising out of the debate has been more intensely discussed in recent years than the (Anglican) priesthood of women. Quite unfairly it seems, the entire theological structure is based on the assumption that only men can be ordained as priests. Thus, when in November 1992 the Church of England Synod voted to ordain women as priests, it brought to an end, at a stroke, some two thousand years of apostolic tradition. Obviously one would have to study the devotional aims that lie behind the feminist leap into the metaphysical which, on the pastoral level, the Lutheran and Reformed Churches had long since ratified and institutionalized. But since reason or equality of the sexes is irrelevant to religious experience, it is possible to see the limitations, in an institution so avowedly spiritual as the theological, of a specifically feminist gnosis which countenances a democratically dispensed interpretation of Christianity and emphasizes its egalitarian rather than its apostolic aspects.

Owing to the inherently static and hierarchic structure of its institutional authority, it is of course convenient to treat the Patriarchal Church as a source of intolerance as well as of intellectual obscurantism and chauvinistic reaction. Even so, the incorporation of the female priesthood into the main body of theological doctrine has given rise to a struggle between the *rationally* contrived plea for feminist equity on the one hand, and the *divinely* received quality of gnostic thought on the other. But whether the Reformed Church stands before us massively and comprehensively as the embodiment of a wasted faith, the most

181

ponderous symbol of the hollowness and inanity of pure reason, or as the potential, and potentially abortive, religious consequence of the feminist revolution, of sacrifice to false idols, the result, in any case, is there for all to see. Christendom has turned out in substance different from anything its founders imagined. For the very fact that we now boast an actual feminist equity and an actual reversal of its Pauline prohibition, makes it none the easier to maintain the sanctity that attaches to its apostolic conventions, not just for devout individuals, but as a way of life traditional to all the great Christian civilizations of East and West, and that is what really matters.

It is true that the feminists' social radicalism does not make them political revolutionaries. Nor is there any evidence that they wish to secure power by force. But regardless whether our concern that the emancipation of women depreciates the role of paternalism today is of any relevance or not, in the circumstances of our time and as an immensely symbolic development it is easy to find ground for pessimism in a reversal of the values and causes that have hitherto ruled a reproductive anthropological society. At the same time, too, one has to remember that it was a long and arduous struggle before it even became possible for women to begin to call attention to the intolerable consequences of outdated social attitudes. To be sure, their victory has been hard-won; there is no need to argue that. The observation, however, which I should also like to make is that although it is important to recognize how much their struggle has determined all subsequent developments, the social emancipation of women as a specifically feminist conception was not due on anything like the same scale to the social dynamism characteristic of the spirit of suffragism as it was to the moral dynamism characteristic of the spirit of reason and enlightenment itself.

Though the evolution of reason and enlightenment has usually been obscured by the particular crusading ideals which surrendered to its incontrovertible consistency, in looking back down the long avenue of social evolution from Mary Wollstonecraft to the first suffragette raid on the British House of Commons, it is noteworthy that even such well-defined social movements as women's suffrage and the important concept of feminist equity, have always evolved as an unvoidable consequence of the growth of democratic ideas. Likewise, whether it was to be the advance from the Age of Scholasticism to Humanism and Enlightenment or the religious emancipation as a contest between Roman Catholicism and the Reformed Faith, or indeed between Protestantism and Calvinism or its various dissenting Puritan sects, on a rational democratic level, the emancipation of women, though of a very different emphasis, too, was characterized by the same evolutionary determination to keep faith with that process of education.

We may conceive what impact these developments had. But if Luther's burning of the bull of excommunication was the beginning of an immense theological catharsis, and the cause of Lutheran reform both true and necessary, the great mistake is to believe that it succeeded in resolving the contradiction between the mystery of faith and the need to dogmatize. There is no such thing as religion without revelation. Indeed, as soon as the principle of religious revolution had been conceded in Germany its immediate result was that the whole issue of Christianity as the carrier of mystical tradition slipped from the essential unity of one Christian Faith to disintegrate and lose itself among the general properties of the various minority confessions that subverted its spiritual outlook. The mystery which surrounded the Divinity was never really restored. Nothing demonstrates this better than the intense evangelical piety of Puritan inspired Christianity which combined practical realism with a capacity for hard work to form that last stage of Christian austerity which was sterile, rational, authoritative and unforgiving – above all, unforgiving. In fact, since the exposition of abstract canonical argumentation is taken so far that it becomes virtually dialectical, it seems a reasonable supposition to make that it may not be *religion* at all. Of course, this has only limited applicability, but some aspects of Calvin's theological system, lacking a truly mystical content, are not so much out of line, ideologically, with the feminist position which seems to have evolved, metaphorically speaking, from that of a convert inspired by a wonderfully moving affirmation of faith to that of a zealot who gives himself over to this new dispensation, precisely because it is susceptible to the aggressive rationalization of an adverse and unforgiving spirit.

Hence the appearance of promiscuity as an act of self-emancipation on the part of the female. Of Christianity governed by the rule of reason alone, and, lacking a deeply meaningful context, becoming as susceptible to enlightened interpretations as it has become memorable for the spiritual retribution which followed.

As one can see from the Protestant Calvinist ethic and its relation to Capitalism and economic power, once encouraged and dispensed in the godless language of dogmatic self-sufficiency, religious mysticism – that celebrated paradox of well-known secrets – itself sank to the level of mere rationalization. Hence the reaction. The blanching of a false dawn and the unfulfilment and mortification which effectively dampened down the type of rational euphoria that believed itself on the threshold of universal enlightenment, but which is but a record of the retributive despondent experiences which have led to this sense of failure, to the spiritual tragedy and to the disgrace, the despair and the shame of the West.

This may well be stretching the topic beyond its original objective, for compared to the progress of this extraordinary demise, feminist liberalism, in the event, seems a very minor affair. Yet, when adapting the spiritual analogy which is so deeply embedded in the heart of the West, to the theme of what has been called 'the living reality of the femine dimension of humanity', we may expect though we may not yet have reached the end of the 'war of the sexes', that the mortification of the original Christian spirit and the promiscuous experience ascribed to the religious freedom of reason, are experiences through which triumphant feminism and its brazen new confidence will also have to pass.

There is one thing, however, about which there can be no dispute. If this gradual abandonment, individually and collectively, inwardly and outwardly, of a natural mystery for the sake of an agreed abolition of the sexual division of labour, anticipates what may perhaps be called the 'discontinuity' of the feminine dimension of humanity, one imperishable fact remains: man's debt to the woman who has deserted him for the pursuit of a task in which she must succeed entirely or fail at her own peril, is still beyond all measure. Indeed, it would be hard to rue an association which so rewarded him. Meanwhile, of course, one has to remember that she has committed herself to a course of action she cannot possibly evade, and that the enticing prospect of sexual and social emancipation, rendered all the more agreeable by the freedom it confers, ceases to express all that life can mean the moment it fails to appease what is, in my judgement, an almost inescapable sense of personal deprivation. Indeed, to note this is to note the loss of perhaps the most sublime form of worship: to love and be loved. I know of no substitute whatsoever, and I very much doubt that anything other will come out of its forfeiture than the psychological consequences of the mental conflicts and stresses which are already fully evident in a modern emancipated society.

There is a paragraph in one of Juliette Drouet's letters to Victor Hugo which forms an eloquent commentary on an aspect of love now more than ever out of place but which here impresses by its very sense of the archaic. The figure of this woman, fascinates by her evident simplicity no less than by her sense of sacrifice. This may not be so easy to understand now, but somehow she was able to make her peace with a love that was the bitter fruit of fellowship with a man who had become the conscience of France in some of her worst moments under Louis Philippe and Napoleon III. Nor is this the place for an account of that, but in writing of it very compellingly there is something deeply touching, almost exalted, in the love of this woman who belonged to an age which, with its penchant for romantic expression, it is difficult to recreate. Remembering their shared moments and entirely convinced of her own true feelings, she concludes on a reflective note:

'Do you remember our moments in setting out, and how we snuggled up under the hood of the diligence? With clasped hands and shared hearts we lost all feeling for everything that was not our love. And when we arrived at the end of the stage, when we visited cathedrals and museums, we looked wonderingly at everything through the mist of love that filled our hearts. At how many masterpieces did I gaze with enthusiasm simply because your words threw light upon the mystery! How many steps did I climb to the summit of interminable towers, *simply because you were climbing them in front of me!*[5] (my italics).

Forever shadowing her man, ever drawing closer to her champion, 'giving up everything, sacrificing everything', as and where the occasion offered; 'always guessing where I was . . . always finding me'(Victor Hugo), it might also be said that this quality of personal sacrifice explains everything else about her love, whether in a positive or in a disparaging sense, not excepting even that marvellous display of stamina which seems to have been a concomitant of her affection, if barely distinguishable sometimes from slavery. From my point of view, however, it was this surrendering force, designed perhaps to be the great conciliatory gesture which, for better or for worse, fulfilled an inwardly conceived purpose and which would, *ipso facto*, function purposively.

The deepness of this attachment brings us back to that disagreeable topic: male chauvinism. Of course, Victor Hugo, had his deficiencies. His faults, indeed, are glaring enough. Nevertheless, we must not take to imposing our own notions and values upon someone else's relationship, nor analyse their feelings out of context. In truth, fulfilling their natural destiny, who can resist such a moving testimony of the feelings aroused by the love of a woman for a man and of a man for a woman which existed between Victor Hugo and his mistress Juliette Drouet. In subordinating all her qualities as a female to her role as a woman, she seems to demonstrate her capacity for striking an essential contrast with the triumphant attitudes, the professional swagger, the ostensible independence, the flamboyant gusto, expensive commitments and intellectual liberties which are *de rigeur* nowadays with so many female militants imbued with the idea of confounding both, human nature and human society.

This is not to condemn the extent or the limits of female influence, nor is it for the 'psychologist of the eternally feminine' (Nietzsche) to set himself up, in her adversity, as the arbiter of her affliction. The modern emancipated woman is not a Juliette Drouet. Nor could she possibly desire to be. To suppose that is ridiculous. But one cannot help thinking that, with the radicalization of the feminist franchise, the progressive and liberating elements struggling to emerge, entire areas of feminine understanding Juliette Drouet naturally epitomized are quite outside her genius. That she often combines feminine attraction with a mind in many respects superior to that of the male, no one will be disposed to deny. But, having cut herself off from the essence and mystery of womanhood as the main source of her power, she rarely appears to us as sexually charismatic. Indeed, there seems to be such a distinct difference in properties now, between the new enlightenment and her former charismatic femininity, that in the process she seems to have surrendered her own inherent genius. Rather in the same final way one is tempted to suggest, that Prospero surrendered his magic wand, resolved never more to make use of it.

We cannot, of course, speak with certainty on such a retributive quality as feminist nemesis. But it is to this declension in her art that I am referring when I speak of Prospero's magic. Nor am I saying that the words of a man living in the past, however committed, should not give away to a cooler appraisal of the cause which, as determined by itself, has to run its course for the best as well as the worst of reasons. But in propounding the ambiguities implicit in that course, indeed, in demonstrating the emotional aspects as distinct from the moral and ethical issues, legal, actual or otherwise, one cannot ask for a better judgement than that of a man, the best servant she ever had. In fact, it is a reasonable assumption to say that he may well understand better than she does the meaning of the mystery which contrasts so profoundly with the attitudes and preoccupations of today's revolutionary womanhood whose brittle sense of attachment, at once less affectionate and notably less secure, seems comparatively unsusceptible to the need of the male for her abiding love and affection.

II Redundant Males

There is little manliness here: therefore their
women make themselves manly. For only he who
is sufficiently a man will – *redeem the woman* in
woman.

Nietzsche, *Zarathustra*

And I will show of male and female that either is
but the equal of the other.

Walt Whitman, *Leaves of Grass*

In any consideration of the history of the movement for the extension of the franchise to women it is obvious that one still has to
distinguish between the advent of women's suffrage – to all
intents and purposes the 'ark of the covenant' – and what might be
called the 'vulgate' view of modern feminism. Though not notice-
ably less radical, it is utterly different in kind. In fact, it scarcely
belongs to the same history except as a progressive,
perfectionist afterthought whose primary considerations are frequently overstrained or even posthumously argued. Unfortunately, however, it cannot be thus dismissed. Indeed, having once
made that distinction, it is rendered even more complicated by a
confusion in the public mind between the concept of feminism
and what is sometimes perceived to be female homosexuality, for
only with the former is it appropriate to speak of any progressive
movement at all.

This situation is not, perhaps, an unexpected one. To begin

with, there are many reasons which explain why, after years of patient constitutional agitation, the enfranchised feminist tradition has been transcending the boundaries of a purely emancipatory movement. Reasons, as we have seen already, which go very deep and involve the rejection of far more than the mere bonds of male chauvinist authority. The patriarchal barrier in a society long dominated by socially conservative conventions, is perhaps less easily set aside. But then, socially conservative realities, too, have been changing as the impact of women's sexual liberation has been affecting them. For if we agree, for example, that there was a definite connection between feminism and socialism in the early parts of this century, might we not also suppose that between the modern liberal feminist and the lesbian or gay activist there is at least a measure of resemblance? Of course, not every feminist was necessarily a socialist and while the description lesbian or gay is recognizably true of a large number of contemporary feminists ('one of the motivating factors,' as it has been described, 'of the extreme feminist movement'[6]), it must also be used cautiously. Its application to the exponents of another social conception, formed by different influences and living a different way of life, may be prejudicial or even misleading. But it is easy enough to see nevertheless that if we take a modern lesbian activist and place her beside her feminist contemporary, vastly different though they may be, the most striking thing about them is not the difference between them but the social and psychological climate they have in fact in common.

Freedom of sex has become the badge of a common progressive identity. The chief ideological expression of this particular sense of unity and cohesion which seems to be affecting all those who share the same general conception of independent sociosexual values. For good or ill it is one of the subtlest and most effective instruments of ideological expression ever contrived. With its constituent libidinous elements in particular, it is a convenient, even compelling, inducement for young men and women moving uncritically in the framework of homoerotic values. A framework, it should be plain, which has been carried far beyond the limits of its proper anthropological use. Barely one more step is needed, one feels, to cause a corresponding change not only in the interpretation of the role of human sexuality but in the sexual etiology of human behaviour itself.

The one clear purpose, then, of the progressive dogmas and

liberalist maxims which made the gay usages and lesbian practices of its exponents not only socially possible but socially
acceptable – recognized in other words, rather than acknowledged – has been the substitution of the homosexual ideal with a
crusading one. Similarly, a combination of factors, both social
and anthropological, led from the very condemnation of homosexuality to a tacit acknowledgement of its demographic significance as a Malthusian preventive. That out of this crusade should
have come the discussion of hitherto unsuspected questions about
the social significance and the constituent nature of homosexual
life is but an indication of how deeply implicated in the work of
liberation the lesbian or gay activist feels himself to be. Besides,
considering how much social grace, intellectual verve and cultural variety the homosexual individual, whether male or female,
frequently imparts to his heterosexual surroundings, it would not
seem extraordinary either that the 'genus' includes so many men
and women of outstanding talent and exceptional ability if not
actual distinction. On this point I totally agree with an editorial in
The Independent, 'only a glance is required at the list of homosexual geniuses down the ages – from Michelangelo to Britten,
Bacon and Nureyev – to show [that] the contribution of homosexuals to making society more civilised and less brutal can
hardly be overestimated.'[7]

There are, of, course, more extended arguments on the subject,
such as human or natural (sic) rights. Nor, in the life of a civilized
man, would one question such claims in law to social or sexual
equity. One could do no greater wrong. But my case is not as
simple as that. For me it is the wider significance of its implications that needs concentrating on. In the first instance, it should
be understood in its strictly anthropological context. To take my
criticism as implying any greater degree of opposition to existing
transsexual views of modern fashionable society is neither justified nor desirable. In fact, my objection is not to the homosexual
but to the *lobbyist*. Nor that he neglects to perform a function
which he never attempts. The reverse, in fact, is true. He attempts
to perform a function which he cannot possibly fulfil. And this
obviously limits the value of a crusade which qualifies as an
evolutionary movement only if, in the event, it antedates a mass
development and initiates universal change. Or is it really true to
say that this conflict over the ethics of homosexual preferences is
a vitalist force, striving, as a movement of social renewal, to

regenerate a decaying and backward-looking society on the one hand and an intolerant and prejudicial heterosexism on the other? That it is not, therefore, subject to the general limitations which apply to certain atypical areas of human sexuality but representative of vital and significant development?

It is well over a century now since Karl Marx described 'The relationship of man to woman as the most natural relation of human being to human being. It indicates therefore,' he said, 'how far man's natural behaviour has become human'.[8] Expressed roughly at the time of the first reform bill, such reasoning lacks none of the attributes that distinguished the moral outlook of the nineteenth-century bourgeois. Which is far from surprising in an age in which the relationship of man to woman was still very much subject to statutory control. Nor, on the other hand, did Karl Marx overstate the case. The one objection one might raise today is that his statement is controversial – highly I think – in its last section, the part concerning man's 'natural' behaviour, for as an index of modern social development it is, I believe, one of the commonplaces of modern social philosophy that patterns of *natural* behaviour have been falling rapidly into decline.

Some would doubtless reply that moral propriety very often has the drawbacks of its merits. And certainly, it can easily lead to intolerance or the kind of righteousness which combines the propriety of a bigot with the morality of a prig. Beyond any question, whenever concerns for social and sexual equality may be legitimately translated into considerations of personal freedom and equity, they should be made to assist the development of those considerations and perhaps even be subordinated to them. As a matter of historical fact, the homosexual is a very old ingredient of even the most cultured societies. Nowhere, in truth, were the peculiarities of the social structure of human society more favourable to homoerotic practices than in ancient Greece. This notwithstanding, few would disagree that the institution of marriage is and has been devised to encourage 'the most natural relationship of human being to human being'. And what Marx meant comes through clearly enough. It is, for instance, nothing short of ridiculous to attempt to use aspects of natural reproductive life, such as full-scale nuptials which have a purpose all their own, as a means of joining men or women of a very different sexual orientation. In such spectacles of marital union, whether civil or ecclesiastical, one is much more likely to stress the comic rather than the social aspect. Indeed, it is embarrassment rather than social achievement one is conscious of. Nor can the fact that such a union is peculiarly barren in its ends do anything but add a note of artificial resolution to a ceremony which only serves to confound so much merit in virtually every other field of cultural and intellectual distinction.

Here the crusade is flawed. It is pure Jeffersonian imbecility. An extraordinary exhibition of social self-delusion. Indeed, one is almost tempted to go so far as to say that no age and no civilization bound by ethical norms has ever known so staggeringly and sustained a subversion of its cultural ideals and of the social, intellectual and spiritual dimensions of its cultural life, by a socially active and legally acknowledged, minority, than the civilized West. And nowhere else, so far as I know, have its exponents been able, on the basis of the most utterly uncritical hedonism to which a period of egalitarian freedom ever gave leave, to canvass their sexual views and consolidate their libidinous ideals on such blatantly brazen and blustering terms.

Let us examine this astonishing development. To begin with, one does not criticize lightly what some of the greatest authorities on the subject have taught us, sometimes with considerable disregard for their own reputation: that homosexuality is as congenital to the libidinous impulse as heterosexuality or any other form of sexual activity in which the carnal desire expresses itself. This is an enticing notion. I am bound to say, however, that even though there has been a fundamental change in public standards concerning the question of sexual relationships, the conventional bias which can be found in various attitudes adopted towards ways in which the homosexual individual experiences physical love, is still one of scorn if not outright condemnation. There is, in truth, a general misgiving that homosexuals are congenitally disposed towards promiscuity. Nor would such misgivings be reversed by anti-discriminative legislation achieved in Parliament. It is all very well to regard homosexuality as genetically predisposed. But the difficulty with this view is that in the overwhelming majority of such cases the sexual preference is neither predetermined nor an 'inclination' but a personal indulgence and, hence, under the influence of conditions which are part of modern sexual history, a perfectly contrived development. At the same time, as a definite group with a certain status of their own, there is no lack of evidence for an anxious quest in search of credible objectives, for a spirit for social conciliation and genuine public self-sacrifice on behalf of many a determined lobbyist who still believes himself in the tradition of earlier reformatory movements, even though it is with a repertoire now of marital travesty and patently unattainable social ideals.

No doubt it is also true that there is a complete absence of contrivance in many, perhaps the majority, of the 'major figures' behind the great artistic, philosophical, literary, theatrical and aesthetic movements of the twentieth century whose affinities are evident and unaffected, who keep their personal sex-life and communal agitation distinct. Who are also, or rather principally, concerned with subjects other than the campaigning issues which are the culminating points of homosexual doctrine. It almost forces one to reflect why, with such a remarkable tradition of creative influence in the arts and intellectual spheres, there should be such a fierce obsession or, as in the case of the lobbyists, aggressive pride about being 'gay'. A doubtful posture if the object is to conciliate rather than stimulate public opposition. Nor, to judge from the manifestations of popular opinion, does the public at large readily accept the connection made between the liberation of women from political, social, economic and sexual subordination and the liberation of gays from heterosexual oppression. Albeit that from the whole character of the homosexual controversy there emerges the impression of an immense emancipatory struggle. Except that now the predominant myth is in the form of a great genetic prepossession which sees the struggle as a necessary step on the way to social reform and sexual enlightenment rather than as a manifestation of its relative significance and importance in the general scramble for sexual freedom.

As part of a process of social transition all this rests exclusively on a growing involvement in the great ferment of a new freedom which is decidedly more libertarian than it is liberal and we may therefore allow that as a credo it sinks deservedly beneath our notice. In any event, one thing is plain, as an aberrational aspect of modern sexual history rather than as the necessary basis for a transformation of modern sexual relations, it deceives no one. At the very most it can attempt to set up a community devoted to limited, largely contrived, objectives rather than succeed in translating the individual experience into a universal truth for popular consumption. And nowhere is this truth more wide of the mark than in a community which, because of its increasing proclivity to convert such specimens into figures of martyrdom and melodrama, ostensively takes pride in the notion – a notion which has become celebrated and continues to be repeated – that homosexuality '*is an inclination as mysterious in its origin as heterosexuality*'.

Nor is this mystery restricted to the homoerotic kind. For here in fact is a formula to which every paedophile would as cheerfully subscribe. To say nothing of a great number of very sensitive individuals for whom the source of its mysterious origin is by no means its moral essence. We are moving, it has been said, in a descending spiral of iniquity, and if this kind of specious reasoning had any force, it would be applicable to a wide variety of very iniquitous circumstances. For astonishing as it may seem, these are precisely the kind of inferences which, as the rallying point of the great liberal morality debate, have become suffused with a large dose of Christian charity and the sense of sin overruled by ecclesiastical sanction.

Naturally, the spirit of reform varies from church to church. It has been especially strong in the Episcopal Church of the United States where, as an exercise in compassion, disaffiliated theologians are attempting to legitimize homosexual marriages. Sweden's Lutheran Church, too, moved closer to accepting homosexual cohabitation after an internal commission recommended a more liberal attitude. By contrast, it is not until autumn 1995 that the Synod of the German Lutheran *Nordelbishe Kirche* will contemplate such a discussion: 'Ehe Familie, und *andere Lebensformen*' (sic). Liberal Domination of the Church of England already assumed critical proportions at the noteworthy 1987 General Synod debate. The traditional position of the Church, to the effect that fornication, adultery and homosexual acts are sinful 'in all circumstances', no longer found favour with liberal theologians. Unsurprisingly enough perhaps in the face of counter moral pressure from her own unrepenting clergymen. At the 1988 meeting in London, in answer to a motion calling for *impenitent* homosexual clergymen to be expelled from their parishes, the General Synod evidently chose the better part of discretion by refusing such a demonstration of its anathematical power. For the Church to probe into the sin, to exegate on its canonical significance, and to condemn the nature of its evil, would be, so it seemed, to condemn herself.

That bad omission apart, we need not here follow in detail the liberal controversies of a Church ridden with morals corrupted by homosexuality or, in the words of the Rev. D.R.J. Holloway, 'guilty of the Gnostic heresy of sex'.[9] The fundamental error in any case, is to believe that the 1987 Anglican House of Bishops ever, in any exact sense, condemned homosexual acts on the part of practising gay clergy. While the individual clergyman behaved pretty much as he liked, the then Archbishop of Canterbury – and spiritual leader of a world-wide institution, nonetheless – merely ventured to suggest that they were 'falling short of the ideal'. An often quoted but seldom decoded line. For those moral conclusions which make ecclesiastical sodomy nothing worse than the pardonable error of the misguided and misled are conclusions which, subject to a little permutation, 'changed the truth of God into a lie' (Rom. 1:25). They certainly did not follow from the more traditional canonical position but once treated with the same passionate fidelity, 'served the creature more than the Creator.' Personally, I could not but regard this as an astonishing self-exposure, as a *post facto* exculpation of homosexuality as the second most completely dedicated form of a Christian vocation. Nor, do I believe, could I possibly have joined in *his* worship. Indeed, if this evangelical view-point of near perfection was ever to be consecrated, it was perhaps most revealing as showing how inevitably theological vacillations of this kind bring every debate in the end to a surrender of the superior values of ethical humanity to the secular needs of the follower of opinion, and that – in a footnote – is the last refuge of a moral coward.

Frankly, one has to find one's way as best one can in the prevailing confusion of evangelical view-points past or present, which are often in conflict if not in actual contradistinction to both apostolic authority and the unceasing and pervasive census of its ethical foundation. Time was when perfect adherence to the religious life required the complete abandonment of all sexual activity. Nor did this requirement stop at would-be priests and clerics in full pontificals. It is true, what may be learned from the strictly canonical debates of the early Christian Fathers no longer tells us anything today. Nor, for that matter, can Jerome's observation that 'marriage differs from virginity as what is good from what is better' altogether escape the practical significance of changes in cultural and sexual attitudes. In particular, it is no doubt perfectly true that what was then viewed as 'falling short of the ideal' is now considered especially good form. But whatever happened to self-denial as the sum of the Christian verities? For without necessarily establishing a connection with the ethics of the past, it is nevertheless true that the essence of the sacrificial character of Christian ethics lies here and that perhaps the most fundamental moral and theological distinctions of a Christian calling can only be derived from a high standard of vocational discipline and personal self-sacrifice.

Ironically, while the authority in doctrine is still prattling on about a *return* to virtues and qualities it bears absolutely no resemblance to, the real problem is that the modern church has been caught in a secular situation which makes it difficult to achieve a balance between the spiritual regeneration of modern man and the ethos and integrity of his oldest theological values. Worse still, where there are too many shepherds and not enough sheep, she has had to fight for the validity of an omnipotent ethos as disseminated by Christ against that of free-thinking liberals who have been distinguished with such epithets as 'modernists' and 'theological minimalists'. Their gift to this world has been a deftly seditious sense of perfection. A trend which has become especially evident in precisely those defiant and potentially irresponsible innovations which the Church in its desperate game of enlightenment has been obliged to condone. There is an established axiom, not unnaturally, which decrees the extinction of any institution that has lost its reason for being. One notices, however, that they have taken it upon themselves to create an organization capable of meeting an entirely new scale of public expectations. And certainly, it vastly extended the scope of the idea that the church may permit what she has usually been known to forbid. As one writer has suggested, 'A Church may win what the world calls success by exploiting the superstitions of the vulgar' – by way of falsehood, in other words – 'and by making unholy alliances'.[10] For that, indeed, could be said of the radical change in the traditional relationship between the First and the Third Estate which saw the birth of the international Anglican Church as a surrogate ecumenical organization capable of exercising numerous functions normally reserved for revolutionary movements and, indeed, as a special left-wing forum for subversive political propaganda, that simply has had no precedent in the past.

The notion that the Christian Church must meet every social requirement and seek to entertain at all cost is a modern development about whose desirability there may indeed be doubtfulness. Could it possibly spring from the assumption that the church is the mouthpiece of popular opinion? That any form of dissociation between her and the populace would be inimical to her standing as a 'tribune' of the under-privileged and their inveterate resentment against the establishment? The reasons are plausible enough. But it is a very grave mistake, nevertheless to think that the spiritual life of a vast community of people can be ministered by a company of priest-theatricals retailing the theological compromises of a church which can never make up its mind about the latest trend in official doctrine. In fact, there is this further to be noted. The theatrical resourcefulness of the Anglican Church in Great Britain, as elsewhere in the world, has been nothing short of miraculous. Of all the followers of Christ, this ardent Virgin has had the hardihood of marketing the Saviour as a proto-Marxist man-of-the-people. Not by words of compassion for the man who died, in his thirtieth year, on the Cross which now merely marks an abandoned outpost, but as a creed of the utmost ingenuity. As a matter of fact, if ingenuity will serve to characterize the attitude of the Christian Church – whether Episcopal, Lutheran, Reformed or Anglican – as a centre both of worship and of social affairs, one might as well say that she has been bought and paid for. That something more like a harlot's finery than a virgin's veil has been the symbol of her calling. That it is always the same promiscuous pledge: Be silent Millions – *I am the people's whore!*

No one appeals to her in vain. Not even for the blessings of the marital union between adults related to one another, what might to all intents and purposes be described, as within the prohibited degree. The idea that homosexual partnership should be put on a par with the profound institution of marriage and thus absorbed into the administrative and legal system, is indubitably the supreme moral contribution to the new world social order of a modern Christian civilization. As we have seen, the Church of England Synod already seemed to be extending potential acknowledgement to the courtship of a man for a man when it raised the validity of homosexual relationships to the dignity of a spiritual contention. But without question the most controversial contribution to the history of this epic can be found in a secret and confidential report debated by the 1990 London House of Bishops. Commissioned by that august body as long ago as 1986, the Osborn Report, it may be stated very briefly, advocated

197

greater understanding of practising homosexuals, suggested that there should be services of blessing for committed homosexuals and mentioned the possibility of placing foster children with homosexual couples – unhappily, so far as the former are concerned. It also, as an almost inevitable corollary, cautioned against too strict a heterosexual bias in primary education.

It matters not a jot that the report was 'not an accepted policy document' of the Church of England but 'advice for the House of Bishops' and as such merely under 'consideration'. It is even more irrelevant that the matter was being treated with the utmost secrecy (and out of sight of the community whose morals were going to be so significantly affected). What matters is that the source of doctrinal authority was, and is, not only used and manipulated by men whose concern for religion seems perfunctory rather than theological, but that these men represent the coercive sway of a world-wide institution. And it is this which gives them their power. Power is unequivocal in this regard. It really makes no difference how minute a virus may be or how innocuous a nucleus may appear at first sight. When even Priests, Wise Men and Law-Givers are ridden with question-begging vacillation, it feeds on something which is, if anything, of the same subversive quality in the popular mind as that which produced their noxious view on political violence, was godfather to their sterile condemnation of unrepenting sinners and has since led to a thousand absurdities – some of them of the most mastering, manipulative and degrading vein – which are our present inheritance.

True, this may be a somewhat emphatic account of the way in which a once great religious insitution, even in decay still the moral custodian of the West, of its traditions and its establishments, has been affected by the shift towards the *social* Gospel. Nor can I readily bring myself to surrender my own conscience to a conditional and consensual authority which presents an absolute doctrinal prerogative in terms of social economy and invites rather than exhorts. Its limitations are self-evident. Indeed, I would dearly like to go along with the *Christian* ideal as a standard for judging religious duty if it were not for the great harm done by that section within the Christian fold which are not in any strict sense exponents of the Gospel but who have transferred the source of their authority from 'the consciousness of God' to the keeping of popular opinion as a new expression of divine good will.

Vox Dei has become *vox populi*, to borrow a significant phrase. As religion declines social and theological objectives are no longer even distinct. The transcendental treatment of religion and theology has given way to a kind of pseudo-religious sociology. Meanwhile, since theology itself rules out the promiscuity implicit in the relationship of men to men, the question of providing a sufficiently remedial principle for what is being sacrificed is evidently problematical. The apostolic necessity for its redemption can be met only by careful circumvention of the terms in which the concept of theological sin finds application. Fortunately for its exegetes, the literal language of the Bible is a peculiarly ambivalent one. To argue along canonical and apostolic lines does not necessarily imply that, as the instance of a general law, all triangles must have angles that sum up to 180 degrees. The matter in other words, because of the difference in the requirements, has to be put into some sort of non-Euclidean perspective. And certainly these requirements have little affinity with apostolic convention, theological or moral. For it must be said that the spectacle of renegade canonists leading the faithful in solemn procession to Christian altars and – as a most diverting footnote to twentieth-century sexual history – of wedding them literally, has to mark the beginning of an altogether new type of Christian revelation.

There has been something of a 'civic' groundswell in recent years amongst the numerous gay and lesbian communities scattered throughout the Western world. It is, for instance, common knowledge that thousands of registered homosexual marriages have already been celebrated – and presumably consummated – on principles of constitutional law in some such pioneering country as Denmark. This hardly seems innovative now. Enough has been said to make that obvious. Of course, the ideal method of solving the problem of promiscuity is to forestall it. But nevertheless, one can have but a poor critical judgement not to perceive that the family is the basic unit of human society and a significant, indeed a critical part of that sense of anthropological and moral tradition which can plausibly be referred to as the most important, the most permanent and the most vitally cohesive factor in public and communal life.

Personally, I find the 'Registered Partners Bill' of 1988 as unlikely a determination of the true social status of the happy participants – and it might be worth diverging at this point – as the

Mad Monarch Ludwig II's unseasonal determination to furnish proof that it was summer by dining out of doors. One would be hard pressed to think of an ass who took greater pride in his ignorance than Ludwig II of Bavaria during the last winter of his life. And yet, to the best of my knowledge, when pointing to someone else's madness, there is no finer example to furnish proof of one's own sanity than the story of *Incitatus*, Caligula's favourite horse, member of the College of Priests and the most unlikely recipient ever of a Roman consulship. Nor – to establish a viewpoint – is there a period or age in the whole of human history whose extreme absurdities, when comparatively examined, seem more nearly concomitant with the follies of Rome (where, according to Tacitus, all things foul and shameful found a home) than the age in which we live.

Few names have come down to us so versatile and prodigious as that of Gaius Caligula, enlightened bungler and the most renowned jester ever to earn himself the laughter of a disbelieving world. But whatever Caligula's royal reasons for rewarding his horse with a Roman consulship, it seems to me – if Incitatus will allow me to say so – that this particular consul so closely resembles Denmark's enlightened Parliamentarians in the quality of *their* horse-sense, that I am very much mistaken if he would not also have made an excellent ass – a distinction I think they have justified.

But I was saying. Fatuity being one of the worst symptoms of our present state of confusion (rather than of decline), or at any rate a power unique for its blinding opacity, the authenticity of the Partnership Act credentials, as distinguished from the passion of its participants, seems to be proof enough these days that not only men's reasoning and intellectual capacities, but their instincts and emotions, too, are subject to two mutually antagonistic conceptions of love. It has, moreover, become something of a commonplace to claim that we are in the midst of a cultural revolution. And so far the emphasis has been on sex, its universal symbol and its most passionate instrument. We can believe, if we like, that the distinction between love and sex has ceased to be significant. But when two standards of judgement, of moral convention, of human perfection no less, are fending for the right to forge the social and anthropological conditions of our future heritage, without question something very enormous indeed appears to be happening. It is not, of course, impossible to imagine that posterity may have a different opinion. We must wait and see. What matters for the time being, however, is the degree to which the ethical content of the Western world itself is being subjected to change; that it is not even clear anymore which standards, whether moral, psychological, anthropological or otherwise, can be agreed upon for good or ill by *all* rational human beings. And this, whether we like it or not, is the crux of the whole perplexing business.

III The Invasion of the Bodysnatchers

> One must admit that it is impossible to show why
> certain things should not utterly destroy and end
> the entire human race and story; why night should
> not presently come down and make all our dreams
> and efforts vain . . . e.g. something from space, or
> pestilence, or some great disease of the atmo-
> sphere, some trailing cometary poison . . .
>
> H. G. Wells, *The Discovery of the Future*

> One should not want to be physician to the incur-
> able: thus Zarathustra teaches: so you shall pass
> away!
>
> Nietzsche, *Zarathustra*

Never in human experience has a date in history and a moment in time been so extraordinarily apt for the totally sudden and unex- pected entry on to the demographic stage of one of the strangest diseases in the history of human epidemics. Not only has if baffled virologists and confounded haematologists by its extra- ordinary complexity and attracted the attention of augurs and prophets, but as an experience as intensely acute as the experience of a slow and terrifying nightmare it almost seems like a living portent of the greatest human trauma ever and as apparent a sign of God's displeasure as ever was visited upon the lands of the Philistines. With the exception perhaps of a massive concern with the greenhouse effect, no single topic has occupied more attention in our day than the theme which can be summed up in the term most often used to denote its key-factor: *Immunodeficiency*, the factor which has a complicated connection to the inability of an organism to resist and overcome infection and which, in its most comprehensive expression, seems all but designed to complete what global warming leaves unfinished.

Thus, the issues are closely joined. What may be said of the greenhouse effect may also be said of the notorious immunological breakdowns. Indeed, what is regarded in some quarters as an act of terrible retribution has also come to seem an almost inescapable consequence of the blessing of the great Industrial and, *mutatis mutandis*, Sexual Revolution, or, in the case of the latter, of frequent, purely hedonistic (and 'alternative') ways of non-procreative sex. Thus, almost within a century – or respectively, a decade or two – man has not only contaminated nature, defiled the woods, and polluted the fields and rivers of the Earth, but the immunodeficiency virus has become absorbed into the very bloodstream of the human race. In fact, it is one of the indices of the acquired immune deficiency syndrome's highly sophisticated nature that it has become perhaps the most representative condition of a society in which protective anthropological taboos and restraining moral traditions no longer play a determining part.

Incidentally, it is with no intention of censure that, in the opening remark above, I have used the word 'apt'. The term may seem gratuitous. But since it is now commonly accepted that the enormous reproductive surge of billions of human beings cannot be sustained indefinitely, this is precisely the moment for saying that, when taken to its logical conclusion, there is only one inescapable end in sight. There can, of course, be no question of saying that a civilization distinguished not only for its system of states, laws, cultures and education, but for morals and ethics as its unifying, even dominant, force, should be made simply to annihilate itself. But it is a mistake, nevertheless, to suppose that the admirable results achieved over the first two thousand years of modern civilization can be continued under circumstances of ever-increasing demographic concentration. Nor, in my opinion, can preventive contraception make a decisive contribution to the real demographic requirements of both the developed and underdeveloped countries of the world. On the contrary, I fear that sooner or later a stage will come when an affirmative answer is the only answer given to the question of whether or not Aids is a preferable alternative for what many believe to be a rather more comprehensible Malthusian argument: ever-increasing military attrition.

For those individually concerned, always under the shadow of a syndrome perpetually impending and perpetually adjourned, I doubt whether it is possible to provide a more abiding torment, to put it at its mildest. But there is a dilemma here. For the remarkable thing, in making this point, is that albeit over ten years now since Luc Montagnier of the Pasteur Institute in Paris first announced the discovery of the deadly virus, the essential facts known about HIV are still medically inconclusive. In spite of massive research into the epidemiology of the disease, there are a great many questions about the precise aetiology of this phenomenon, its enormous expansive power and preventive treatment or therapy, which even today have remained very largely unanswered. The reason for this is by no means obscure. An agent can be effectively treated by another agent only if it is consistent in itself, and that HIV is not. Nor, as to the initial stream of hypotheses with regard to the inaugural stages of the syndrome's virological evolution, is it possible even today to deny that, beyond the fact that immunodeficiency and homosexuality are jointly and closely associated with one and the same condition, science itself is quite incapable of dissecting it into the varied potentialities it originally affiliates. Isolating the molecular structure of the infecting agent is one thing, but proving what caused the virus to evolve, as one might suppose, over many years, possibly decades, is another matter entirely. All of this is elementary, of course, and it is unnecessary for me to recapitulate the full history of Aids research into the cause, detection, prevention, treatment and cure of the disease, when it is long apparent to anyone knowing the facts that even though a definite correlation between homosexuality and immunodeficiency cannot be seriously denied, the plain truth of the matter is that the principal disseminators of the deadly virus today are predominantly men and women with heterosexual inclinations.

To speculate, then, on ultimate causes, is to plunge into imponderables. In the unorthodox case of Professor Hoyle, I concede, one must be sensitive to the uncommon nature of his contention that 'terrestrial life is a phenomenon which originated outside the Earth.'[11] But, Sir Freddy, at all events, also made the startling assertion, though with what accuracy one cannot tell, that the germ strains which have caused the outbreak of diseases, plagues and epidemics in the history of the human past, have all been infiltrated from outer space. Though most scientists would disagree with it, some of them such as flu-epidemics, are even said to be caused by sun-pots. Nor is there an easy way to judge whether Sir Freddy's firmly pronounced conclusion that we are 'the descendants of life seeded from the depths of space',[12] has any scientific basis in fact.

Are we supposed, then, to take this seriously? As a matter of fact, Fred Hoyle may well have been resurrecting the concept of 'panspermia'. The idea that living matter is universally diffused in space had in fact been circulating ever since the Swedish scientist and Nobel laureate Svante August Arrhenius (1859–1927), one of the founders, incidentally, of the modern science of physical chemistry, first propounded it. The view is no longer held, but in many ways Arrhenius' notion that organic matter is constantly emitted from 'habitable worlds' in the form of microscopic spores that traverse space for years or even ages, is not a bad description of Professor Hoyle's and Chandra Wickramasinghe's formidably held opinion that space is full of viral germ-strains and that life in its earliest form, which is to say, during the first two thousand million years or so of the earth's biological evolution, did in fact emerge through continuous absorption of organic compounds from space. Nor has this theory ever been entirely discredited. On the contrary, there are now tolerably good indications that the organic molecules necessary for the formation of life may well have been introduced with an earthly bombardment from space by comets and asteroids some four billion years ago. There is one feature, however, that distinguishes Hoyle's and Wickramasinghe's idea of free organic distribution. They are probably alone in their belief that the earthly biochemical evolution necessary for the organization and formation of most living cells, has been selectively controlled, not as one might have expected by biochemical agents and physical laws, but by some cosmic intelligence that has interacted with mankind throughout its terrestrial history.

One does not have to be a votary of science fiction to see that this captivating conjecture may give rise to many an ingenious theory for anyone wishing to ponder the invasion of the planet Earth by beings from a distant world. Beings, if it were feasible, from which primitive mankind is not only considered to have received its molecular code, genetic information and basic evolutionary knowledge, but, subsequent experience may suggest, the human immunodeficiency virus which, assigned to us from afar, has entered the earth's atmosphere at a crucial demographic moment to play a decisive role in human affairs. Hoyle wouldn't have put it in just those terms, but as the authors of *The Search for the Virus* have said, 'if we could play at being Satan for the day, charged with the task of designing an epidemic to undermine both the developed and underdeveloped countries of the world at the end of the twentieth century, then the blueprint for the design would incorporate many of the features of AIDS'.[13]

But whatever its origin, it is sad, tragic, even catastrophic, but not perhaps coincidental – to speculate on proximate rather than primary causes – that hundreds of thousand, perhaps millions of people who would not otherwise have fallen victim to lethal infections should now be doomed to premature death as a consequence largely of sexual promiscuity. Indeed, the factor of promiscuity is considerable and – even though I am not for the moment concerned with whether or not this is a moral issue – the classification into higher and lower risk groups no more inappropriate to the special nature of the disease than a division into homo- and heterosexuality. From 'the cult of anonymous and almost incredibly frequent sex', as one critic put it when describing the homosexual 'liberation' in the United States of the 70s, to an acute sense of being discriminated against.

Much righteous indignation has been expressed by homosexual activists that we are being preoccupied with morals rather than with strategies for fighting Aids. This is not wholly unjustified. Nor can recriminations alone produce moral purpose. It is important to recognize, nevertheless, that even though it is going altogether too far to say that moral laxity is the essence of the matter, contagion at this rate and level has everything to do with the theme of licentiousness as we have become familiar with it in the spheres of theology and ethics. The entire history of mankind, incidentally, has been conceived in a highly principled and fundamentally moral imagination, even though it is true that as a moderating force, the moral veto that imposes constraint is today of academical rather than of an ethical interest. One may disagree, but at issue is not so much the question of homosexual culpability (which may or may not be significant) or the struggle for homosexual rights (which will be enlarged upon in the course of this argument) but an uncomfortable presence, in the heterosexual paradise, of the serpent of promiscuity. What ultimately defeats us, in other words, is the inevitability of a disease that spreads with the aid of actual procreation. And the real problem facing us is not pathology as such, but a characteristic and significant lack of personal responsibility on the part of those who seem to conceive of life primarily as a playground for the exercise of the libidinous faculties. Someone very effectively summed up the role of the serpent when he said that man was too highly sexed for his productive needs, so nature was killing off the most highly sexed – the promiscuous.

Inevitably, this means a fresh look at deeply held moral beliefs about men's natural leaning towards social responsibility or other collectively felt values as the predominant basis for a healthy morality. Moral perfection of any kind is rare, and though it may be pleasant to be told of the right to make personal decisions, it is in the human character that without a certain sense of collective responsibility in public life, its moral values easily become contemptible. Collective responsibility, moreover, applies particularly to the individual. It means, in principle, that the individual member of society, in sexual relationships as in all other things, is subject to a golden mean; not to prescriptive moral proprieties as a relatively circumscribed or ethical creed, but essentially to the transformation into ethics of biological relationships.

Moral exigencies are never purely man-made compositions of the human will. Rather they tend to arise spontaneously out of a natural anthropological need. To obey them is in fact to obey a law of nature. To disobey them is to have severed a natural bond. The truth is that even though this relation to natural laws was not invariably a religious relation, the dependence of morals upon biological attributes may, in the early stages of social evolution, well have been the driving force behind the development of all organized metaphysical systems whose restraining influence on the individual life, on a wealth of sensual appetites and physical relationships, should always be kept in mind in order to fully appreciate the *organic connection* between moral ideas and the men who so held them.

It is, moreover, a common assumption that a great variety of taboos with respect to sex, food, or drink, must have a scriptural basis; that social virtue cannot, in truth, be separated from religious, or Christian ethics. In its fully developed form, however,

207

the reason for the moral taboo has changed just as the rationale for individual responsibility has undergone a variety of institutional and social transitions. That was inevitable. Conscience no longer recoils. The taboo has lost its sacred attribute. Religion, it is now being contended, is primarily a social artefact, an aid, no more, to secular or individual living rather than a moral-metaphysical concern. But virtue is transient and the pursuit of pleasure persistent. And if his ritual observances of the sacred taboo, which had both an occult origin and a moral justification, were important for the aboriginal as a code governing his anthropological childhood, they appeared to follow a rule for which parallels are not hard to find throughout all major systems of totemistic worship and social customs as an interdependent way of life.

All civilizations, without exception, whether Christian, Judaic, Islamic, Buddhist or Hindu, were conditioned by the presence of certain social and anthropological needs. Orthodox Jews must abstain from the consumption of meat which has been improperly slaughtered. Muhammad, as a reading of the Koran makes clear, prescribed the strictest laws of prayer and both, as an Islamic code governing social behaviour and as a rigorous system of hygienic laws, imposed abstinence from spirits or wines, periodical fasting, sexual temperance and (ritual) cleanliness. Untouchability is given prominence in a system of Hindu beliefs or social customs and is as near in importance to chastity as anything in the Old Testament where the concept of sin is given an almost predominantly sexual interpretation. But at no point should the Oedipus taboo be quoted with reference to any particular system of religious or totemistic laws, linked as it is also in Greek myth and tradition, with both sexual immorality and the universal significance of the degeneration of biological barriers and anthropological laws.

It is easy to question all, or very nearly all, of this as outdated, exotic or a matter of purely religious concern, as obsolete cultural archaisms even, pertaining to the remote or primitive past. But the plain answer is, that nothing we know of taboos and their prohibitive nature on the one hand or of their unforgiving retributive powers on the other, makes our having acquired a new and unconditional immunity at all likely. For the time being, therefore, we may simply take this 'immunodeficiency' as adding to the evidence of the retributive power of the biblical prohibition of the sexual sin which appears not to be entirely without a certain poignancy directed at a sense of moral propriety that we ought to preserve in even the most emancipated circumstances. So general indeed was this appreciation of the dangers set forth in the comparatively florid context of the New Testament, as may be seen for example in Romans 1:24–32, that the moral laws which subjected men to the principal significance of its apostolic authority became a distinctive characteristic of a civilization which had inevitably absorbed sacred canonical attitudes in order to impose a measured judgement upon all its legal and constitutional actions.

On it depended, for instance, Henry VIII's 'Acte for the Punnyshment of the Vice of Buggery' of 1535, which transformed what had for previous centuries been an ecclesiastical offence into a felony punishable by death, even though when Civil Law ousted Canon Law it was still measured by such standards as the canonical system of ecclesiastical jurisprudence demanded. The law against 'the most horrible and detestable vice' was vigorously confirmed in the reign of Elizabeth I. In both cases the statute had been designed to uphold a long-standing ecclesiastical prohibition against an offence which was punishable by burning to death in France and, either singly or in combination with adultery, still carried the death-penalty in some parts of seventeenth-century Germany. Subject to gradual later adjustment, including a royal warrant against 'vice, profaneness, and immorality' in the reign of George III, the law remained on the statute books in the overwhelming majority of – intending no value judgement – civilized countries until the twentieth century took a somewhat more benign view of the vices of an earlier civilization which in more characteristic eighteenth-century accents, were said to admit of 'no palliatives'. Insofar as that was true, in 1780 two homosexual offenders were actually stoned to death in the pillory as a unique mark of popular disapproval. And it is precisely for this reason that, in a climate of opinion opposed to these things, emancipation was gradual rather than sudden and dominated almost entirely by the need to balance so much popular distaste with certain fundamental civil liberties. This is particularly true of the former USSR where, plainly, even as late as 1989 homosexuality was still a serious offence carrying a penalty of five years in a labour camp for consenting adults, whereas in the remarkable case of the USA, 'this mad penetration into the very dregs of liberty' has flourished as in few other countries of the civilized West. Here 'everything has its rights', as Peter Ustinov so acidly said of a similar matter, 'even pornography'.[14]

In China, not usually considered an evolved society of a highly sophisticated or cosmopolitan culture, gays are still vulnerable to arrest and sporadic beatings by the police. Curiously, this treatment does not mean that homosexuality is illegal. It is more probably the continuation of the social consensus by the public at large of what they have traditionally denounced as 'abnormal', the expression, it might be said, of the true instinct of the great mass of the people. So if our own social emancipation has brought corresponding generic changes and a new set of sexual relationships, we cannot, without contradiction, speak of a form of behaviour which must once have been *natural*. I do not say that one is worthier than the other. But I do think that what is 'natural' is validated by its congenital *norm* and by that alone. So if there is a suggestion here of moral default, as if the granting of a greater measure of sexual freedom had been decisive in its influence on the pursuit of happiness as a hectic and hedonistic way of life, its relevance here is negative precisely because it pretty much offends everything of natural or normal value and therefore can scarcely be considered inoffensive or even held dear. The briefest way of illustrating that, in principle, the sexual offender is an outsider is to cite Freud's quotation of Northcote W. Thomas, the anthropologist, who states flatly that 'the violation of taboo makes the offender himself taboo'.[15] His behaviour, in other words, becomes distinct from that of the simple tribe and, consequently, fundamentally harmful to it.

Here then is the heart of the matter. The taboo was not only a normative form of law but also, like a fervently held religious belief, the guiding code for modes of behaviour that were its biological counterpart. A society has been well defined as 'a moral community held together by shared values'. Some societies are more 'evolved', of course, than others and, in any case, few taboos still exert their original spell. But no community is favourably disposed towards the apostate who is seeming to compromise the communality of the group, and if it cannot bend him to its own purpose it obviously becomes preferable to ostracize him in what is essentially a manifestation of the communal faculty for self-regulation – properly speaking, the jurisdiction of the man in the street – which is fundamental to all anthropological thinking. Conformity to the tribal habit expresses communal integrity. Transgression is tantamount to apostasy. The logic is subtle, but it is also compellingly simple. In a word, to throw in one's lot – in the mythology of anthropology (which is neither stale nor out of date) – with the proscribed forces of the universe, is simply to perish with them.

To some this might seem an attitude of extreme paranoia. But if it seems unduly doctrinaire in defending the value of traditional thinking or unnecessarily reactionary about the cause of (homo)sexual liberation, it seems no less extraordinary that a society whose most pressing duty it is to overturn a sexually transmitted epidemic should look upon the mandate for upholding a conflicting sexual prerogative as a matter of equal concern. Time was when the need for religious precepts and the fear of divine retribution built into them, served as an indispensable anthropological purpose, when it was the taboo which secured the success of the moral objective. Today the willingness to accept moral constraint is greatly diminished and the demands made upon it far less exacting. In a similar fashion, a confirmed social habit of continually creating 'taboos' by moral customs and conventions has long since been abolished. Our morals, therefore, tend to be more and more arbitrarily derived from a number of anthropologically conflicting interests – whether it is the rule of the pithy prejudices of the 'primitive mob' or that of 'progressive self-righteousness' in a pressurized cosmopolitan society – without anyone once admitting how far this compromises the responsibility of humanity as a collective concern.

I will not labour the point that the public liberation of gays, as a social and and sexual accomplishment, is neither congenial to popular views of morality nor congenital to the struggle for human rights. By which is meant the struggle of man striving upward and asserting his dignity through certain natural or inalienable rights, precisely because these are held to be self-evident and not because they are held to be destructive of these ends. Nor is it for me, perhaps, to deny that the desire for happiness is an inalienable and legitimate aspect of every human existence, and not as such invidious or a cause for rebuke. Even so, I doubt that the presumed right of an increasingly assertive minority to force the silent majority to accept it on its own terms, bears resemblance to anything but the lip-service that virtue has paid to vice. Vice has been turned into virtue because we are no longer conscious of the contingent character of the organic connection with which the moral intention began.

There is no need to go further. Unless one takes an unwarrantably benign view of the present immunodeficiency, any reasonable inference from the excited and over-stimulated behaviour patterns of those closely connected with homosexual mass-rallies and metropolitan gay-migrations, must lead to the conclusion that they have become the victims of an irrational herd-instinct. A most suicidal instinct, if at all closely examined. For it is this, I believe, together with an almost desperate, death-wishful expenditure of pleasure, which has singled them out for precisely that end they largely appear to have proposed for themselves. Not unlike the drowning-act of the Lemming, it is certainly one of the most striking examples of death-wishfulfilment in humans. At least one would think so from their almost deliberate acceptance of all contributory causes.

If the contention seems extravagant, it cannot be for the reason that proof of it is provided many times over at a time of massive homosexual urbanization. As I have said, the desire for happiness is not in itself a cause for rebuke. It is the very essence of life and liberty. There is a time, however, when the pursuit of Life and Liberty may well become excessive and that of Happiness precisely one of those deviations from the necessary 'striving to surpass' without which civilizations inevitably begin to disintegrate. Nor is it 'Gay Pride Week' which matters in the present context but, to make a final assertion, the hedonistic dissolution of the West.

'On that note I will end,' as a certain man of letters said upon quite another occasion, 'proposing no remedy for there is none, save by such as can make the deaf to hear, the blind to see, and the incurably vulgar to hold communion with the gods.' Which is a sobering reflection, if he is right about the deaf, the blind, and the incurably vulgar, for all those whose sad and cheerless misadventure may furnish a lesson for these terrible times. Times which have a large and troubled theme. It certainly involves this author's sincerest appeal. For even if not everyone is entirely happy with the conclusions I have drawn, my reservation is that problems are not removed by being unacknowledged. And, without necessarily concluding that it will be heeded, my appeal is to those very anonymous victims whose numbers by now must be millions or more and who, if figures can prove anything, are indistinguishable from millions of others whose ultimate fate may largely depend upon their being convinced of its *moral* truth.

PART THREE
DEATH OR
IMMORTALITY

I wish preachers of *speedy* death would come!
They would be the fitting storm and shakers of the
trees of life! But I hear preached only slow death
and patience with all 'earthly things'.

Many die too late and some die too early. Still
the doctrine sounds strange: 'Die at the right
time.'
Die at the right time: thus Zarathustra teaches.

Nietzsche, *Of Voluntary Death*

11

THE PLANET OF DR MOREAU

"Curs'd wolf: thy fury inward on thyself!"

Dante; *D.C., Hell, c.vii.*

'*Damn that howling!*'

Wells, *The Island of Dr Moreau*

The number of people who nowadays sense that
something is fundamentally amiss with society is
not small, but sadly they dissipate their energies in
protesting against one inconsequential matter
after another. The correct thing to protest, as I
propose to do here with something approaching
mathematical precision, is the cosmic origin and
nature of man.

Fred Hoyle, *The Intelligent Universe*

The great Sir Francis Bacon, lawyer, philosopher, Lord
Chancellor and perhaps the most unequalled thinker of the
Elizabethan age, frequently and implicitly affirmed his belief that
God, being the divine Creator and having bestowed upon men the
capacity for imaginative thought and rational inquiry, in return
expected rather more than mere proficiency at prayer or a high
degree of religious devoutness. Being no ascetic himself, and
deserving of some very small and contemptible things as well as
of some great and distinguishing thoughts, that, on reflection,

seems reasonable enough. Indeed, in an age unused to such freedom, there were few Elizabethans more gifted. And not surprisingly, as a pioneer of intellectual reform Sir Francis had some rather precise ideas of his own about what he himself felt to be a thoroughly original and previously unthought of method of rational inquiry.

The one example he pointed to when calling attention to the inadequacies of the academic practices and usages from the age of Aristotle downwards was the drawing of logical inferences from deficient or insufficient premises. It was no good thinking that facts could be made to fit the theory. The problem was to determine a method for the classification of knowledge and for eliminating errors until, so far as might be possible, only one causal consideration remained. And as a matter of principle to have made the concurrence with experimental fact the chief determining consideration for or against the falsehood of a theory was in truth a merit to which the rise of experimental science in the seventeenth century was essentially due. The choice of method determines its result. Indeed, the new method of *induction*, with its findings based on verifiable facts, was generally and intrinsically a process of elimination. It demanded that every hypothesis must be subjected to the test of scientific experiment and is probably the first and closest approximation to our modern notion of science as a formal concept. Its importance to science in general, quite apart from presuming to challenge the Olympian authority of Aristotle, thus derived from the experimental approach to scientific questions as the only analytically viable method.

The effect of this on science was marked. Indeed, it is a striking indication of the genius of this extraordinary man that he managed to escape not only from the intellectual climate of his own time but also from the vast prevailing system of medieval philosophy on which every one else drew for evidence of the soundness of their ideas. In a sense, of course, Francis Bacon was interested in the practice rather than in the theory of scientific inquiry. For when he turned his back on the method of deductive reasoning which essentially looked for facts that fitted scientific preconceptions, he decisively took the view that the pursuit of knowledge for its own sake was at least as meaningless as the false scientific plausibility which had been generated by a speculative mixture of unverified data and inadequate premises. It was clear, in view of the obvious lack of appreciation of the true nature of science and its real aim, that knowledge must aim at progress and seek to re-establish the *imperium hominis*, the sovereignty of man over nature which had been lost with the growth of an extensive system of false dogmatic principles and blind medieval theories.

As a factor in the advancement of knowledge, science bulked large. And the advancement of knowledge as the noblest of all possible endeavours, was a subject to which he would continually return. At the same time Sir Francis believed that his new scientific method ought to be complemented by an equally serious concern with the needs and requirements of human existence. Indeed, one important function of the new science would be to alleviate social distress and to exploit scientific discoveries for the general benefit of human progress. It also meant that no responsibility could surpass the responsibility of applying knowledge 'for the benefit and relief of the state and society of man'. In Bacon's words: 'To teach men the use of their knowledge so as to command nature', was, if one had to direct a guiding principle at the institution of science, a more worthwhile contribution to the requirements of the new age than a method which was valueless, because inapplicable, unless it commanded the support of a significant scientific context. Once that context was lacking, the danger as set forth in a mythological metaphor was that 'knowledge that tendeth to profit or profession or glory is but as the golden ball thrown before Atalanta, which while she goeth aside and stoopeth to pick it up she hindereth the race.' Taken at the level of the metaphorical explanation Sir Francis' words are in fact unequivocal. Without a deep and determined purpose as a vehicle for its imaginative powers, even the most brilliant intellect is certain to drift into waywardness, or, to keep up the analogy, 'all manner of knowledge becometh malign and serpentine'.[1]

One does not have to keep reminding oneself of Bacon's enormous genius in order to see that there are strong reasons for trusting in his wisdom. The scientist, like the philosopher, believes in boundless possibilities of improvement for the human condition. Unfortunately, being in search of personal recognition as much as anything else, he is subject to allurements of his own. Hence, there is an enormous contrast here between the glamour that modern scientific exploration has acquired during the past fifty years or so, and the kind of questions Sir Francis himself had felt were important. Other dangers are less apparent. But inevitably, so far from being the free subject of frank scholarly communication, science has increasingly become the object of intense professional rivalry. Especially of the profit-oriented variety. A great many scientific developments of the twentieth century are not only distinguished by a marked absence of – to quote once more the line from *Valerius Terminus* – 'the benefit and relief of the state and society of man', but by a sense of scientific sensationalism running far ahead of actual research. Which is the more true, of course, among researchers receptive to a sense of personal distinction. And that is a pity – especially when the alleged break-through fails repetition in other laboratories.

This is not to say that modern science lacks either the capacity or the industry to grasp its social or evolutionary purpose. Nor is it true that such a purpose is notoriously difficult to define. Indeed, the most resolute charge to be brought against science, particularly when considered as an institution of progress and enlightenment, is that such a purpose has not been allowed to assert itself, that it has been modified as a result of developments which in themselves may adversely affect the prosecution and pursuit of discovery. Quite conceivably so. And indeed, when it comes to assessing the comparative merits of a wide range of scientific innovations which are about to unchain a technological revolution potentially as universal as that which inaugurated modern industrial society, the possibility of doubt and error must at least be admitted. This is especially the conclusion prompted by the enormous importance ascribed just now to what has also been called 'the most astounding prospect so far suggested by science.' The very prospect namely – as determined by the laws of DNA and the molecular biology of the human gene – of being able to engineer our own biological future.

This may work satisfactorily enough for so long as the scientist's creations are kept within a well-defined ethical and experimental limit. But turning to the matter of moral concern (and that of all concerns is the most difficult to balance) the scientist will give us nothing in time to come which we now recognize as ethical. Nor is this to anticipate. But I think it sufficiently clear that societies become unstable precisely because the relationship between evolution and purpose has become unstable. And where well-defined evolutionary patterns no longer exist, as I have argued elsewhere in this book, there is nothing left to correspond to the former consensus of ethics. In fact, following a line of

218

thought owing largely to H. G. Wells, if moral censure is to be apportioned it ought to be directed not against the scientist as the explorer of a dangerous art or against his overpowering desire to extend the frontiers of knowledge. That is nonsense. It ought to be directed against a society which is showing signs of an incipient irrationality because an exceptionally recondite technological civilization has reached a state of perfection that demands an outlet in some major evolutionary development. All collective irrationalities, sexual deviances and sociobiological anomalies are therefore the consequence and outcome of the contradiction between the exigencies of social progress as a major evolutionary requirement, and the facade of complete social harmony as constructed by social scientists. And in my view, indeed, all ought to be seen alike as the pathological disorders of a severely destabilized species.

It is easy to get carried away into confusion as to what in fact this implies, and it is important therefore to survey the forest as a whole rather than see individual trees. As an example, however, there is no way to improve on the kind of possibility, whether it was ever seriously intended or not, that test-tube baby technology should make it feasible one day even for a man to become pregnant. This may seem quite an innovation. But actually, there is a double unwholesomeness here. To begin with, I particularize this flight of fancy – as I might particularize a number of others – because, as any experienced midwife would have told its authors, it takes something rather more than the self-indulgence of a wayward scientist to actually *rear* the progeny that might derive from it. 'These people are bored', says Margaret Mallon of the Union of Concerned Scientists. And as a serious scientific statement, seen in the context of a healthy reproductive society, the suggestion is of course ridiculous, contrived with no regard to viability. Yet, by a curious paradox, there seems to be some degree of support for the context in which this idea has come to fruition. A context in which the switch from male to motherhood has been so subtle that we are probably not fully conscious of the ethical conversion. Nor is it nearly as far removed as it could be from some of our present ideas of what constitutes the struggle for human rights. It has genuine prophetic power because it epitomizes the truth, not about a categorical evolutionary imperative, but about the sheer ambivalence of the marginalizing evolutionary process. For the rest, I can only say that if the extraordinary possibility of male motherhood owes almost as much to its appearance at the 'right'* moment as to its undisputed biological possibility it also demonstrates that the madhouse of the modern mind is never quite able to examine itself with any degree of detachment.

It is a reasonable inference, in any event, that the transition from male to motherhood is an exertion that few men would make with grace, and none without finding himself involved in a confrontation which touches on the entire relationship between the sexes. On everything which has given a procreative anthropological society purpose, identity and motivation. In fact, though we might be hard put to it to say exactly just what it means, the problem of motivation for a superior technological civilization and its own sense of anthropological significance, is at bottom, and fundamentally, a very serious matter indeed. That much is perfectly obvious. What is perhaps less obvious is that, because the tale of the pregnant male is of all bio-technological feasibilities by far the most preposterous, it is also the kind of feasibility that would furnish the strongest argument in support of an otherwise uncertain truth; that the absence of evolutionary purpose compounds the causes of evolutionary decline. When science leads to travesty it is in a state of manifest decay. It is time to question the values which allow their possessors to perpetuate the kind of society in which the desirability of our very survival becomes dubious, if not desperate, because it is perverted by the excessive consequences of fruitless and futile living.

This brings us to the essence of scientific responsibility. For the fact is that the error of giving false judgement of what it means to be a scientist or to pervert the ethos one should try to sustain, is by no means a new one. And if we bear in mind that evolution deals in ends and not in means, we may well doubt whether the 'eugenic' enlightenment of a new scientific alchemy will ever make innovative cultural transformations in the sense that Newton, Darwin, Faraday and Clerk Maxwell, or Einstein made cultural transformations. We have already noted some of the views of Sir Freddy Hoyle in the preceding chapter, and even though they cannot be admitted without a prior denial of Darwinian biology, there is no denying Professor Hoyle's opinion

*The possibility of male pregnancy was first raised in 1986 in an article in *New Society*, a now defunct publication.

'that it is not so much a case of biology influencing the state of society as it is one of the state of society controlling the thinking of biologists'.[2] Nor is it always apparent, perhaps, that evolutionary and human purpose can never be other than reciprocal. As for the interpretation of that purpose, I do not believe that reasoning is a matter for the intellect alone.

It is likely that no such misgivings governed the surgical skill of an aberrant scientist such as Dr Moreau. Which is precisely why his story deserves to be read, both for its peculiarly symbolic value and because it affords a striking illustration of a wide range of issues in ethics that must ultimately be faced by all such representatives of scientific progress. H. G. Wells' *The Island of Dr Moreau* is in many ways a fascinating book. Not only is it one of Wells' earliest successes, but no subject could have offered him a greater or more varied potential for possible ambiguity in our own moral attitudes than the force of its inspired madness. There, however, the ambiguity ends. For obviously, even when the more apparent failures of Dr Moreau's surgical and vivisectional experiments with ursine, feline or bovine creatures, i.e., with bears, cats and oxen besides apes, swine and other such beasts, are disregarded, it needs little imagination to see that the grafting on of human characteristics to creatures which retained the souls of beasts, their lusts and their savagery, and which are neither instructed in the ways of virtue nor sensitive to moral values, had to remain a misguided anatomical concern.

But it is unnecessary to go into detail. What chiefly concerns us here is that if its absurdity is immediately apparent, the chief objection to turning beasts physically into a semblance of human beings is not at the level of the physiological transformation. It is that it gives a false representation of what it means to be human. It is true, all this is hypothetical enough. But, conscientious objections permitting, from the moment that point is conceded there is actually no objective way of saying what distinguishes the means and ends of Dr Moreau from the means and ends of the modern geneticist who, to pass beyond theoretical discussion, seems to have brought to a new stage of perfection what in the case of Moreau essentially amounted to a moral difficulty over the corresponding concept of ethics. That Dr Moreau's purpose was absurd is a prospect we need not, in fact, even discuss. As a necessary step towards forming hypothetical human beings out of a hybrid array of savage beasts, his creations inevitably became conditional on unreasonable contingencies. The Beasts, it was plain, were so innocent of any human criterion of ethical knowledge as to be quite unassailable by moral or rational argument. As a matter of fact, such differences in mental constitution as would be expected of beasts not humanized by 'psychic inheritance'[3], made total obedience to 'a series of propositions called the Law' absolutely indispensable. Clearly and definitely stated: 'Not to go on all fours; *that* is the Law. Are we not Men?' etc., it had the merit of being so simple-minded as to require no further reasoning or imagination for its understanding. But it utterly subordinated the Beasts to a great deal of indoctrination and thought-control. And that precisely was Moreau's purpose.

Dr Moreau was the absolute lord and creator of the Beast-Folk who feared, obeyed and recognized him as such. And then there was the Law. Ritually endowed with incantatory powers and especially created for their own protection, it would exalt his personal deification, magnify the momentousness of – in the terms of this special case – the Creator, and impel the beasts to join the *Sayers of the Law*, such as the Ape-Man, in ritual obedience to the particular instances of the general litany:

> '*His* is the House of Pain.
> *His* is the Hand that makes.
> *His* is the Hand that wounds.
> *His* is the Hand that heals.
> *His* is the lightning-flash.
> *His* is the deep salt sea.'

Behind these words, to which all other considerations were subordinate, may be read the calamity of the Beast Folk, the fear and the agony of their limited powers of reasoning and their desperate desire in some small way to transcend them. One recognizes that such transcendence was absolutely necessary for the victims of an irrational instinct. For their physical metamorphoses, though designed to simulate those of men, did nothing to relieve the tragedy of their position. As a matter of fact, the outcome was never in doubt. From the moment they began to taste blood again this strangely effective analogy ceases to deal with their sporadic progress and turns to the reversion of the Beast Folk as their lust to gratify themselves becomes too strong for the Law to parry.

222

As one can see, it may well have been considerations as conflicting as these that persuaded Charles Darwin to declare 'that man with all his noble qualities ... with his god-like intellect which has penetrated into the movements and constitution of the solar system ... still bears in his bodily frame the indelible stamp of his lowly origin'.[4] And it is perfectly true, if only because of his highly ambivalent attitude to himself, that from the very birth of his existence, *homo sapiens* has had to brave the contrariety between the animal he was and the man he wished to be. That, at any rate, is what one might call the prophetic aspect of Darwin's natural history, the conviction that any flagging of his moral or intellectual standards, or as Charles Darwin put it, of 'his noble qualities', inevitably causes man to relapse into his 'lowly origin' which, in many ways, still has retained an enduring presence. What Darwin said was not new, but it was prophetically said. And whatever view may be taken of man's double legacy, it defines his limitations exactly. Between the animal's wants and his own needs it is a testing time for a race of humans. For a species of half-gods whose remarkable genius and boundless intellectual passion is about to evolve to a staggering degree of scientific ingenuity and, wherever diminished – and here the excellent Charles Darwin must be conceded his point – a breed of half-savages whose aboriginal herd-instinct appears so utterly unaccompanied by the high seriousness of moral and intellectual purpose which alone makes his 'god-like' existence possible.

'God-like', of course, is the relevant term. In actual fact, it seems clear enough that before we even consider this necessary and transcendent development, the transcendent principle itself is much more important than its actual attainment. Not that I suppose it to be unattainable. But the real target in any case is not so much a new understanding of men's potentially almost unlimited greatness. It is to find the means capable of solving the intractable problem of motivation, and that is not just a question of technology but of philosophical and ontological method. Nor is it easy to define either, but either may well become the object of a form of worship, a vast dynamic force, which could prove both inspired and effective if we proceed in a strictly scientific and business-like way to attain it. 'Worship' is a somewhat misleading way of putting it. But expressed in purely scientific terms, homage on those terms, even at the most rationalistic level, is entirely compatible with the overwhelming evolutionary significance of a charismatic utopian dream. For it is precisely here that man's essential genius lies. And it would certainly seem, given unlimited technological freedom in an appropriate setting, that the resulting conciliation of science and metaphysics – to invoke the anthropic symbolism already present in quantum physics and general relativity – could well lead to the creation of a new evolutionary consciousness under a galvanized cosmic perspective.

Freddy Hoyle intimates as much in *The Intelligent Universe*: 'Space and time may not be truly fundamental concepts, but may be a kind of perspective resulting from the particular aspect of the universe which happens to fall within our experience'. Stephen Hawking expresses the same thought: 'We see the universe the way it is because we exist'. Strangely evocative words but, as both Hoyle and Hawking appear to intimate, it is left to us to suggest some sort of mental image of the means to further advance. And that advance is important.

It is, in any case, as difficult not to be overwhelmed by the tremendous advance of human knowledge as it is useless to try and depose the conquest of space from its rightful place at the top of scientific endeavours. 'It may frighten us a little by its loneliness; it offers no threat. A new world beckons. The trial should be made. *Not to try is a greater hazard than to fail.*' The italics are my own, but the words are Francis Bacon's. As it happens, they have the unexpected tone of a veritable declaration of cosmic intent. In fact, the passage quoted stems not, as one might have supposed, from a contemporary commentary but from Bacon's *Cogita et Visa* or 'Thoughts and Conclusions on the Interpretation of Nature' in which he so splendidly describes the 'glory of discovery' as the true ornament of mankind. Nor, if it is necessary to choose between death or glory, or more appropriately perhaps, between death and immortality, can we afford to believe in prudence. The most that can be said of it with any degree of certainty is that if human immortality is a subject on which contentious speculation is possible, mere ignominious survival or other equally salving concerns are entirely pointless to any evolutionary thinking. As for the terms on which immortality may actually be achieved, it is at least arguable that if to some fundamental degree such objective should fail, one may confidently trace such failure to caution rather than audacity, and nobody can tell me any different.

From one angle or another, these are far-off developments, very far off indeed. We are talking about a future that cannot be predicted and the date and conditions of man's ascent into heaven will depend upon various unpredictable circumstances. But in cautioning against the dangers of delay I am not only thinking of an image of greatness patterned on a Promethean vision of man. I am also considering that the laws of the jungle are more inflexible than those which govern human civilization and a useful reminder, moreover, that without the higher significance of the last, neither man nor beast is sufficiently unequal to merit distinction in other respects. It is as simple as that. Nor, in view of what is known about the laws of the jungle, is it difficult to understand that the prerogative of the fittest is unquestionably more in accord with the facts of evolution as we know them than with a great many detailed laws which are ineffective, not merely because they are uninspired, but, as will be seen in the next chapter, because the Sayers of the Law – particularly those formed in an arid academic tradition – do not have the kind of vision which the expanding cultural and spiritual life of a great technological civilization requires. Clearly, despite men's avowed intention, there is no short-cut to human perfection. There are no simple-minded rules in terms of charity, equity or the very provisions of the legal system which can be laid down for setting forth a model for the development, perhaps better expressed 'domestication', of the human animal.

Here, then, it seems is the fruition of the very train of thought which might have been at the back of H. G. Wells' own mind, that without some objective fitted to their genius, men will either relapse into idiocy or revert to bestiality. Which merely completes and endorses the general impression. For it is now certainly possible for us to see that for all the obvious mastery with which scientific ingenuity has been absorbed into a pleasant way of life, that pleasantness does not extend to the categorical millennarian imperative necessary for saving men from the catastrophic (rather than cathartic) consequences of the unintended misuse of their own immeasurable powers.

In the case of Dr Moreau, the idea of exercising a measure of discipline over the Beast Men by means of laws he had them obey, obviously remained the strongest element in his conception of the evolutionary process. Matters are even grimmer, of course, when the social theorist has to invent a social order which, potentially at any rate, is self-defeating because it binds its possessors to the rules and proprieties of their frequently ineffectual existence rather than give rise to the kind of incentive which requires scope in some major achievement. One may dispute the wisdom of this conclusion. It is, however, an accurate summing up, derived in part from the simple laws of plain common sense and in part, albeit with a strictly symbolic significance, from the hero of Wells' prophetic narrative. Having made good his escape from the terrors of the island, he sums up the whole affair when he points out that the lessons he drew from his experience with the despairing island misfits were none too remote, in fact, from those which he drew from similar encounters with the men and women he subsequently meets. Or, as he himself has noted: 'I could not persuade myself that the men and women I met were not also another, still passably human, Beast People, animals half-wrought into the outward image of human souls; and that they would presently begin to revert, to show first this bestial mark and then that . . . Then I look about me at my fellow-men. And I go in fear.'

There is a fear here which is neither irrational nor even remote from human affairs. As Nietzsche has argued, 'The enlightened man goes among men *as* among animals'. When Wells' narrator, Edward Prendick, returns to civilization he could not repress a strange recurrence of the uncertainty and dread symbolized by the island and the coarse and brutish creatures clinging on to it. Contradictions in human nature induce a psychological sickness in man, epitomized as often as not by an atavistic regression to compulsive elements in human behaviour over which Sayers and Makers of laws nowadays exercise very little effective control. Prendick neatly concedes the point with the admission that 'I have withdrawn myself from the confusion of cities and multitudes, and spend my days surrounded by wise books, bright windows in this life of ours lit by the shining souls of men . . . My days I devote to reading and to experiments in chemistry, and I spend many of the clear nights in the study of astronomy. There is, though I do not know how there is or why there is, a sense of infinite peace and protection in the glittering hosts of heaven. There it must be, I think, in the vast and eternal laws of matter, and not in the daily cares and sins and troubles of men, that whatever is more than animal within us must find its solace and its hope. I hope or I could not live'.

And so, we live and hope. Hope, that man will not deny himself the very destiny he has been called upon to claim, hope that the rewards will justify his efforts, that

His are the Stars in the Sky!

12

THE SAYERS OF THE LAW

O my brothers, with whom does the greatest
danger to the whole human future lie? Is it not
with the good and just?

Shatter, shatter the good and just! – For the
good – *cannot* create: they are always the beginning of the end?

Nietzsche, *Zarathustra*

All beings have created something beyond themselves, and are you going to be the ebb of this
great tide?

Nietzsche, *Zarathustra*

*'The truth remains that today **nothing** stands in the way to the
attainment of universal freedom and abundance but mental
tangles, egocentric preoccupations, obsessions, misconceived
phrases, bad habits of thought, subconscious fears and dreads
and plain dishonesty in people's minds – especially in the minds
of those in key positions. That universal freedom and abundance
dangles within reach of us and is not achieved, and we who are
citizens of the Future wander about this present scene like passen-
gers on a ship overdue, in plain sight of a port which only some
disorder in the chart-room prevents us from entering'.*[1]

Thus, in terms which are almost trite the great visionary of the
future ventures to express the commonplaces of his 'belief in the

perfectibility human society might attain to *if* it ceased to make war, gave up its national consciousness, and joined in the brotherhood of man'.[2] 'If' is certainly the operative word here. Nor, bearing in mind the long tradition of statements such as this, would it be true to say that Wells' theory of universal freedom would be anything more than a repetition of the humdrum. Nothing is said that has not been said by another writer. Indeed, what else could still be added that would be more than reiteration? That nobody likes war for war's sake? Nothing very innovative emerges from that. Nor does it tell us very much about the actual complexities of a frustrating world of alienated individuals unwilling to serve the cause of peace except on terms as favourable as possible to themselves. In particular it does not explain how to harmonize the principle of the greatest possible good with the difficulty of applying it to the greatest possible number. And since not everybody prefers butter to guns, and not all men of good will are allied against the same evil, the conclusion is inescapable: not in ways agreed upon by all for the common and mutual benefit of all.

The great mistake, then, of H. G. Wells in asserting that '*nothing* stands in the way to the attainment of universal freedom and abundance but mental tangles, egocentric preoccupations, obsessions', etc., was to underestimate how substantial the trivial, the trifling and the tiresome can be. Likewise, the fundamental error of moralists and philosophers in developing the claim which it has equally been the fashion to make, that every single war in the history of human civilization has in fact been avoidable, was to overrate the extent to which national governments, in the face of the overwhelming preponderance of the trivial, the trifling and the tiresome, are in fact the actual masters of events. In truth, if all are agreed that human nature ought to play no part in considered assertions of political doctrine, then, in a sense, they are denying the existence of any problem at all. Conflict is easily provoked and easily continued. And when one looks at the complex world of human personalities, attitudes, opinions and motives – and not only of 'those in key positions' – the implication seems to be that even though there may be no obvious statistical correspondence with respect to the destinies of men, inasmuch as every collective activity is an amplification of statistical averages, far too much depends on such extended amplifications to be governed by individual personalities or be determined by single events. For like the random movement of molecules or of vast and uncontrollable sub-atomic events, they too seem to have the kind of certainty, to round off the analogy, that the laws of thermodynamics have. And that makes the whole business of 'individual freedom' much more uncertain of universal attainment.

At all events, since we have here risen to the level of prophetic analogy, it would not perhaps be inappropriate to add that, as a conflict of principles, the relative concepts of good and evil, too, permit of some considerable differences of interpretation. I say this with the certain conviction – and anyone may question the validity of it – that even though warfare has enjoyed a poor histor- ical press on all possible occasions, it would be both unintelligent and difficult to deny the moral resources which are inherent in it as a form of catharsis. It is true, nothing can mitigate the cruelty and brutishness of war. But merely to assert that, on a more hope- ful note, warfare is incompatible with human nature is not to deny that it was to a great extent by the deliberate resort to arms that the desired state of 'the greatest happiness for all', has largely been brought about.

I say so with no intent to invoke dangerous thoughts or to flatter the profession of arms. No insinuation could be more misleading. Modern warfare has virtually every possible fault. It is quite definitely not heroic. But since it is impossible to ignore that history's great 'wars of truth' signify nothing less than the problem of evolution, they may be interpreted equally well as great deeds of penance. It certainly is no accident that they have also led to enormous strides in moral awareness and – purchased at the price of so much affliction – to the kind of scientific and technological advancements which now testify to the enormous significance military evolution has had for the general progress of science. One can see, on the other hand, why this can give but limited comfort to the moral philosophers and social theorists for whom the natural rights of man and the laws of historical evolu- tion are not meant to be opposites. Nor, to attempt a clearer and more explicit statement of the case, would such considerations have been appropriate to the men and women of the 1950s and 60s who came to believe – unsurprisingly enough at a time when Russia and America seemed firmly set on a collision course – that there was no salvation except in nuclear disarmament, and des- perate attempts to outban the bomb became their overriding concern.

To be fair to Bertrand Russell, when he was so careless of his dignity to sit down on wet pavements he was not setting out to be a serious moral philosopher. A fanatic could have done as much. Nor would it be true to say that that most unequal little man, Jean Paul Sartre's method of dragging philosophy on to the barricades was wholly his own or that it was entirely irresponsible. Decisive action has before, and since, proved to be the best protection at times against the authoritative tyranny of resolutely reactionary minds who prefer 'organic social development' to the controversial methods exercised by the exponents of democracy by deed, or, to enlist the title of an article in which Russell debates the question whether workers should or should not engage in political strikes, of 'democracy and direct action'. In a measure, though he was not as yet the controversial, often notorious, figure of his later years, his standing at this time as a social conscience and political agitator was very much akin to Sartre's, even though it is to Sartre that goes the credit for best defying the political orthodoxy of his time with the introduction of revolutionary statements of principle. Statements that, largely owing to his personal efforts, were to 'revolutionize' contemporary treatment of social questions even though the social revolution itself belonged to an earlier age.

One of the most notable figures of his time and, in his biographer Ronald Clark's judicious estimation, the world's most persistent propagandist for peace, Bertrand Russell was, at any rate at first sight, a much less obviously extremist type. An upright and dignified man with an enviable prose-style and great stateliness of manners if apt, at times, to express himself precipitately, his mastery of rhetorical expression and epigrammatic wit somehow always contrived to appeal to the individual rationalism of forces both much more and far less radical than himself. The contradiction, perhaps, lay in his extreme hatred of fanaticism. How did he put it? 'I think fanaticism is the gravest danger there is. I might almost say that I was fanatic against fanaticism'. Yet, for some reason, perhaps having to do with the fact that his fanaticism and his hatred of fanaticism worked to a common end, nothing was as it ought to be and difficult, in consequence, to be treated with any measure of detachment.

'The proportion of abuse to argument', says Alan Ryan,[3] '[was] very high'. And certainly, under the circumstances, to become an associate supporter of the Campaign for Nuclear Disarmament which reverberated in the consciousness of the time, and seemingly the natural choice as its president when it was founded, in 1958, under his prestigious patronage, was not only illustrative of his political convictions but actually expected of a man who had no equal in the art of lending dignity to certain fields of political activity which more usually suggest a very close connection between a man's intransigence and his radical philosophy. At all events, when he put himself ostentatiously at the head of the movement, there was no mention of the conspicuous fact that much of the rising tide of nuclear protest which he so skilfully knew how to orchestrate, was inconsistent with Russell's own qualified advocacy of nuclear weapons and with the special sense in which he had previously countenanced their use in 'justifiable' or pre-emptive wars. In actual fact, we look in vain for a definitive comment, explicit, implicit or otherwise, on twentieth-century world politics which throughout a lifetime pledged to every variety of personal notoriety he never faced consistently. It is impossible not to admire the ease with which Russell managed to bring his many contradictory convictions under one hat. He could preach appeasement, and even defend defeatism, throughout the 1930s as readily as he would encourage American policy-makers in 1945 'to think of using their nuclear weapons to bomb the Soviet Union into a greater respect for the values of civilization'.[4]

When one first encounters a statement such as this, one is apt to dismiss it as the bluster of a madman who is out of touch with everything but the cause of his own convictions. To this bene-factor of the human race, who advocated the doctrine of nuclear 'deterrence' with all its genocidal consequences, a policy of restraint was simply humanitarian fiddlesticks. This may be a posthumous point, but one well worth making nevertheless. For when Russell accepted the need for a pre-emptive nuclear war, he was accepting the condemnation to death – by his own estimate[5] – of approximately five hundred million human beings (ninety-nine per cent of whom were probably anti-Communist and allied, therefore, to Russell in spirit). Nor was he concerned with the more abiding values of human existence. The majority of his writings are so flimsy in the ephemeral sense, so much involved in the inferior issues of his day, that they are interesting now only to people with a biographical interest. Some, in fact, are not only inconsiderable to all but those who are well conversant with con-temporaneous topics and events, but much more limited than one might have supposed from the sheer size of his reputation alone.

232

As for his work on mathematical logic, it would be even more distinguished if we did not have the extremist to stand beside it. Nor is it wholly surprising perhaps that anyone with as much capacity for such purely abstract subjects as symbolic logic or epistemological theory, indeed anyone at all who proposes to undertake to demonstrate whether 'the class of such classes which are not members of themselves is or is not a member of itself',[6] should also otherwise contrive to invoke a great mass of political subtleties and ideological contradictions.

Closely linked to his class but not a member of it was a man of very different temperament. A universally admired individual and by far the best known of the world's leading physicists, Albert Einstein was famous rather than notorious. He also, on this occasion, supplied the motivation for a statement Russell was preparing in the hope that it would be signed by a panel of the most important scientists and eminent persons of the day. Indeed, of all the scientists holding influential positions, Einstein was perhaps the most closely identified with the genesis of the Bomb less than half a century after he first propounded the Mass-Energy equation, even though nuclear physics was one of the few branches of modern physics to which he did not contribute.[7] But however widely he might have differed in his political views, he did not hesitate to subscribe to the common principle of saving the world from the drift towards nuclear destruction.

Issued in the name of signatories whose impressive roll-call included six Nobel laureates, the Russell-Einstein Manifesto of 1955, obliging the world to take note of its impending destruction, was largely inspired by these two men, if not without a certain divergence of their methods and aims. While Einstein had quietly been building up credibility with the men who mattered, Russell seems to have been careful to make himself as conspicuous as possible. It speaks volumes for his histrionic genius that he could behave like a ten-year old and still get world-wide approval. Indeed, though some might feel the conclusion to be extreme, as I have said, it was not peace he craved nor war he abhorred, but notoriety he craved and anonymity he detested. Nor was he concerned with preserving the peace, if anything he was going to *fight* for it, if only to prolong the quarrel.

That Russell would have been capable of personal violence seems unlikely. The covert desire itself, however, has the support of a respectable psychological tradition on the sublimation of the aggressive impulses into useful social activities. It may be obscured by pacifist histrionics, but is fundamental to them nevertheless. 'Love of peace', in other words, is a common psychological substitute for the love of war. William James appreciated this fully when he said 'that civilization needed activities which were the "moral equivalent of war"'. In actual fact, if Russell's own writings on the relationship between individual psychology and social or political events scarcely dispose of the ambiguities and contradictions in his own psychology, they do explain the intensity with which his convictions projected themselves. In truth, to say that their real strength lies in their significance when applied to the author himself is as apt as such a proposition can be. More particularly so, when conceived in terms of the redeeming power of those parts of the human personality which are intensely and continuously aware of the need to counter the destructive force of their own negative ambitions.

When the signatories demanded to know 'shall we put an end to the human race; or shall mankind renounce war?', they must have known that the second part of the question did not have any viability even though they may have convinced themselves that they were asking the obvious. Indeed, the assertion once made by the historian Cecil Chesterton that 'war is always the result of a conflict of wills' is perhaps as concise a statement of the objection to this kind of question as one could possibly make. In this respect the whole nature of human life is charged with conflicting activity. A person's moral quality cannot be weighed or measured; it is not a matter of good people or bad people. It is bound up with the conflicting circumstances of both, and in both cases the redemption can only be relative. 'Whoever fights monsters', as Nietzsche has cautioned, 'should see to it that in the process *he* does not become a monster'. What precisely this means is best understood, perhaps, in terms of Russell's own performance. For the indictments he drew up against modern militarist society so resembled the nature of activities which are the 'moral equivalent of war' as to replace the entire action, making conflict justifiable rather than reducing the occasions for conflict.

It may be that such ethical justifications are both necessary and impossible to avoid. It may even be that 'one of the great heretics in morals and religion' happened to be in pursuit of objectives that strike us as being admirable. Unfortunately, admirable though they may have been, to pin one's faith upon the patently unobtainable is also absurd. As he grew older he became more and more prone to experience fantasy as reality. If he was a fool, he was Cervantes' fool, never attaining to wisdom but, like the honourable man of la Mancha, continually being unhorsed. Frankly, one is bored by it all. Not for want of respect for the honour of his Dulcinea, to be sure, but because the patterns of alienation which set people at odds and lead to divisiveness are too easily rationalized in terms of idealism or fanaticism, of socialism or capitalism, of racialism or imperialism, of pacifism or chauvinism, according to our voice of conscience or in obedience to our inner law of being. Whichever the case, but certainly depending on our particular and personal opinions which always separate us – shall we say, like the river Rubicon?

This pattern at any rate, though completely contrary to his accredited wisdom, if otherwise in perfect character, Lord Russell foisted upon a world whose benefactor he averred to be. His idea of a progressive society was one that would abide by the arbitrary judgement of a man like himself. The right to impose peace by force, having been touted by Russell as a matter of life and death was not in itself very innovative, if a matter for moral opprobrium and precisely the opposite of its purpose. This view has been bluntly if appropriately put by Kingsley Martin, editor of the *New Statesman* who made the same statement of fact when he wrote in some alarm to the great man that his idea of an international ultimatum read 'like the beginning of war, even though you say that its intention is to stop one'.[8] It may in fact have been true that Russell's redolent criticism of 'wicked men in power' and his censure of official nuclear policies which led to such widespread national protests in Britain were rather less destructive than they were constructive. But it remains the case nevertheless that he tended to give predominance to radically directed ideas and was prone to seek violent, even genocidal, solutions to his problems. In truth, the real irony of the situation lies not so much in the peculiar satisfaction with which he performed his double function of 'social conscience' and 'political agitator' – the 'World Ombudsman', as someone pronounced him to be (apparently with no sign of sarcasm) – but in the fact that his dialectic at times sank to a depth of absurdity that makes one wonder how he ever managed to convince even the most gullible of spectators. Very likely, some people find themselves even now believing that this reputation was merited, giving him a moral authority for which he was never

235

endowed. Believing, in other words, that Russell was fighting a noble cause, when in fact *he* was 'becoming a monster', arrogating moral 'prerogatives' to himself, to use the most inoffensive word available, which would have enabled him to destroy half the civilized world.

This, then, was the dignified and altruistic being who was as determined as any of his scattered followers to close his eyes and ears to any voice of reason that might confound his quarrelsome assaults upon the political and social establishment. And yet, Russell's conception of a political theory was not quite the theory of universal revolution. The true idol of the radicals was in the contemporaneous France. Here the intellectual and social prestige of his political counterpart – a symbol of the same order of magnitude – Jean Paul Sartre, was decisive in *les evenements* that led to the May Revolution of 1968 in Paris, even if it produced no lasting results. Of course, there was no real fellowship between the two prophets. Sartre was not, like Russell, a professed 'lover of peace'. He was the great 'tribune of the people' in all but legal recognition. 'The academic godfather', as Paul Johnson has described him, 'to many terrorist movements which began to oppress society from the late 1960s onwards'.[9] What Sartre was right about, of course, when he refused the world's most coveted literary prize, the Nobel Prize for Literature in 1965, was that his intellectual creations ought to be judged on their own merit, and not merely be upheld by literary honours or laureate tradition. 'A writer must refuse to allow himself to be transformed into an institution, even if it takes place in the most honourable form . . .' However, since proof of their merit was a simple pragmatic one – success was demonstrated by the irresistible attraction his works exercised upon the inflamed psychology of Western middle-class *sans culottes* – whether Sartre liked it or not, an idolatrous movement based on the concept of *l'existentialisme* had rapidly begun to emerge. As one aspect of the intellectual revolution, if an inexpressibly dreary one, it was at least as important in giving rise to the fertile history of twentieth-century left-wing radicalism, as was the radicalized intelligentsia's oppositional campaign to overthrow the world. In the philosophy of world revolution as Sartre conceived of it, existentialism was a necessary prerequisite for the circumscribed but nonetheless identifiable right to violent action which presented itself as the appropriate vehicle for this kind of social suggestion. In short, for a vast and insatiable variety of special interest groups in search of the world's true cause, to whom it never occurred that what the philosopher says is no evidence of the truth.

One could go on with considerations of this kind. But it would be impossible to understand the peculiar and very complex nature of the intellectual radicalization at the peaks of Western culture, without understanding that it was characterized by a widely, perhaps universally, prevailing class and status antagonism of the kind that actually related it to the spirit of social radicalism of the nineteenth century, an age peculiarly given to such extremist convictions. Indeed, it is a wretched culmination of its triumphant onward-march that the vast intellectual labours that went into the making of the nineteenth century should have given birth to nothing more substantial than a historical prevarication in the twentieth. One sees a clear progression, moreover, from the revolutionary tradition of nineteenth-century thought to an increasingly arrogant intellectualist intervention through manifestoes of social danger in the name of social reform. But when all allowances have duly been made for the political negativism, social radicalism, philosophical atheism, moral pessimism and intellectual libertinism on which the spirit of conflict rested, in a word, for the trivial, the trite and the tiresome as disseminated by our two sages, I am quite willing to believe that these two men, so different in their origin and their class, in their work and their versatility, had yet one thing in common. They shared precisely the characteristics that are found to be chiefly remarkable for reducing such paradox as 'the class of all classes which are not members of themselves', to a species of French mules and English jackasses. And that, between ourselves, is probably as near as one can ever come towards actually resolving it.

I do not claim to grasp their mental processes, nor that of mules and asses in general, but undergraduates, as we know, took them literally. Most men might have wished for a finer tribute. For with all due respect to Quartier Latin *sans culottes* and students at Cambridge and Oxford, to prefer the excitement of spectacular action to the tiresome tuitions of tedious dons, need not be indicative of serious revolutionary developments. Truth to tell, if philosophically it was the tragedy of the intellectual revolution that it lacked the saving grace of a truly transcendent cause, I can only say that the philosophic impact of Russell, Sartre, and many lesser known Illuminati, upon their age was not the happiest of gifts. There is little point in repeating that the basis of human ethics is

237

the belief in the transcendent power of man. Pointing to their enlightened rebellion, however, one can certainly say that it never achieved more than the bogus intellectualism which it held forth as an ideal. In fact, one can scarcely point to any achievement at all. What we have instead is the new fanaticism: the absurdly unconvincing bequest of *political correctness*. For that it is possible to regard this latest and strangest demonstration of the intellectual genius for radicalizing social and cultural trends as a legacy of the 60s, seems to me to need no proof. Indeed, in terms of its formal continuity, the after-effects of a decade of politically correct activism, are more incisive perhaps than were the original intellectual challenges themselves.

There are enormous challenges in the world at present, notably in environmental terms and in terms of the inevitable reorganization of an industrial society. Indeed, the reality from which springs the peculiar significance of the greenhouse effect is so cataclysmic and so far-reaching in its ecological consequences, that few will deny the profound importance, practically and philosophically, which a universal programme for the environmental restructuring of the earth's ecology is bound to have. More intrusive and objectionable – to respond polemically to a polemically expressed request – is the sinister and foreboding tone and the dramatic emphasis on social reform as the necessary prelude to the creation of an utopian future. Nor is it difficult to see that such a future can only lead to a highly morbid ideality. It may be objected, for example, that social control and moral compulsion, fundamentally, are nothing more than techniques for manipulating human beings. And therefore to accept an all-consuming social discipline, whether it is the legislative control of the forces of nature or, fifty years on, of our genetic endowment, is to do violence to the earth's ecology as well as to humanity.

If the habit is an old one, using terms and tactics which have a familiar ring, it is not moral compulsion as such, or even techniques for social control in general that dominate the thinking of a new generation of 'ultras'. Rather it is a well-founded concern for a great many ecological issues which – apart from being spuriously egalitarian – do not lend themselves particularly well to the enhancement of the freedom of the individual. Nor to easing the intellectual difficulties which the individual has in escaping from the doctrinaire climate of these times. And I am fully conscious of the irony that one of the most important weapons in the armoury of intolerance and social control is in fact the language of genuine concern. Nor are any of these developments intentionally proscriptive in the same sense or terminology as the minority right campaigners or social egalitarians, gay-liberationists, animal protectionists, the feminists, the crackpots, cranks and new-ageists are proscriptive. Yet, such is the logical flow of compulsory thought and effective thought control that, whether through its stifling effect on human motivation or through the troubled relationship of logic to life, it imparts as powerfully as any of these pressure or special interest groups a whole sequence of attitudes whose repressive eco-intellectualism is becoming increasingly dominated by the social politics of pedantic middle-aged bureaucrats who never risk a noble thought and whose conception of a social equilibrium chiefly requires that one type of intolerance should be replaced by another.

It is a matter of contemporary experience that the Earth is becoming smaller and smaller as a result of industrial and population growth. Unfortunately, however, for these Friends' of the Earth total commitment to a staggering programme of preventive demographic checks – which, among other environmental reasons, is directly relevant to this problem – it is very much a fact of life that too strict a discipline of contraceptive repression can never have a lasting appeal for the great mass of human beings thus deprived of their procreative endowment. It might be justifiable, but it can never be just. Even to accept the necessity of the contraceptive principle as something that cannot be avoided seems to me to misconceive the natural function of human society. This, on the basis of an anthropologically healthy existence, has at all times been to produce offsprings. Where the progenitive conditions are becoming artificially restricted, it is easy enough to foresee that a society cannot become evolutionary retrogressive or reverse the process which engendered it, *and* stay healthy or even alive.

In historical terms, then, this development denotes the rapid fading of a major anthropological tradition and its veneration for evolutionary fitness. In allegorical terms, even the most cursory glance at the acronym FOE – in no very uncertain meaning of that word – goes a very long stretch indeed to suggest that in some way they seem far better equipped to become the enemies of the human race than they can ever be the friends of the planet Earth. It would be quite wrong to imply that what the eco-hawks did manage to achieve, particularly under Greenpeace's uncompromising leadership, was anything less than the raising of an environmental awareness that might conceivably have saved our globe. But even if that came to be universally admitted, certain key characteristics of the ecological revolution, so incurably unseeing in its onesidedness, have clearly come to be the objects of an exercise in brainwashing which sometimes seems to lack all corresponding virtue. Indeed, the first thing to be noted is that 'wind and water power were the main energy sources of post-medieval industry',[10] that they represent the least efficient form of energy production, a form of power in its declension, no less. Perhaps the clearest indication, therefore, of this declension is to be found in the fact that our Friends are actually willing to exchange the prospect of certain prosperity for the subsistence of a wind-and-water economy; that, I repeat, they have actually succeeded in placing fidelity to the Earth – which instantly confounds their benevolent stand with its deeply pessimistic philosophy of the powers declining from nuclear to 'alternative' fuels – before the ability of a highly technological civilization to master its own central and salving destiny, its conquering vision and cosmic ambition.

Public opinion, on the whole, has followed the retrogressive judgement here, but I am not so sure it is right. For if the world's verdict endorsed that judgement, it would represent a highly improvident depreciation of the skill and ingenuity offered to it by a technological civilization. One thing, in any case, is certain, we would be left in no doubt where its spirit resides. For the pessimism conveyed in the demoralization of an age whose judgements no longer embrace transcending or even confident standards, is not merely ecological. It is evidence of deep changes in the orientation of the collective psyche. It is fundamental to a world lost, in more recent times, in impossible ideas of a new intellectual darkness. In an illusory nostalgia for a remote and rustic past. A mellow eventide of butterfly and thistledown as the great concluding age of peace, or what is held to be the last and most perfect phase of human existence. Without regret and without ambition. Even though it can accomplish nothing except the petrification of all that which lies at the basis of a healthy and progressive civilization. And the triviality of much of it, rather than the propensity for windmills and hydro-electric power, explains why the Great Green Manifesto which seems to have become a kind of highly charged panacea for the correction of all social ills, reads remarkably like a repeal of the principal contents of Magna Carta or of the original Bill of Rights.

These are perhaps trivial instances, and I do not mean that all Greens are oddballs. On the contrary, the manic phase has almost elapsed. As someone said, 'long gone are the days of the bearded, sandal-wearing, muesli-crunching green', for their real influence is elsewhere. It has passed out of their hands into wider and more pervasive strata. Ecology is now on virtually every political agenda, and much of its eco-intellectualism is indeed necessary and supported by the best of apparent reasons. But that is to confuse the issue. I may be wrong, but ecology is hardly an adequate replacement for the loss of history's surpassing objectives. 'The most careful ask today: "How is man preserved?" But Zarathustra asketh,' and the question will tolerate a great deal of examination, *'How is man surpassed?'*. And that, it seems to me, is the infinitely more important consideration.

The last words, at any rate, proclaim the weakness of the ecological movement. If it hopes to salvage the Earth it has no measures for saving humanity. Which leaves things pretty much at an impasse. What it comes to, in the final analysis, is the exclusion of any reasonable thought about preserving the balance between ecological prescriptions for a brave new world and the total legislation of human life. As for the rest, one soon wearies of such prattle. Indeed, the banalities vary. But whether ecological, pacifist, eirenic or activist, and however irreconcilable in their ideologically different ways, we are provided with no central purpose upon which to extend our future hopes. The initial impetus spent, clearly and unmistakably they all rest on a compulsory sacrifice of what is perhaps the most dynamic heritage of human evolution: its transcendent genius, the true bestower of all our noblest values.

And so we arrive at the Sayers of the Law, the various high-flying legislators who are unable to think up any alternatives for the coercive provisions of the legal system; the sundry commissions on social justice who praise it for the same reason; the dull and pompous academics who have nothing to put in its place; the ubiquitous Nobel laureates and morally high-minded altruists who add their own invariably bleak contributions. Indeed, all the ethical monitoring fraternities, advisory or select committees and learned conventions of fools who *would* be the conscience of humanity when the trouble is that no one can be quite sure what that in fact might be.

Wise men we find in plenty. But whether they are zealous and well-meaning iconoclasts or purveyors of good causes, amenable, kind, unselfish and just, beyond all possibility of doubt at the heart of the confusion is the inevitable fact that good and evil is common to both. In time, perhaps, wise men will learn. But since no certain method has ever been devised by which wisdom can be made to discriminate between the appearance of evil and the reality of its opposite, it has been legislated out of existence. The most we can hope for is an appreciation of the laws which carry the greatest promise of material happiness. For that indeed is the condition forced upon us, the individuals, so that this sedentary subsistence world, may offer itself as a sufficient explanation for the fact that it has never risked a worthy challenge. Indeed, what the individual may think or feel about the thoroughly unheroic spirit of an age whose social idealism is progressive in one situation but retogressive in quite another, does not matter in the least. He does not, on that account, transcend it. How did H. G. Wells express it? 'Don't inflict visions upon us, spare our little ways of life from the fearful shaft of understanding. But do tricks for us, little limited tricks. Give us cheap lighting. And cure us of certain disagreeable things, cure us of cancer, cure us of consumption, cure our colds and relieve us after repletion . . .'[11]

The theory is that all men are infinitely perfectible; the fact is that up to the last moment in the consummation of this tragedy they are confined by rigid judicial imperatives, buried under the dead-weight of legal prohibitions, and held down by 'the good, the true and the just', as the sardonic Nietzsche wrote of ignorant men and 'the incurably *mediocre*'. Bluntly stated, by social dignitaries, noble legislators, religious pontiffs, Eminent Persons, men in periwigs, immensely erudite immortals and, to mention the most obvious case, by keepers of insane asylums.

The 'death of a species', wrote Charles Darwin whose view on natural selection I have no wish to misrepresent, 'is a consequence of non-adaptation of circumstances'. And whatever else may have been said since, as a statement of fact, actual or potential, it seems remarkably in accordance with the need for the species to fall in with the rehabilitated forces of evolution. And nobody ever made this more clear than the admirable H. G. Wells when, in *The Fate of Homo Sapiens* he issued a 'last' resounding warning to mankind: 'Adapt or perish, that is and always has been the implacable law of life for all its children. Either the human imagination and the will to live rises to the plain necessity of our case, and a renascent *homo sapiens* struggles on to a new, a harder and happier world dominion, or he blunders down the slopes of failure through a series of unhappy phases, in the wake of all the monster reptiles and beasts that have flourished and lorded it on the earth before him, to his ultimate extinction. Either life is just beginning for him, or it is drawing rapidly to its close.'

We should, with perhaps equal plausibility, also remember that the meaning of Life – even in its most ill-conceived moments – is by no means confined to the extreme monotony of our quotidian existence on Earth, nor exclusive to the problems of an organic, environmental, or social kind which have held the stage for so long. That would be utterly to misconceive its nature. It is manifest with the same decisiveness in the concept of *nuclear energy* as one of the most dynamic catalysts of a highly indeterminate stage in human development and, we may add, of hope. Less dynamic perhaps but none the less relevant since the whole of human civilization was based on its universal and redemptive power. Indeed, it may be taken for granted that if we fail to take the necessary steps to preserve either of these Promethean gifts and keep alive for all time the two most powerful forces known to man, we might just as well give up the quest for the stars and enter a period of universal retrogression.

Thus, in all their different manifestations – distinguishable in form perhaps but not always in essence – throughout the evolution of man, hope and fire have never ceased to be the fundamental embodiment of what its philosopher meant by the Will to Power. To make a single, lasting symbol out of it and to rationalize this Will into the prediction of a new and charismatic age of the future, was bound, of course, to create great fools – and madmen – and no one has better anticipated this aspect of his teaching than the prophet of the New Age himself: 'My enemies have grown powerful and have distorted the meaning of my doctrine, so that my dearest ones are ashamed of the gifts I gave them.'

'My friends are lost to me; the hour has come to seek my lost ones!'

Clearly, there can be no mistaking these if we may judge by the historical proportions of the power struggle that will mark the next hundred years; by the ideological split between men and

Supermen, by the estrangement of those who are increasingly committed to their eco-socialistic friendship with the Earth from those who are, above all, historically motivated and whose new way of thinking can best be understood by placing it in the cosmic and evolutionary context of a major biological species, where the struggle between death and immortality makes much more historical sense. To be sure, from everything we know of the technological, ecological, cultural, and even spiritual development associated with the former's so-called friendship with the Earth, we need look no further than this obscure bridgehead in Space, drifting limply among the stars, in order that we should witness the last inert moments in the gentle, uninspired life of that race, long since become insignificant and meekly dragging out its languid, remote existence on the extreme periphery of the Milky Way, rather than remember it – and perhaps this is the correct and proper view – as the birthplace of the most dynamic, creative and inspired race ever to open up a whole New World.

13

THE WILLERS OF THE WILL

'Is it possible to extend a higher civilization to the lower classes without debasing its standards and diluting its quality to the vanishing point? Is not every civilization bound to decay as soon as it begins to penetrate the masses?'

Michael Rostovtzeff, Russian historian

Tell me, my brothers: what do we account bad and the worst of all? Is it not *degeneration*? – And we always suspect degeneration where the bestowing soul is lacking.
   Our way is upward, from the species across to the superspecies.

Nietzsche, *Zarathustra*

'To be bred in a place of estimation, to see nothing low and sordid from one's infancy; to be taught to respect oneself; to be habituated to the censorial inspection of the public eye . . .; to be habituated in armies to command and obey; to be taught to despise danger in the pursuit of honour and duty; to be led to a guarded and regulated conduct, from a sense that you are considered as an instructor of your fellow citizens in their highest concerns, and that you act as a reconciler between God and man; to be employed as an administrator of law and justice . . .; to be a professor of high science . . .; to be amongst rich traders, who from their success are presumed to have sharp and vigorous under-

standings . . . these are the circumstances of men that form what I should call a natural aristocracy, without which there is no nation.[1]

Thus Edmund Burke, moralist, political controversialist and influential man of letters in the English literary tradition as well as in its particular tradition of polemical writings. Perhaps the greatest publicist of his period, Burke was an acute observer of the radical excesses of the French Revolution and, when the issue had to be put fairly and squarely, an eloquent and astute politician. Indeed, though tradition has it that his speeches were not always well delivered, as a great parliamentary rhetorician he nevertheless raised political oratory to the level of a fine art, and never more so as when he devoted himself to discrediting the republican overthrow of the Bourbon monarchy in France. In fact, one of the major polemical objections to the French Revolution came from this learned Irishman, author of the *Reflections on the Revolution* and, on the spur of the moment, of the arresting designation 'swinish multitude'. The violent attack of a disordered mob upon the economic, political and social prerogative of an elite he saw as the true keepers of law and liberty, could not be reconciled with his conservative love of order and, writing in 1790, he may be forgiven perhaps for deploring the drift towards a revolutionary egalitarianism that was to be in many ways as authoritative and repressive as the power-monopoly of the *ancien régime* it had gone on to replace.

There are of course unkind critics who would suggest that Burke defended law and order because he loved being a member of the privileged establishment, or that this led him to place political self-interest before a direct and unprejudiced reflection of what he conceived to be the evils of the French Revolution. It is however unfair to his reputation as a man of letters and a conversationalist not to allow that it may have been civilization at its height which he defended, the vitality of its cultural and intellectual life, as well as the stability of its national and constitutional institutions. Institutions which depended on rather more than the reasonable man's concept of law and order. For apart from racial and temperamental distinctions, doubtless, it was considerations such as these which explain the success of a constitutional monarchy in England, the more remarkably so in view of the strains and stresses imposed upon the Divine Right of Kings by the sudden decapitation of the hapless Louis XVI.

Unfortunately – to state a commonplace of popular political thought – only the evils of hereditary rule, the undue concentration of political power in the hands of a ruling aristocracy clinging to hereditary prerogatives, survives in popular memory, whereas the moral authority of an aristocratic elite or the historical significance of this elite in any development of national character, culture or political nationhood is, and will probably remain, very generally ignored and forgotten. Readers of English history are, of course, well enough acquainted with such elementary facts as noble rebellions and baronial wars. In actual fact, as perhaps the oldest feature in the political aetiology of a statehood whose social structure proceeded from and rested on that institution, the old feudal nobility not only served as a bulwark against the prerogative of the Crown, but effectively determined the limits of sovereign power. In fact, the feudal system itself was something like a voluntary balance between the central monarchy and a landowning baronial class. It is a matter of historical indifference which power one gives the attribution 'stronger' or 'weaker'. The important thing is that it was mutual, that it made an accurate understanding of the rules of political reciprocity the supreme test, if not the necessary condition, of a nation's continued survival.

So what was the result? Magna Carta, trial by jury, the writ of habeas corpus, parliamentary monarchy, the Bill of Rights, civil liberties, freedom of speech, constitutional division of legislative and executive, the rule of the majority and, closely following it, what has also been called the 'democratization of culture'. We are mistaken, however, if we think that the triumphant movement towards egalitarianism or classlessness was either a necessary means of *culture* or a manifestation of it. Nor, insofar as the struggle for democratic freedom has largely been fought from the lowest level, was the entire upward movement of the common classes anything less than a powerful social catalyst. But as an order with a definite social identity and a culture and tradition of its own, they finished the class-war with a hierarchical paradox that has never been wholly resolved. This can be seen very clearly in the peculiar relationship of class distinction to wealth. That is to say, once prosperity took over, the cultural tradition of a working man's pride showed extremely little resistance to corruption by the values at whose service it had been placed. Populist sentiment would not keep pace with more 'titular' ambitions. Pride of social status was not the value the working man choose to pre-serve. Class distinction was increasingly substituted by admir-ation for wealth alone. Nor is it any good pretending that the concept of social hierarchy, as a rise in status and standard, does not now tend to manifest itself in the more affluent social position of a class of moneymakers or what is perhaps best defined as an aristocracy of wealth.

So there is the paradox: 'Mob above, mob below! What today means poor or rich?' Then comes the practical argument, for the basic issue remains as it has been defined all along: 'Where I found a living creature, there I found the will to power; and even in the will of the servant I found the will to be master'. No, there is no difference in kind, no genus of men called 'aristocrats' nor a genus of men called 'commoners'. There is only the impulse of their respective genius. Merely because high birth and nobility, rank and gentility implies a status or class distinction, it does not necessarily imply that there is also a natural or indigenous divi-sion between a 'sovereign' and an 'inferior' breed. No argument is needed to assert that. In such a comparison all one can do is to weigh their respective merits. Of course, when the first demo-cratic societies emerged from classical antiquity, as in the manner of the fifth-century Greek *polis*, they were still completely domi-nated by the political heritage of a traditionally governing class. And even though the actual concept of democracy is a thoroughly Greek one and *Ecclesia* and *Boulé* essentially constitutional forms of government that were open to all social levels, only a constitutional purist would deny that the traditional upper classes still retained considerable executive power. Indeed, what most impresses the reader of history is the fact that a privileged magis-tracy who may well have been Archons or Areopagites, neverthe-less provided the constitutional framework for the great legislative reforms and enactments that ultimately were to culmi-nate in the aristocratic imposition of a fully-fledged Greek democracy.

Thus, once we have conjured away the familiar anti-aristocratic connotations, together perhaps with the ethos, which modern reaction has no difficulty in deprecating, of a genealogical institu-tion that almost leads back to mythical or divine ancestors, there are very obvious cultural and social accretions in the dynastic processes by which we can trace the origin and the evolution of the world's political, religious and legal institutions. Yet, it is clear from the eventual debasement of aristocratic power, and the increasingly less absolute nature of kingship, that an hereditary nobility, too, was bound to meet its political end with the rise of the lower classes who had different gods, different forms of social organization and different ideas of political and economic development. Inevitably, their claims and concerns would sooner or later have to be accommodated within the parliamentary process of social change.

Obviously, this line of argument does not intend to be complete. Nor is it meant to be a celebration of a ruling elite at the expense of their less elevated subjects. But regardless of what their subjects have chosen, historically, to regard as morally valuable, to say that there is more to history than the noble art of leadership is not to deny the value of historical leadership. Indeed, it is as significant an indication of the quality of this leadership that the whole civilized world derived its inspiration from an aristocratically dispersed formulation of Greek democratic enlightenment, as it is bound to be true that the history of the West began with the quest for knowledge. It is not even philosophical inquiry that I have in mind, or a society where speculation and research lay midway between science and philosophy. Indeed, where art had a perceptivity, a peculiar intimation of knowledge which even expressed the characteristics of both. With regard to exploration as a creative activity, moreover, it was by no means directed exclusively towards an examination of the world and its cosmic processes. Once removed from such matters, the diffusion of knowledge also encouraged trade and the traffic not only of goods but also of ideas.

What we now call the post-Mycenaean period demonstrates the mutually advantageous situation attached to this development. Particularly at a time when the Greeks embarked on a campaign of wider conquests to the West and combined an exchange of products with journeys to the ancient lands of the East. Ancient exploration placed a premium on commerce and exchange. Trade and traffic was in fact its umbilical cord. As it gathered to itself an immense variety of artisans, craftsmen, merchants and scholars from all quarters of the world, or of the civilized world at any rate, this Golden Age of Greece already anticipated that wonderful body of men, the trader and the adventurer which, two thousand years hence, would lay the foundations for the Golden Age of Discovery with its expanding skies and its escorting stars. Both shared the same psychology, each in its own way, of an elite or an avant-garde. Both were conscious of a certain superiority, of a powerful impulse to penetrate the unknown, if none more justifiably so than the men who put out in frail vessels which carried prospective empire-builders on voyages across horizons not so much unheard of as mythical, and who succeeded in stimulating a scale of historical activity that might otherwise have remained utterly insignificant and inert.

The odds that had to be met, their wide range of intricacy and variety, may best be judged by the past five hundred years of exploratory accomplishment. The crucial test of course only comes now, with the universe itself as a technological catalyst. But it is significant nevertheless that in spite of so much technological naivety and geographical inconsistency, the whole subsequent course of modern history was thus to be initiated, indeed made possible, by the very determination of those rare individuals who, if not easily classifiable as a definite type, can nevertheless claim definite merits of achievement as a rather special people. For here, if anywhere, among pioneers of this stamp was the raw material for that iron body of men which constituted, if one may risk a commendation, what Burke would call a *natural* aristocracy, even though they were more likely to think of themselves as having derived from the most oppressed segments of society.

Thus, in a fundamental sense, nobility must be understood literally. If they were not recruited from the same social level as the aristocratic patrons of geographical exploration, these astonishing men and women who so profoundly effected the course of modern history, were nevertheless aristocrats in the most exclusive sense. Not only were they derived from the most qualified and enterprising selection of all social levels, but rarely falling below a high standard of personal achievement, they lived congenitally and habitually in an atmosphere of truly ennobling activity. An activity which was naturally selective of the best. Which is to say of individuals who enjoyed a challenge and were deadly serious about imposing their own special identity upon the lands they found and inhabited. In fact, as they and their successors gradually settled down to the consolidation of vast and new-found domains, they also and inevitably shaped themselves into the nucleus of that great historic movement whose American heirs – 'consisting in the North of the old New England families with their mercantile wealth and their Puritan traditions, [and] in the South of the great slave-owning squires'[2] – still continued to be found in a modern Patrician Establishment.

'I am tempted to believe,' the Swiss *philosophe* and physiocrat Isaac Iselin once suggested, 'that North America is the country where reason and humanity will develop more rapidly than anywhere else.' Coming from the late eighteenth century, this is as fair a sample as any of the sentiments that we are here called upon to remember in considering the messianic role of America during the great age of the democratic revolutions. I have already mentioned the pursuit of happiness in the American context and illustrated some of the most comprehensive retrogressions of human values the civilized world has known to date. I must return to it again for a moment in order to catch the more distinctive tone of what the Fathers of the Republic had so specifically and carefully in mind. For such ideas of the primacy of the Rights of Man as were to be transformed into the socio-political ideas of Life, Liberty and the pursuit of Happiness, also strongly informed the Marquis de Lafayette's discerning appreciation of America as 'the safe and respected refuge of virtue, honesty, tolerance, equality, and of peaceful liberty'.[3] And if that indeed is as matters stood when the Marquis was a Major General in Washington's army, even now it may be said that the majority of people begin and end with a generalization about the almost legendary reputation of America as a land of wealth and endless opportunities.

It is difficult perhaps to decide which, if any, of the most obvious generalizations reveal the true forces that were at work in the making of this astonishing land. The odds are, however, that at least some of the ideals which America adopted for herself and practised for humanity's sake, have been indissolubly fused into an object of worship that has become in more than one respect a symbol of America's utter and shameless surrender to her own infatuation with the overriding power of wealth. To keep the record straight, it seems hardly unfair to give America the chief credit for the deference with which the rest of the world has submitted to the evident and observable signs of her 'greatness'. There seems to be every inducement to take that course. Nor can common disapproval be expected of the country which, for fully two centuries now, has been synonymous with the best in the West, when its commercial progressiveness and sustained material success is probably the most superlative effort ever to exercise its magnetism upon a world which itself seems to have found little difficulty in overemphasizing this particular aspect of the pursuit of happiness into a kind of pleasure principle based on the maximization of profit.

When the Marquis de Lafayette said that 'The fortune of America is closely bound up with the fortune of humanity', he meant it literally – and significantly, as I myself believe – and what he meant deserves consideration. Nor need one argue the specifics of an influence so consistently displayed that it has become one of the most obstinately pervasive symptoms of modern material society. An extraordinary illustration of its want of a more solemn purpose, if not of a defective historical sense. Perhaps the only guarantee, if a monstrously poor one for the continuing fortune of, according to Walt Whitman, 'a new race dominating previous ones and grander far, with new contests', of a race once admired the world over albeit chiefly interested now in the pursuit of *material* Happiness and no longer in the sense once developed so carefully and significantly in the articles of the American Constitution, is precisely that: the predominance of the material point of view.

It is indeed appropriate here to add that no negative implication should be drawn from the possession of wealth itself. It is pointless to blame money for the emphasis we place on its corruptiveness. The acquisition of a personal fortune, whether as a primary purpose and a 'leading principle of action', as a habit of outperforming one's peers or as an exercise of the instinct for self-preservation, so far from being invidious, is one of the last great individual events of this egalitarian age so uniformly lacking in any element of 'heroic' enticement. As an established way of life it is in many ways of overwhelming significance, if not central to the thinking of men who judge their achievement less on its own merit than by how it competes with the achievement of others. For here, and only here, can be seen in its common and unchanging foundation the secret of our true regeneration: the force of our own ambition.

It is an ideal that I do not disagree with, no matter how corrupt or invidious the way of the world. Truth to tell, it has never been apparent to me why it should be 'easier for a camel to pass through the eye of a needle than for a rich person to enter the Kingdom of God', easy enough though it seems for such a charge to be made. Nor do I for one moment doubt that Christ was addressing himself as much to a desirable state of a worldly society as to the secular controversies of his own time. On the other hand, if the tender of a just and reasonable man rose above temporal questions to the level of a theory of grace, there might well appear to be a good case for striking a reasoned balance between what Adam Smith referred to as our 'self-love' and our 'humanity'. As he put it, he was not concerned with the benevolence of the butcher, the brewer, or the baker but with their regard to their own interest. 'We address ourselves, not to their humanity, but to their self-love; and never talk to them of our own necessity, but of their advantages' (*Wealth of Nations*. Book 1, Chapt. 2).

Adam Smith did not thread needles as well as do clerics and canon-lawyers, and his 'self-love' was somewhat doubtfully relieved perhaps by its ambiguous appeal to a moral intention. Nevertheless, as we thread our own way in and out between the wealth of nations and their social responsibility there is nothing in the difference that separates poor and rich which would allow us to claim the spiritual preponderance of the one over the other. Nor, when we compare his economically solid statement on human self-interest as an inherently productive function with the central dogma of the social welfare state, can we fail to notice how much is being forfeited in terms of a socially dynamic purpose. That is to say, individual ambitiousness also deals with a moral challenge; the social welfare state can hardly claim the same kind of purpose. Following Adam Smith, Thomas Malthus, too, insisted that 'if our benevolence be indiscriminate . . . we shall raise the worthless above the worthy; we shall encourage indolence and check industry; and in the most marked manner subtract from the sum of human happiness'. Especially, as far as one can tell from the negative power of inertia as a distinctively human attribute, since the beneficiaries of open-handed and high-minded conditions have a natural tendency to continue in the state they are in.

Take Sweden for instance, that colourless model of all social virtues. Widely considered the supreme exponent of social care and progressiveness, one of the results of some six decades of barely interrupted social democratic rule has been a level of general affluence and conditions of social service that have for long been the envy of the rest of the world. The Swedish judiciary system, too, has long been renowned for its humane and benevolent approach, for its policy of rehabilitation rather than that of applying punishment. In truth, what has been especially notable about Sweden's enviable claim to being the perfect society with no status distinctions between different occupational categories, is the fact that the criminal fraternity has been by far the most under-employed professional group, to say nothing of the widespread, if hopeful, perception that a society under socialism is a society united by a body of universally shared values.

On the academic level all this is perfectly sound. The decisive flaw in this rendering of an egalitarian and democratic utopia is that the demand for a single cultural value which features so prominently in socialist theory, points straight to a society in which the citizen, sociologically and psychologically, would be permanently implicated in the supreme duty of being a member of the State. It is an ideal which finds its most characteristic expression in the dubious social ethics of making the lowest common denominator the highest standard of collective excellence. That is to say, the best in the state is expended on the most mediocre. For his total reliance on its social aspect also adapts the citizen perfectly to the needs of a political democracy which gives the greatest advantage to those who have the least aspiration, whose attitude to social excellence is, in fact, one of supreme indifference.

With the best will in the world, is it possible to imagine anything less inspiring? The question seems to have a ready answer, because the demand amongst ordinary men continues to be made with overwhelming consistency, whether ideologically, politically, economically, academically, artistically, creatively, scientifically or otherwise, *for*, not against, the social rise from democratic unexclusiveness. The struggle for the highest is the process that engendered them. It is its own and the only solution to the riddle of the purpose of creation. It is the key to the mystery of life. It makes no difference whether their lives are sheltered, cared for and administered down to the last detail, or controlled, in every meaningful aspect, from the cradle to the grave. To subordinate the will of self-seeking individuals to the idea of social well-being as the sovereign subject of their genius is to define genius in terms of what it is not. In the end, all that is left is the extraordinary rational but totally unreasonable degree of social organization which, as a description of its specific conditions, social and socio-psychological, leads to the Hegelian State in its most tyrannical form. It also arrives at the most compact and concise expression of the idea of an individual's limitation. As Nietzsche has noted, 'there is nothing to make better, nothing to make worse'; he might with equal truth have added, and nothing even to pray for.

The Scandinavians were never a numerous people. Yet, as a race of almost providential audacity their prowess was remarkable. Indeed, if any single trait may be taken as the key to Norse expansion it was that same spirit of enterprise which subsequently recapitulated itself in the history of the central Europeans, carrying them too into virtually every other corner of the world. No one could match the ferociousness of the Vikings or the sheer gusto of the Normans. They fought simply for the perils and adventure of warfare, annexing what they could by the right of the stronger. In fact, from the eighth century onwards when Danes and Norsemen first raided the coasts of Dorsetshire and Northumberland, their influence as builders of nations was to become far more widespread than their nomadic existence seems to have warranted, sweeping over almost the whole of Western Europe and penetrating as far afield as Sicily and the Holy Land. As Normans they settled in Gaul, founded Normandy and adopted the French tongue, thus anticipating and inaugurating an entirely new epoch in the history of France. At the same time they annexed new lands by right of conquest from the peoples they overawed in the course of their southward advance, equally ruthless towards the strong and the weak, and perpetually victorious. Although as invaders they may have seemed unequal to some of the mighty kingdoms they raided from the sea, measure for measure, the historian Charles Oman said, they 'were always able to hold their own'. In truth, so ferocious and powerful was their nature that this lively and rapacious people actually became Europe's dominant military dynasty. Having invested northern France in AD 888 and conquered England in 1066, signs of Norman influence still abound in Ireland, Scotland, England and Wales. As Winston Churchill said of the Vikings, and his words may equally well be applied to the Normans: 'When we reflect upon the brutal vices of these salt-water bandits, pirates as shameful as any whom the sea has borne, or recoil from their villainous destruction and cruel deeds, we must also remember the discipline, the fortitude, the comradeship and martial virtues which made them at this period beyond all challenge the most formidable and daring race in the world'.[4]

As for the rising power of Sweden, it was crowned by a soldier of genius, the Lion of the North. A man of destiny, he could amplify and expound her history as no other man alive. Ever since the Thirty Years War Sweden was the leading power of Northern Europe. Under the influence of such inspired rulers as Gustavus Adolphus, carrying on the great imperial tradition like a new Pericles behind the rising power of Athens, and the gaunt and striding Charles XII, hero of the great Northern War, she had reached the acme of her proud imperial history. Charles had enormous resilience. Never, in fact, has a man seemed more superhuman than this king of Sweden during the time of her greatest struggle. An audacious and indefatigable horseman who could spend weeks in the saddle he was certainly the greatest soldier his country produced, the most irresistible ideal of the soldier-king to bear comparison with any and a genuine Spartan to boot. It is no exaggeration to speak of the most relentless spirit ever to be spurred on by an almighty dream. Nor could anything but a dream have unlocked for Charles the horizons on which he had come to thunder. But since it embraced his death in its adversity its real result was that it set Sweden at nought, even though it is still possible for most purposes of this particular argument to say that upon the powers exercised by these two men and their Homeric sense of destiny a great deal of modern European history has come to depend.

Now of course, not a single dream remains. For what is chiefly remarkable, given the long and special supremacy which raised this Baltic land from obscurity to a central place in European history, is how very little of it all has been retained in the national outlook of a society no longer rated for its leaders. I say this not because I am here concerned with bemourning an imperial tradition from which greatness has departed – none of that has any validity now – but because this tradition appears to have been turned into nothing more substantial than a succession of generations that can pass through the history of mankind without leaving so much as a trace of their existence. What more to the point, at any rate, could be said about an historically nebulous sociopolitical *organization* which creates idols in the image of public spending but which has neither visions nor dreams to add?

There is no trace of magic in this barren land, no deity, no demon. Purpose is but a vaguely defined sentiment. Insipidity is at a premium. And when we have reckoned up all, the hollowness, the emptiness, the colourlessness, it is difficult to escape the conclusion that this hinterland of Europe has none of the solicitude for destiny of the men who linked the history of medieval Europe with the full flowering of her Viking past, the historical spearhead of Norman colonization. Nor, I dare say, is there anything terribly inordinate about that. The modern Anglo-Saxon, to take a comparative view, has very little in common with the Anglo-Norman aristocracy that gave nobility to England. In fact, the exceptions to this rule are few. It is easy enough to show that with the greatness of Empires went also their vigour. It is necessary, however, to keep these comparisons in mind, for the single and most sovereign factor, and one that has more than a genealogical validity, to account for the rise and remarkable power, nationally, socially, culturally, of a changing society, was the intrusion of a Scandinavian population into the Anglo-Saxon realm.

There can be no reasonable doubt that ever since 1066 Britain traces much of her rich store of cultural heritage, national characteristics and special racial attributes to the influx of 'an exceptional aristocracy [from] an exceptional province'.[5] This influx, as we know, goes by the name of Norman Conquest. Elaborating the same essential point, the memorandum of Thomas Carlyle on the Anglo-Saxons as 'a gluttonous race of Jutes and Angles capable of no great combination'; makes memorable reading, particularly when he speaks of them as 'lumbering about in pot-bellied equanimity; not dreaming of heroic toil and silence and endurance. *such as lead to the high places of the Universe . . .*'[6] (my italics).

These are euphonious words. And thus weightily intoned we have the testimony of a man whose capacity for distinguishing between greatness and greediness was, if anything unmistakable, and whose love for 'silence and heroic toil' was very patently an abiding passion. Beyond that it is probably safe to assume that it was only under the Norman kings and with the skilful blending of the men who had confronted one another across the narrow sea, that is to say, with the intermingling of Normans and French with Angles, Saxons, Jutes, Britons and native Celts, that they began to aspire to that many-sided genius which we call England and which, over a considerable course of time, raised her to a position of greatness unequalled, it may be said without too much inaccuracy, in the entire history of the world.

'Greatness' hardly needs an explanation. Whatever else it is, it can generally be held to be at the opposite extreme from greediness. Though one may desire to turn it into a central principle of economic organization, into an economically productive function even, one may also wish to perpetuate the significance of its origin. And that would be to extend its possibilities into the release of creative energy and the growth of the whole operative force of the human will to power which is at the heart of everything. For that, in effect, is precisely where it is. Meanwhile, the essential point to emphasize is that for all the encouragement the problem of growth and creation has received in the painful process of past evolution, much of it is obscured now and overborne by the conviction that the *social* need, according to the philosophy of Life, Liberty and the pursuit of Happiness, is the greatest of all needs. Essentially, therefore, I have endeavoured to state in a fair if personal manner the nature of the consequences of taking the pursuit of happiness as the only goal in life. As a matter of fact, it is the basis of my claim that we have neglected the importance of greatness in human affairs and overrated the importance of an implied social contract. For with this development, there can be no doubt, we must associate a loss of resoluteness, a degeneration of purpose that leads one to question its implicit evaluation of a universally held sense of egalitarianism and classlessness as the highest of social virtues. In sum: 'The *collective degeneration of man* down to that which the socialist dolts and blockheads today see as their "man of the future" – as their ideal! – this degeneration and diminution of man to the perfect herd animal (or, as they say, to the man of the "free society"), this animalization of man to the pygmy animal of equal rights and equal pretensions is *possible*, there is no doubt about that!'[7]

Thus spake, not Zarathustra, but the prophet of the Superman himself. In the event it would be a serious mistake to find fault with the copious derision of Nietzsche's way of expressing what is still true, except that the degeneration of man into a pygmy with equal rights and claims can now be further extended to cover other points. Inevitably one is reminded of some equally categorical opinions on the subject of 'pygmies' and 'giants' of which H. G. Wells delivered himself. Unlike Nietzsche, Wells did not envisage a new division of the people based on men and supermen. The distinction between the two is important nevertheless, for on it, as a kind of analogue of the shape of things to come, Wells' vision of the future had to rest. In fact, the problem and a similar possibility of stunted historical growth in some way resembles that of the profoundly antagonistic 'little people' in

Wells' *Food of the Gods*, who had only one aim – both as a measure of their own limitations and as part of their perennial anxiety in the face of greatness – and that was to 'cut down all the giant plants, kill all the giant underlife [and] burn out the traces of the *Food*'.

Significant in the light of Wells' purpose is the use he makes, for instance, of *Herakleophorbia*, or 'the nutrition of Hercules' as he describes the Food in the first chapter of his narrative. As things are, it certainly is representative in its way – if not necessarily representing it – of the physics of nuclear energy. As representative, one might say, as 'the power that fuels the stars' is commensurate with the awesome requirements of a future whose ultimate purpose is technological emancipation rather than an excess of technological surfeit. In fact, the Giants had grown to such extraordinary heights because they believed that the proof of the Food lay in the eating. The 'little people', however, seemed to share the full violence of the anti-nuclear mood that has been so fanatically embraced over the past ten years or so by the hundreds of thousands of pygmies whose instinctive understanding of greatness and growth is so necessarily and so avowedly devoid of 'higher' purpose that in this respect political leaders were actually obliged to fall behind rather than lead the rout of political opinion.

The consequences are incalculable, 'for in spite of the slow conversion of progressive ideas into the fact of history, the Dark Ages have a way of coming back. Civilization – the world of affection and reason and freedom and justice – is a luxury which must be fought for, as dangerous to possess as an oil-field'[8] or, indeed, a nuclear power-station. To survive, therefore, the question which we have to ask is whether an enraged horde of little people who recognize nothing great, who are not historically creative, and who are inspired only by the everpresent fear of ambivalent and dubious evils, have the right to interfere and tamper with an entire way of life committed to the rehabilitation of precisely those powers in question – now that space travel is a reality and the physics of nuclear fusion an imminency – and thus, in the climax of our hopes to throw away the fundamental principle of further evolution if not the essential condition of our future liberty and our moral dignity.

It may safely be said that it is impossible to render the answer better than in the words of the little Giant H. G. Wells himself: 'Then the little pygmy world would be safe. They would go on –

safe forever, living their little pygmy lives, doing pygmy kindnesses and pygmy cruelties to the other; they might even perhaps attain a sort of pygmy millennium, make an end to war, make an end to overpopulation, sit down in a world-wide city to practise pygmy arts, worshipping one another till the world begins to freeze . . .'[9]

What more can one say about one of the most unendurable nightmare visions of a brave new world, except that nothing worth preserving would survive. Nor am I concerned here with people who prefer to be pygmies rather than giants. What I am more genuinely concerned with, in fact, is not so much that lesser men are essentially like their leaders or the levelling process foisted upon them, but that their leaders themselves will tolerate no more great ideas, that their vision is not one of men's 'divinity' but of their overwhelming futility, their spiritual insignificance and their social distress. The essential point to remember, therefore, is this: a society which combines utter hostility to every form of supremacy with an extreme solicitude for happiness as the most substantive way to deny its own genius must eventually become both the agent *and* the object of its own degeneration. And in conclusion, therefore, one may agree with Nietzsche that it has 'turned a means to life into a measure of life: instead of finding the measure in the highest ascent of life itself – in the problem of growth and creation.'*

* *The Will to Power*

260

14

THE DREAMERS OF THE DREAM

'Men are not equal'.
And they should not become so, either!
For what were my love of the Superman if I spoke
otherwise?

Nietzsche, *Zarathustra*

And as the lesser surrenders to the greater, that it
may have delight and power over the least of all,
so the greatest, too, surrenders and for the sake of
power stakes – life.

Nietzsche, *Zarathustra*

*'If a name were to be given to impartiality and firm resolve, to
indefatigable activity in words and deeds, and a determinate
ardent pursuit of victory or honour, if to that cool courage, which
peril cannot daunt, misfortune cannot bend, and success cannot
intoxicate; it must be that of Roman fortitude . . .*
*Their generals stride like giants from one quarter of the Globe
to another, and bear the fate of nations in their prompt and powerful hands. Thrones are overturned by their foot as they pass, and
they determine the life or death of myriads with a word. Perilous
height, on which they stand! Ruinous game, where crowns are at
stake, and where the wealth of nations, and the lives of millions,
are played away!*
On this height they walk as simple Romans, disdaining the

pomp of barbarian kings; the helmet their crown, the coat of mail their only decoration.'[1]

'. . . determine the life or death of myriads with a word' – that great Roman word, worth the whole of the *corpus juris*, the famous Roman Code on which so much present-day legislation in almost every civilized country of the world has come to rest. Few men, and none in modern times, have written so masterfully on 'the great character of the Romans', their pride, their glory, their rise and decline, as Johann Gottfried von Herder, one of the most eloquent and erudite men of the eighteenth century. Such magnificent acclaim, of course, is no longer possible, or indeed desirable, now that the Roman legionary has discharged his duty and the ethos of empire been disparaged everywhere. Despite its great accomplishments in law and administration, all we are presently justified in affirming is that a Roman code of ethics was important in its own day, both as a conception worthy of free men and as a vehicle for transmitting genes of moral development to the men of the future. Nor must we assume that the rise of the Roman Republic was predatory in any simple or primitive sense. That would scarcely be fair to the Romans. Conquest, after all, was their business. And if *we* speak of diplomatic duplicity as one of the indispensable principles of successful Roman government, it remained an axiom, with Herder at any rate, that at the same time the Romans attached great importance to the value of an oath, to the inviolability of *fides Romana*, which it is not in fact hard to identify with the general concept of 'good faith' or *pistis* of the Greeks and as such with a general assurance of respect for a given pledge.

Personally, I find it absurd not to insist on Western Civilization as a historical achievement of the very first magnitude. It is much more absurd, however, to suppose that it could ever have been achieved without the 'duplicity' whereby Rome appropriated to herself the lucrative monopoly of the Mediterranean trade, an enormous field of private enterprise for the great financial syndicates or 'societies' which were extravagantly involved in public affairs. Or indeed without the vast corpus of Roman law which promoted a more equal, freer, progressive, prosperous and dynamic form of society – a very different kind of society indeed from the point of view of a lawless world which was brought under the rule of the *pax romana* and shielded from any rapacity but her own. In actual fact, it is not difficult to recognize the continuity of classic Imperial tradition if we see its survival not just in Greek marble or a Roman sense of world-citizenship, but in the progressive cultural unity which provided the historical basis for the rise of the West until the diplomatic usages laid down by Graeco-Roman civilization were again to occupy a prominent position in British imperial history with 'the "yea, yea" and "nay, nay", of a British envoy' whose word was current at the value *he* put on it.

Thus esteemed by Macaulay (other historians may have been less categorical), he at least was convinced that 'English valour and English intelligence have done less to extend and to preserve our Oriental Empire than English veracity . . . the one power in India on whose word reliance can be placed'.[2] And ever since then one of the orthodoxies guiding the theory and practice of Western statesmanship has been an overwhelming need to impose its own moral idealism upon international principles of a political obligation. In truth, as already hinted, such principles are long-lived and one can see no break in the continuity of Greek philosophy, Roman law, Christian humanism and the democratic evolution of Western moral enlightenment which is as much a legacy of classical antiquity as it is at the source of the constitutional, juridical and social evolution of the major Western powers over the past two thousand years.

The age of what we call Imperialism is now over for all of us. That much is certain. But in returning to the point with which I began, it is hard to imagine a political creed more likely to encourage the natural development of a sense of mutual obligation in the political thinking of nations, than the parliamentary creed which is representative of all countries that have been reared in the high moral tradition of the imperial West. Nor do I find it a temptation not to deny that that tradition has long since been vindicated by its own inherent idealism. In fact, it might be plausibly urged that an idealist programme of economic and administrative measures and a concern with the protection of international rights, also established the basis, in an atmosphere of democratic freedom and equity, for a single, coherent system of international law. That this law, too, contains principles to which nations may appeal against other nations, indeed, which are binding upon nations strong enough to resist the law, is a remarkable tribute to the power of a consensus which is secured by a network of constitutional devices, strengthened by judicial independence, and founded on

263

considerations of national freedom and international good-will.

It is in this essentially rather orderly way that national and international laws have determined social attitudes rather than military strategies or political survival. That the concept of international law is too limited in its concern with the complex causes of social unrest, too lenient in its toleration of various types of disruptive political behaviour, too ineffective in its application to the conditions of many a systematic genocide, and too indeterminate in its fundamental distinction between a moral and a legal obligation, cannot stand in the way of the fact that it is the medium which more than any other defies the calculated venom of political ambition. Of course, under most circumstances the State must be protective of national rights. The theoretical priority of the International Court of Justice can, it is true, override national parliaments and the international law supersede national statutes. But it is a mark of the integrity of the national community as an autonomous political unit, nevertheless, that the very idea of international interference in internal affairs of state has in all normal circumstances been judicial anathema. And nowhere, in fact, is this more clearly apparent than when the world community, despite its ostensible preoccupation with international principles of a moral obligation, declares itself incompetent to inquire into the circumstances under which the dogma of state sovereignty becomes the pretext for despotic or sometimes genocidal governments to corrupt the very principles which ought to be the real motivating concern of an international legal authority.

It is sometimes said that the failure of the post-colonial past has been the undue emancipation of various spendthrift dynasties with a vast relish for theatrical magnificence, of governments which aspired to international hooliganism and whose judiciaries surrendered one legal principle after another, or of power-drunk rogues who massacred, evicted or transplanted entire communities at will. More recently there have been worse examples, the most notorious being a policy which was based on the permanent eviction of ethnic minorities by their own belligerent governments. Nor is this a very adequate description of the feelings we experience when we see the spectacle of drunken paramilitary troops enforcing a policy of 'ethnic cleansing' whilst the international community (to avoid scandalizing the lawful perhaps) runs a determined no-involvement policy.

264

Of course, so far as feeling goes, there is no schematization of the legal process. Belief in lawfulness is sanctioned by belief in stability and tradition, and the definition of its terms is the covenant of that tradition. Because of its many dependent clauses, legal theory is concerned with ideal situations. It embraces varying levels of interpretation and often blurs the fundamental distinction between judicial military strategies and conditional political attitudes. The one lesson one can certainly learn from it is that of political improvidence rather than inconsequence. Truth to tell it is the misfortune of twentieth-century humanity that the architects of international legal theory never understood a fundamental limitation of their craft with its implied suggestion that the dignity and equal rights of men and women everywhere and of nations large and small requires not only to be upheld but also seen to be upheld, for a great deal of it is nullified by an exhibition of justice whose chief merit often seems to lie with the kind of appeal it has for the spectator. One objection is therefore that it is less important in some cases to do justice than to seem to do justice. Which certainly explains why the survival of tyrants, their aggressive domestic hostility, may well depend on nothing more than restraining a vacillating international authority from 'exceeding its jurisdiction'. And with that in mind it is one thing to inspire those who believe that they have learned their lesson as far as Hellenism is concerned, with a noble purpose aimed at a comprehensive and civilized comity of nations and to organize their faculties into a common channel, but quite another to yield the ground to a vigorously prosecuted, if as yet undeclared, post-colonial global disaffection as an independent branch of political theory.

Small wonder, then, that the ancient art of Western condescension does sometimes have its prejudicial air, for the lesson is clearly – and I have no wish to be unpleasant – that this is neither surprising nor disreputable given anticipations as dispiriting as these. More straightforwardly, what is of importance in any discussion of international jurisdiction is that its enforcement is not merely a moral necessity but a humanitarian requirement of civilized society and therefore obligatory and a very grave responsibility to disparage. Besides, we have needs other than the mere rendering of judicial deference to recalcitrant third-world power-brokers. Needs which I shall discuss later. Here I am concerned, if I may, with trying the readers judgement and, between the problems and solutions of the Roman universe and the impulses governing the modern world, with amplifying his moral experience.

To begin with, it is certainly true that if ever there was an undisputed master of the civilized world, it must surely have been in the first half of the second century BC when Carthage, Greece and Macedonia had all been conquered within a few eventful years and Rome was setting up kings in Egypt and the lands of the East. And not only by force of arms, but as will be seen, by 'bringing them to heel with a walking stick'. It is impossible, in following what that means, even for an admirer of the 'plainer' virtues of Roman fortitude, to deny that the Senate's attitude in attempting to impose some sort of order on the chaos of international behaviour was nothing if not arbitrary. Especially where fortitude combined with cupidity and Rome, like the West, was most ready to display it. There is, however, a difference here. In fact, the Roman concept of power differed from that of the modern Representative Parliament precisely in a way in which a body of Roman Senators sufficiently powerful to be able to stop at nothing must necessarily have differed from the contemporary parliamentarian who more usually bolsters his case by quoting legal precedents.

At any rate, what actually happened is that at roughly this time (168 BC) Antiochus Epiphanes was encamped somewhere in the desert before the gates of Alexandria. A somewhat megalomanic sovereign of the Seleucid dynasty, he had gone to war with the Ptolemy infant king in order to annex Egypt. This, to do him justice, was foolish enough. And precisely to emphasize this point, Popilius, a Roman envoy, had been dispatched by the Senate with peremptory orders for the king to withdraw at once. Doubtless this was an act of the political will personally typical of the immensely powerful magistrates who in little more than half a century had brought nearly the whole civilized world under the rule of their government. But who ever said anything so preposterous as that it was their given right to order kings about. Antiochus said he would consider the request and communicate his answer. But more than such a statement was required to make Popilius acquiesce. For it was then, we are being told in any standard work of Roman history, that the Roman took his staff and, by a gesture almost of condescension, traced a circle in the sand, challenging Antiochus to step out of it before conveying his reply. The King understood at once. It was a very direct and very far-reaching challenge, and it inevitably produced two effects – Antiochus capitulated and relinquished Egypt forthwith and Rome, at a stroke, assumed the virtual hegemony of the East.

The rest of the story is soon told. In point of fact, in the interest of historicity it should be remarked that there was nothing improvident or inconsequential about the moment when, according to a press report of the time, 'A line was drawn in the sand, operation Desert Shield put into action and unprecedented international co-operation sought and won'.[3] It can probably be said that this moment had something of the same condescending and peremptory significance. The Second Gulf War was clearly not a war of conquest but a punitive expedition intended to remind the erring Hussein of his duty as a member of the international community. Exactly which differences of opinion between states ought to be settled by an impartial arbitrator and which precisely are a matter for military intervention is of course a subject on which views may vary. What is certain is that Saddam Hussein as the propounder of a theory of Islamic revolution based largely on ideas of personal hegemony, had opened hostilities with a military attack upon the tiny Gulf nation of Kuwait. What motivates such men is far from doubtful. But a more prudent man, or a man less intent on personal power than Saddam Hussein might have been alarmed by a display of unanimity very rare in the history of the United Nations. International response was total and uninhibited, America very decidedly taking the lead. There was no one on Capitol Hill or in Congress who did not know perfectly well that the prevailing public mood was one of extreme indignity. Thus, the practical first-fruit effect was the surprise pre-dawn raid of Thursday, 17 January 1991 which commenced the Allied air offensive. Its ultimate but inevitably logical result was the reduction of Iraq.

It is not my business to incite altercation or to advocate the waging of pre-emptive wars on behalf of the Western democracies. I believe in freedom and I admire equity. But, in all, I beg to point out that anyone who believes that the West found its highest nobility in its significance as disseminator of the most fundamental humanitarian principles, both moral and political, owes it to himself to reflect upon those principles and to prevent his own sense of their importance from being penalized by the calculated fury of some mad and avenging *Jihad*. Stated more precisely, the

267

vigorous prosecution of the Second Gulf War and the successes of the united forces of the Coalition, so obviously marked the beginning of the business which ended the proclamation of high moral principles from a position of military vagueness, that it must have seemed to most of us, in equity as well as law, that it should remain the fundamental principle of the new order of things or – the term defines its scope – of the New World Order.

Anyone who is familiar with the famous words *ceterum censeo Carthaginem delendum* ('for the rest, it is my opinion that Carthage must be destroyed'), is familiar with Marcus Porcius Cato, 'the Censor', in whom this implacable viewpoint overrode every other consideration. His political opponents, led by Scipio Nasica, refuted it on the grounds that the continued existence of the disputed city was a prerequisite for a reactive moral energy, for a spirited foreign policy and, whatever its own endemic evils, for the preservation of a vigorous society at home. In short, when it was proposed that Rome could only retain her highly dynamic qualities for as long as she retained her potential enemy, the principle of it was almost certainly sound. But Cato's view – a characteristically simple view – prevailed; and whether or not his judgement was wrong, three years after his death the unhappy city, too, had practically vanished from the face of the earth.

That Rome ultimately profited from what at first seemed a severe disadvantage – the life-and-death struggle for national existence – has been shown with great force and poetic clarity by Johann Gottfried von Herder in the opening passage. Herder's great vigour of expression, particularly impressive in quotation, is fully equal to the business of doing justice to the Roman's greatest moral asset: plain fortitude. As a purifying and regenerative force it was a contagious one, and its fruits appeared almost inevitably in every country of the Mediterranean world. Indeed, if anyone doubts that the real inspiration which made America a global power was derived, not from the creed of Thomas Jefferson that all men are endowed with equal rights, but from a spirited foreign policy and the aspiration for global expansion, the following may safely be said: If the American Republic ever decided to accept defeat on the original issue of its bid for world hegemony – the imposition of the principles of liberal democracy on all the nations of the world – it would instantly deteriorate as all nations deteriorate which fail to take their reason for being seriously. One such instance, to which I do not wish to refer at any length now except to say that the USSR did not merely deteriorate, it fell inevitably and instantly apart, we were able to witness for ourselves.

It is said that Cornelius Scipio Aemilianus, the conqueror of Carthage, wept as he watched the burning city crumble to ashes in an infernal display worthy of Cecil B. De Mille. Nor was it compassion that he felt for the once proud, now broken foe, but an awesome foreboding of Rome's own tragic downfall. With a prophetic clearness he perceived the death of Rome precisely as it was to be. A perception only equalled, in a more mythical medium, by the tragically expressed foreboding of the Trojan, Hector: 'For in my heart and in my mind I know that Troy shall fall.' Once again, therefore, this prophetic myth of Providence seems to lie at the base of the necessity to prevent the West from becoming a victim of the ideological vacuum which has ensued with the sudden extinction of the Soviet Union as an aggressively expansionist state. It is certainly not an invitation to self-complacency. One should, on the contrary, expect that America, and by implication the West, would find it necessary to replace a forfeited cause with a *raison d'être* that can force the national will back to first principles and convert an erstwhile war of doctrines from an ideological into something which – to give due force to the contention – one might call an evolutionary struggle, a doctrine of conquest, nevertheless.

No one should glory in power, not even in the most righteous situations. But no one could possibly say that it is better to be the victim than the hangman. With 'marauding bands of gunmen; starving children and grieving mothers; shell-shattered homes and vicious killings', the humanitarian invasion of Somalia certainly was a case in point. The adoption of Security Council Resolution 688 in April 1991, too, was an unusually enlightened policy decision. But subsequent developments presented no such enlightenment. Possibly, there were other reasons. Perhaps, there were too many expectations associated with the new order and America did not wish to put too heavy a burden upon our sanguine hearts. 'The hostage, the losses and the horrifying pictures of Americans being dragged through the streets of Mogadishu caused the US to announce that it was pulling out of Somalia'.[4] Said Richard Dowden: 'This was the day the new world order finally died.'

'These are the times that try men's souls.' Thomas Paine's way

269

of putting it seems an accurate summing up. 'The summer soldier and the sunshine patriot will, in this crisis, shrink from the service of their country; but he that stands it *now* deserves the love and thanks of man and woman.' Reading this, it is not hard to remember when first Americans fought for the rights of man. It is, moreover, a significant fact that for the first time in modern political history the West is not fundamentally challenged by the East. The two main contenders for world leadership having accommodated each other, giving the USA something like a walk-over, the dispute no longer survives. What this means is quite clear. It means that the West is faced with a profound problem of readjustment, a new sense of motivation deprived.

'At the end of the Second World War', Paul Johnson writes in a Chapter entitled *The Flight of Reason*,[5] 'there was a significant change in the predominant aim of secular intellectuals, a shift of emphasis from utopianism to hedonism'. It is of course possible that no such corresponding development, no general shift towards US withdrawal from international affairs, or even isolationism, will mark the birth of a New and substantially Hedonistic Age. Nor does the end of the Cold War necessarily mean a *pax americana* in which *the pursuit of Happiness* preponderates. But whatever scepticism Mr Johnson may have expressed, it takes no imagination at all to see that young men and women in search of felicity, and mere rogues in quest of profitable enterprise rather than the defenders of the New World Order are the distinguishing and representative features of the incursion from the West.

Let us therefore make the assertion that the fundamental problem of our time, the toughest problem in the entire venture of a technological civilization is the problem of motivation itself. Looking back, it is but a truism that the problem central to the deepest psychological trauma in the history of man is essentially a crisis of evolution; the ongoing collapse of an entire tradition of values to say the very least, a sweeping away of convictions, a denunciation and adieu to every metaphysical implication since spiritual certainty has been replaced by its opposite. Nor is this the sum of the argument. It is bad enough that young men and women who are endowed not only with economic resources but favoured technologically, should be seen to succumb to a tangible sense of their own stagnation. But it is a remarkable situation by any standards that a civilization which is deeply if incomprehendingly conscious of a very perceptible void should be insensitive to the fact that it will never succeed in renewing itself from within. Real change can come only from without, from the emergence of a new perspective, a new dream, and new leaders prepared to consider the problem of our future regeneration precisely in terms which have not, so far, occurred to any single one of them.

That might seem extravagant. But as Wernher von Braun once said about the importance of a deeply committed leader, 'There is something inevitable about the Space Age, just as there was something inevitable about the Renaissance, or the Age of Steam, or the Air Age . . . (and) the personal interest that political leaders take in these new contemporary ideas has a great effect on the *speed* at which these new ideas take hold.'[6] Certainly – and this is a fact which we must always and firmly bear in mind – the Earth is not merely a Garden of Eden to be made fruitful. It is a 'footstool', in the metaphorical language of H. G. Wells, from which to reach out among the stars, rather than the realm of beasts and men, perhaps even supermen, if in any case allegorical in its development of the familiar subject of man's expulsion from Paradise because he was incapable of enduring the trials of a perfect existence. Men take no comfort from an orderly state of creation, as distinguished from hopes of improvement or redemption, without sacrificing some essential feature of their humanity. In actual fact, I happen to think that both these hopes are closely affiliated with the laws which regulate our moral life. Even in the limited sphere of scientific investigation any man who ventures to penetrate the unknown will always look for some gleam of genius that might exceed ordinary human dimensions. Genius, in fact, is much more than an instrument in our method of survival. It is closely bound up with the question of moral will and, whether in the form of a mystical sense for moral redemption or a talent for social, scientific or technological improvement, with the transcendent resources inherent in both.

It is perhaps inevitable, then, that the problem of genius should become an essential part of the larger issue of the redemption of man as an immortal being. Significantly, it is now that Western man is crossing the threshold of his severest test in world leadership and of the problem of genius that marks another important change. A crucial change in our social, scientific and technological development. The simple fact of the matter is that Western statesmanship has entered a period which makes it practically impossible to maintain its political supremacy, perhaps for a century to come, and to impose a certain discipline of international obligation upon a complicated pattern of different states, peoples, races, cultures, ideologies and religions, without a new source of moral authority. A new kind of inspiration which has the force of human action behind it in a way that will carry conviction. Without, in fact, demonstrating this capacity for leadership in both its science and its *super-humanness*. Nor is this to devise a lofty manner of saying that I am a strong believer in a revolution in leadership analogous even to that which has taken place in the natural sciences. The challenge of Space is incomparably more inspiring and infinitely more powerful and pervasive than the purely social terms from which the utopian evolution of the world has so far been made to proceed. Besides, it is issued not to a dying civilization but to a potentially immortal one.

Even if we do bear in mind that almost all futuristic discussions are discussions of an inherently theoretical nature, there is more than enough here, I believe, to convince us that with the development of modern science and technology there has been a genuine trend in recent times towards the recognition of man's significance against a background of order which, because open-ended, is ultimately in the nature of a cosmological development. But given the ever-increasing financial commitments and political obligations the West has incurred in the cause of civilization, one might well be pressed to admit that its energy and resources are necessarily deflected in directions other than the conquest of space. It is, on the other hand, impossible to overstress that the financial cost for the move into space might be a small price to pay compared with one cogent, inescapable reality: the ecological expenditures and demographic consequences which, otherwise, will inevitably result. Certainly, it is true that in the light of our present interests even the preliminary preparations for that move are still incomplete, if not actually superimposed on a context of social reality to which they do not as yet belong. But more serious from the scientist's point of view is that in the long run the real limit to technological growth may precisely be the lack of the financial resources which alone can enable him to proceed effectively.

On this point no compromise can be made. Nothing in between will do. It is likely enough, on the other hand, that the conquest of space is a project – as someone has said in a related statement of the same case – which has to be funded by the century, not by the fiscal year. This is the more plausible since the problem is only partially one of human ingenuity. Much more problematic, as I said, is the amount of money that can be made available precisely without denying the fundamental claims of human society itself. I am well aware that, even though it is far from being composed of fellow humans in a single cause or motivated by a 'single will', we are all fellow travellers on this space-ship called Earth, and as a basis for a more balanced equilibrium in international relations it is, and will remain, essential to relieve a mass of human suffering and distress. The Earth, said Homer, is the property of all. But let us be frank, insofar as humanitarian motives are still a valid force for peace, it is far more rewarding to unite the world's peoples in a common cause and to make the chief propulsive force of human civilization the transition from Earth into Space, than to see to it that nations of no great importance or standing – the point, it will be remembered, with which I began – should have the foreign policy of a major power or the advanced weapons capability to initiate a major nuclear war.

It may strain credulity, but it is an astonishing fact that the total military expenditure for the whole of the year 1990 has been estimated at some 900 billion dollars worldwide, or just under 'two million dollars a minute'.[7] This is the more remarkable when it is remembered that the total cost for the American Apollo space programme which put the first man on the moon was less than twenty-five billion dollars spread out over nine consecutive years. Nor is it part of my case to deal with the unlimited and scattered objectives of innumerable sets of partisans, races, cultures, nations, societies, dictators and feudal chiefs too interested, in any event, in their own immediate destinies to feel any enthusiasm for the creation of worlds in so remote a region as Space. But at the same time it is important to realize what a tragic and calamitous step it would be to arrest the development of space research on the mere pretext that it is hindering Third World development or the advance of social progress.

But all this is irrelevant without some competent and sufficiently powerful international authority willing to act on its own humanitarian theories. Nor can it be denied that the destiny of every nation of European origin and, having found herself burdened with world-leadership, none perhaps more than of the United States, is ultimately controlled by the national pride and confused ambitions of precisely those nations who do not believe in moral conscience as a source of either political responsibility or democratic accountability. More pointedly, one is perhaps justified in saying that only the toughest and most stalwart defenders of Western values against those who are opposed to liberty and democracy, resentful of foreigners and infidels, loath of meeting a white man or congenitally incapable of a single self-denying act, can ultimately provide the authority necessary to save the world of human civilization from this aggressive and disunited species.

This, however, is an involved and intricate way of expressing a simple point. The practical fact is that today we have a turning point in scientific evolution. A revolution of man's view of himself and of his function in the universe which is perpetual self-overcoming. Raised to the highest possible level one might elevate this function by using mythic ideas and images, even by stimulating the gloomy optimism of the Son of Man which, as one of the few unbroken threads in the tissue of Christian philosophical thinking over the past two thousand years has borne and shed its finest fruits, to yield fresh fruits with a new dispensation of Man: the *Superman* in whom scientific and ontological understanding are combined – in which case the ultimate test of genius is conceded – to deliver the world from the world. There is no mysticism in this. Nor is this to say that science should proceed as much by faith as by reason, or that it should reject reason for intuition, but from the point of view of our present state of knowledge it is no longer possible to deny that, within certain well-understood limits, science itself is subject to the same uncertainty relations as is its peculiar power to render life into logic and yet retain its mystery.

At such moments we are apt to solve the riddle of creation. Then, of course, there is the question of scale. For such evidence as there is in quantum electrodynamics by no means disposes of the necessity to believe that – according to Freddy Hoyle – 'astronomers will eventually discover that much of what they currently believe concerning the behaviour and formation of galaxies has to be modified to take account of intelligent control.'[8] Henceforward, too, I suspect, they must take account of the external and internal terrors revealed to men who are subjected to the most probing trial of self-knowledge to which the mind of man can possibly be exposed. These days are far off, but one imagines substantially similar experiences when men of flesh and blood for the first time offer themselves to face the awful hazards of interstellar travel, of a loneliness almost unendurable. We commonly say that no man may trespass on the boundaries allowed to mortals. But the simple fact of the matter is that to transcend and trespass on boundaries of that sort would require the manifestation of a rare confidence, of an act of faith so fundamental that the individual who could live with the solitariness of that potentially timeless condition, would have to be considered a new kind of man, or indeed Superman, whose life lay in the stars, who raised self-sufficiency to a level which not only meant the inception, to all intents and purposes, of an altogether higher or superior species, but the total expatriation from ordinary human society.

Elaborating at greater length, Karl Gustav Jung scrutinizes the mythological argument and concludes that 'every step towards greater consciousness is a kind of Promethean guilt: through knowledge the gods are as it were robbed of their fire, that is, something that was the property of the unconscious powers is torn out of its natural context and subordinated to the whims of the conscious mind. The man who has usurped the new knowledge . . . has raised himself above the human level of his age ("ye shall become like unto God"), but in so doing has alienated himself from humanity. The pain of his loneliness is the vengeance of the gods, for never again can he return to mankind. He is, as the myth says, chained to the lonely cliffs of the Caucasus, forsaken of God and man'.[9]

I am fully conscious that it would be going too far, on present evidence, to suggest that the physicist is beset by anxieties about his own hubris of discovery. One hardly supposes that. But when the process is considered in detail, one cannot help feeling that anyone who is introspectively transcendent as a scientist is likely also to point the way for a transcendent future, even if so far as one can tell that future measures in millennia rather than centuries or decades. In fact, it is more than just a guess that the future spaceman would be rather intrigued at our present image of him yearning for the pleasant climes and life of this Garden of Paradise. He may never have known the Earth or the Moon. Nor is this man-worship or a repudiation of God. But left to himself and alone in space, man has no chance insofar as he is merely human. As for a repudiation of God, much depends on what kind of god he is. It is a commonplace of science, that 'God' is a forbidden word. Nor are we obliged to take it literally. But, until it ceases to be a mere metaphysical expression, it is important to state succinctly what it does and does not mean. For when we are on the point of being able to see quantum-dynamic effects as a function of our own senses rather than as a probable consequence of the laws of physics, we have no choice but to believe in the transcendent power which is common to both.

Seizing on this fact, nothing strikes one so forcibly when trying to fathom the new frontiers that physical science, both pure and applied, is beginning to reveal to us, how completely the scientific conception of genius has become the greatest mystical force of our time. But for his genius the most important thing about man is his science. For here is renewed that quest for the meaning of genius and the dream of the dreamers which, for thousands of years, has enlivened the minds of astronomers, mathematicians, explorers, geographers, merchants, adventurers, poets and philosophers, or, if that fails to establish the general infrastructure which made human civilization possible, of anyone else who might have inherited the instinct for destiny in human nature. In ordinary words, it is unnecessary to stress that civilization has produced results not just through single individuals but through the varied and collaborative efforts of joint action, which is to say, through the great mass of men co-operating with one another towards a single all-embracing end. But to say that professional science is based on teamwork rather than on the power of super-human genius is not to say that the transcendent reality of the physicist might not come into conflict with the transcendent reality of his universe or that, true to his own reality, he may not be god and deicide in one.

So when we ask whether God is well and truly dead, the idea as hitherto understood, is quite meaningless. But one thing would certainly follow from the continuous nature of this kinship: the technological provisions which may one day enable men to escape from the planet Earth or, more properly, from space, time and gravity, are not the project of a megalomaniac illusion of illimitable power. This fact, I believe, emerges not only from the long-range objectives for interplanetary travel which, though scarcely formulated as yet, are remarkable evidence nevertheless of the immense preparations for the most colossal task of any kind ever undertaken by men, but from the broad sense in which this is true of the transcendent character of the facts of evolution. More specific than that, one is struck by the tendency of evolution as an almost perfect mechanism through which a species can actually overcome itself. Something of the sort is already implicit in the process of natural selection as a product of contest, for by the very act of surrender as a law of self-conquest, life itself is made the object of renewal. I would now add that there is much in men which is still cruel, savage and predatory, more bestial in truth than god-like, and if the facts of evolution seem to suggest a compulsion over which men seem to have little control, it is all the more essential not to abandon the 'higher self' or to turn away from the will to power as a principle upon which natural selection operates, towards paralysis, stagnation and evolutionary dead-ends.

But, as I have said, the important thing to remember is that the future belongs to the scientist and his all-powerful need for knowledge. Science alone can lead the world out of its difficulty. No other institution can. Science holds the key to the greatest age of faith in the history of the world, even if we cannot define it. For the problem is basically a psychological one and involves a spiritual recrudescence and enhancement of human values. This consideration lies at the root of everything. Indeed, the Promethean assault upon Space, both absolutely and relativistically, is not simply a technological feat, but a psychological revolution. It is an attempt, is it not, to rediscover something profound and deep-rooted in the human psyche, an expression, I believe, of both a penetrating utopian recognition and a desperate search for a new identity on the part of the men and women who are plainly in need of a more transcending and persuasive experience than the outdated religious idealism to which they can no longer relate. But the chief importance of a new psychological dimension lies precisely in the fact that ultimately it gives redemptive power to that irrepressible desire for intellectual scope and physical activity which has always been, as it remains today, a fundamental part of human evolution.

Nor is that all: the question now arises once more whether 'the first of the human race' will prove to be the last, the Nemeses and destroyers of the world, or whether they will actually begin to take their own future more seriously in hand? The 'white man' of today must bear his burden. It may even be necessary for him to surrender the very way of life that the precursors of our own day found so congenial, the very planet, perhaps, from which he commenced his assault on the heavens which the rest of mankind may be too improvident, indifferent, hostile or hungry to participate in. There appears after all no reason why, faced with the blank incomprehension of men with no real understanding of the vital needs of future generations and assuredly inspired by no desire to meet him on terms of equal co-operation, he should submit with whatever patience (and resources) he can command to those who wish to have no part in 'a species higher than man'. That would be an ignominious surrender. Ultimately, I am persuaded, the world will triumph over the legacies of ignorance and inequality, provided its assets are employed and its efforts synchronized to this end. But that those at the bottom end of the scale cannot participate in such efforts should not descredit those who do. In fact, it would be invidious not to excuse 'the meek and the poor in spirit' (especially, to be sure, where meekness is compounded by blindness) who are merely struggling with the basic problems of life. Above all, one must distinguish them from the products of surfeit, as we know them in the West, whose loyalties are to social equality and material happiness rather than to humanity and the collective future of all.

Even so, this is not perhaps the place to expound Darwinian evolution, but its operative formula that evolution not infrequently proceeds through the elimination of 'specialized types' and the survival of the simpler and more adaptable forms of life, is really a good summary of the irreconcilable antagonism of the principles upon which it is based. Much would depend, of course, on the nature of the decline. On whether for instance it is caused, in the language of the evolutionists, by 'a new vigorous society overrunning a senile one' or though 'the total collapse of the more advanced technological societies, and a reversal of human life to the primitive subsistence level'. No doubt the two are related. But with the latter in mind it is not perhaps unreasonable to say that a condition of their pre-eminence is that 'the first of the human race' – and technically at least this may be true – establish new claims to immortality or else, whatever their other claims, make room for supercession.

I do not mean to overrate men's desire for immortality. None of us is superhuman. But man's essential purpose, one can feel tolerably certain, is of a kind that gives us a new meaning of the idea of immortality and its power to liberate without relying on metaphysics. In fact, the more one discovers about the essential contradictions of that sense of human immortality which has been the inspiration of so many celebrated metaphysicians anxious to reflect upon its transcendental foundations, the more likely it begins to seem that practical effort not abstract metaphysical speculation may well be at the heart of the puzzle, or – to give this idea an added emphasis – may well be the best way to pass from one dimension into another, into a level beyond that of time and history, and to leave the meek and the poor in spirit, who are so busy ravaging each other, to dispute the inheritance of the Earth and of our own hard-won and honourable place on it.

15

THE STAR WHICH RULES THY DESTINY

The star which rules thy destiny
Was ruled ere earth began by me:
It was a world as fresh and fair
As e'er revolved round sun in air;
Its course was free and regular,
Space bosom'd not a lovelier star,
The hour arrived – and it became,
A wandering mass of shapeless flame,
A pathless comet, and a curse,
The menace of the universe;
Still rolling on with innate force,
Without a sphere, without a course
A bright deformity on high,
The monster of the upper sky!

Byron, *Manfred*

Many Communities there will be who will hide
themselves and their young and their victuals
within gloomy caverns, and there in dark places
will sustain themselves and their families for
many months without light either artificial or
natural.

Leonardo da Vinci

Of the stars it may safely be said that even the most powerful optical telescope cannot magnify them into anything more spectacular than mere points of light on a dark background. Even our knowledge concerning their size, mass, temperature and chemical composition or, in equivalent terms, their nuclear reactions and thermodynamic properties, is derived almost entirely from a careful analysis of their electromagnetic spectra. 'A spectrum contains more than a rainbow of colours' Isaac Asimov has written, 'much more'. It may, all the same, have its limitations. Nor, by analysing starlight spectroscopically, is there any enhanced prospect of solving the apparently insoluble problem of bridging the gap between our spectroscopic data and some more tangible knowledge of the Universe. Moreover, to assume, as the ancients seemed to assume, that the movement of the heavens could best be explained by supposing that, once every day, its immense dome turned on its own axis, was not perhaps as paradoxical as it may now seem. To us who know the facts, it might seem like a superficial judgement. But it was natural enough considering that not only the stars but even the galaxies are so far away from us that even though they may be moving in different directions at different velocities, they appear as if permanently fixed in their apparent positions. Hence, few of those with a full comprehension of the problems and limitations of interstellar transportation find it easy to imagine that our apparently limited technology will ever succeed in reaching the point where it can send exploratory probes, let alone manned craft, to even the nearer galactic stars. To be precise, this is hard to imagine even of the nearest system, Alpha Centauri, which is visible enough to the naked eye but, being some four and a half light years away, effectively inaccessible.

By these observations I do not, of course, suggest that this exhausts the function of the stars. The stars are our timekeepers. Their claim on our attention is profound and enduring. As far back as we venture to go in the history of the great civilizations of the ancient world, vanished already when Rome was built, they have always played a central role in human affairs. Timeless and archetypal, it is the hidden purpose of the stars to be gazed and wondered at as witnesses of our existence, indeed to be catalogued and computed as living and oracular symbols in which men recognize their doubts and their dreams, their destinies, and perhaps even themselves. Of course, like most attempts to describe the heavens, these are romantic stereotypes. But if one is to ascribe a particular design to the stars for reasons other than purely scientific, it is to provide a rationale for the human imagination and thus to enhance the sphere of association and to waken and give guidance to man's capacity to evolve. This detail has importance since nothing yet discovered during the long history of human civilization rivals the charismatic conception of the stars as a principle at once of energy and organization, as a living mythological symbol of metaphysical redemption, an object of wonder, veneration, awe and speculation, and even as a guide to the human psyche itself. It might have been thought perhaps that modern men would seek to disaffiliate from their archaic commitment to the eternal and the mythic, or in some measure sacrifice psychological susceptibility to certain demands of logic and exactitude. But for all our rationality, the impulse of the imagination cannot be purged or refuted by facts. In our hearts and minds the fundamentally active rather than the specifiably refractive, life rather than logic, has proved itself a force of undiminished power.

Nor is it a question of physical measurement. Stellar evolution unfolds against an authentic spiritual background, the ultimate incomprehensible perspective from which everything has to be viewed – pure and unconscious space. Because the universe we seek to fathom, in its spiritual essence as in every aspect of its physical appearance as an impersonal force, uses the principle of first causes as a means of conceptualizing itself, it would also seem capable, on these terms, of grasping itself as a purpose. Intelligence involves self-knowledge. In fact, even without introducing the concept of intelligibility, if there can be anything like a first cause, it might just as well be the representation of the Universe as the object of its own contemplation. An object, particularly with regard to the genesis of man, which generates and extends itself by an ongoing process of self-realization. Nor is it an abstract theory to suggest that what is in fact a crisis of modern civilization is not so much indicated by the fact that the world's ecological life-support systems are under serious threat – for in spite of the accompanying retrogression of values the notion of crisis cannot be reduced to a mere socio-demographic dilemma on the one hand and to certain climatological peculiarities on the other – but by circumstances which, at a time of acute spiritual transition, appear to be the direct consequence of an increasing vacuity of metaphysical purpose.

Thus, to future generations, as indeed to ourselves, the whole logic of the scientific approach to the Solar System, to adopt a more technical terminology, is not just consistent with a new belief in science and technology, but compatible with a cause as immutable, as abiding and as permanent as the stars themselves: men's concern for new ideals and new patterns of existence. For whenever men have thought seriously about inaugurating the next major phase of human existence, it has always been a natural step to go further and, at the threshold of new and greater undertakings, to resume as a means what had been exhausted as an end. 'Man', said Nietzsche, 'is something to be surpassed.' Nor is it difficult to show that it is usually at the actual moment when the most highly advanced civilization is finally beginning to corrupt or alienate its own instinctive destiny, that this must either signify the death of all *natural* human values or – as I prefer to think – inspire it to reproduce its highest conceivable genius. And that is what we must now consider.

It is of course the easiest thing in the world to sneer at proposals to industrialize the Solar System or to establish settlements throughout when, as many people seem to believe, such a purpose would not be justified. I freely admit that the more closely one examines the matter, the more such difficulties as the technological transition from the most favoured of planets, the flourishing garden of the universe, on to the harsh environs of the Solar System where conditions are very, very different, tend not to resolve themselves but to proliferate into an obstinate, costly and protracted challenge stretching far, far into the future, both in space and in time. A tremendous effort is required here, nothing less it is plain than a universal revolution in scientific imagination. In point of fact, even the best informed scientific expertise would probably not at present stand up to it with any determination or outright conviction. This being so, the most sensible thing perhaps would be to accept defeat and to plan the future accordingly. Let me point out, however – and I hope I am not without a due sense of the complexities here involved – that despite the enormity of the task, such reservations simply do not meet the exponential character of potential technological innovations and that, as time goes on, even the most intelligent condemnation of what is undoubtedly going to be the most sustained technological challenge in the entire history of civilized man, cannot prevail over the tremendously accelerating effect of human ingenuity once it is applied to the full stretch of its considerable powers.

Few things are more surpassing than the rapid and complete

changes wrought, at its conclusion, in the socio-economic foundation of what we now call the Industrial Revolution. The first and most obvious of these was the shift of emphasis from agriculture to industry. Nor, as far as a shift of emphasis goes, can we seriously maintain that, in a different medium, such a revolution would not be significantly diminished by the sheer size and enormity of the obstacles involved. But since the process also entails the coming into existence of a new civilization, or at least a new type of society, more important perhaps than the complexities of what is, in any case, an over-simplification of a vastly involved situation, is that nothing concentrates the scientific imagination more effectively than the tendency in human nature which is inherently inquisitive. The acquisitive capacity, too, is uniquely and characteristically human. Indeed, it is specifically worth remarking that such transitional periods have traditionally been the most financially rewarding in human history. The New World, of course, broke all the records. But even though it is premature perhaps to speak in terms of interplanetary cost-effectiveness or of the establishment, at a foreseeable stage, of the commercial infrastructure that would make interplanetary space-flight economically viable, there is nevertheless already tremendous scope for big private organizations capable of undertaking large and important projects without risk to public funds.

The most telling argument, of course, for the conquest of Space (however remote from the commercial interest) is the need to dispose of our chemical or indeed, nuclear, waste. This has been one of our fundamental concerns during the past few decades, and never more so than at the present moment. Freeman Dyson has summed up the situation very clearly in *Disturbing the Universe*: 'There are three reasons why, quite apart from scientific considerations, mankind needs to travel in space. The first reason is garbage disposal; we need to transfer industrial processes into space so that the earth may remain a green and pleasant place for our grandchildren to live in'.[1] Nor can we go here into an extraordinary wealth of additional reasons for such cosmic resource productivity and its vast ramifications in terms of an ever-increasing social and economic enterprise system. New examples occur almost daily. Nothing, in sober fact, argues against the technological advance into space as an economically productive revolution – even though it is inevitable that in any extended discussion of the subject the question of public finance should invariably be reintroduced. As I have repeatedly said, the need for funding – or to state it categorically – the lack of it, stands out with all the realism of a sentence of death. If the conquest of space is the most Promethean of all the conquests of man, it is also an immensely expensive business. Most importantly of all, it is rooted in a shrewd appreciation of commercial realities.

There are, however, other ways of meeting the problem. As we have already outlined in Chapter Four, irrespective of the conventional role ascribed to public money, empire-building and the territorial acquisition of new worlds in America, Africa and the Far East, was almost a private undertaking. It was dictated by no municipal necessities, created no fundamental objections on the part of the ordinary taxpayer and saved the Exchequer from the difficult and costly task of defraying the fiscal strain of equipping and maintaining the Empire. Apart from all other objections, it would simply have been inexpedient on economic grounds (and politically out of the question), that large sections of the British Empire, to name just one example, should not have been profitable, self-financing, or under Company control. We can see the beginnings of this process already manifesting itself in the specific historical context from which such companies arose. Not everyone agrees with it today, but the revenue producing potential of Crown Patents and Chartered Concessions gave its recipients a share in political decision making which, it is true, not infrequently extended far beyond their original brief as merchant-adventurers, but which, as a money-making process, remained an economically productive function and inseparable from the condition of historical growth.

In addition, of course, there was another reason why the single-minded pursuit of an entrepreneurial activity that would have done credit to any conglomerate of modern industrialists not only changed the face of Europe, but, in the act of discovering new worlds, projected Europe far across the seas. Conventional or fiscal resources of revenue were not, it will be recognized, always commensurate with the needs of an empire. That budget left little room for expansion. And if empire-building became a general commercial enterprise whose common symbol was, in the case of England, the red cross of St George, it is not usual to find that to the commercial incentive for conquest was thus appended military bluster and the arrogance of nationhood. Nor does the common criticism that this particular period of adventurist imperial policy formed one of the most lawless chapters in the history of European statesmanship, affect the validity of the assertion that, as many a discomfited historian has justifiably pointed out, it also provided the economic foundations for the political rise of the West.

To the best of my knowledge, it remains an established fact that the condition of human self-esteem at the national level affords real opportunities for transfigurative international projections. To put it bluntly, it was no parochial pride whereby J. F. Kennedy secured for himself and his nation an everlasting place in the history of space exploration. Intentionally or otherwise, Kennedy struck a major blow for the future of interplanetary flight when, just over a quarter of a century ago, he delivered his celebrated promise to put a man on the Moon. That promise contained little immediate economics[2] perhaps, but a great deal of history nevertheless. If it was also a challenge – or, at any rate, duly acknowledged as such by the Soviet Union – so much the better, that would be the finest tribute to an incredibly historic event, to a priceless experience of a new and surpassing kind which has never as yet been equalled. Thus, during the period in question and in circumstances reminiscent of the famous race to reach the South Pole between Amundsen and Scott, a truly dynamic vision began to transform itself into one of our epoch's most astonishing and significant exploits.

There are, of course, other ways of looking at the merits of manned space exploration. Unhappily, not everyone understands its real significance. For instance, 'by 1979, there were to have been more than 200 people in space – 150 in space stations (50 in geostationary orbit); 25 in lunar orbit, 50 on the lunar surface, and 12 *en route* to Mars. It was a beautiful programme,' according to Duncan Lunan, the schedule's faithful chronicler, 'destined to vanish like snow in the sunshine.'[3] Saddest of all, there is a very considerable section of scientific opinion in America even today which defends the belief that the whole *manned* space-programme is but a glorious event of the past, an experiment not worth going on with. Nor is it worth commenting on the more fundamental objection that NASA's financial resources are always stretched to breaking point. True, one way of circumventing this chronic predicament would be the use of remote controlled mechanical and robotoid probes or, in more exotic terms, of 'cybernetic anthropomorphous machine systems'[4] which, it has been postulated, can conduct the same experiment much more cheaply, more reliably, and with results that are equally satisfying (to some at any rate). What is not clear is precisely how enthusiastically the totally mechanized conquest of space is going to be responded to in the public mind when the process entails the destruction or at least the reduction to potential insignificance of any human interest in the matter. Except, perhaps, for the technology that grows out of it.

Doubtless there is great merit in all of these austerity programmes directed at the cautious deployment of funds. But much more is involved here than the mere economy of resources. No conceivable incentive could possibly be derived from assuming that some instrumented technological mechanism is present to convert aspects of space flight which are specifically and uniquely human, into a mere function of the difference between men and machines. In spite of what some of its theorists may suggest, the whole idea would cease to be a human concern in any meaningful sense. It may furnish a species of technology, but it could not pretend to offer a philosophy. No stimulus is offered to the imagination of the human mind. And without such a stimulus, i.e. without such an inducement in their visionary life it is something of an open question, perhaps, whether men with souls are to remain human or whether, after all, they themselves need to become humanoid entities, a species of 'Cyborgs' so to speak, in order to secure their own extraterrestrial future.

Thus, if we are at all serious about creating a new age, what is needed is an act of the scientific imagination as fundamental as the meanings and values by which it is to be sustained. In other words, the conquest of space will succeed as a human conquest or not at all. One may take as an indication of this that, at least according to former President George Bush, America's resolve to send people to Mars is to be unshakeable because – in words that the most parsimonious Senator could not fail to understand – 'it is humanity's destiny'. This, I too, believe to be the case. Yet, as we have already seen, the resolve 'to strive, to seek, to find', though attributes of the heroic, the sublime and the pioneering, is only one aspect of the New Order in Washington. Quite another, it may be recalled, was Bill Clinton's inauguration. This particular President's resolve, understandably if unfortunately, still appears uncertain and liable to be shaken (especially in sticky situations) by the cordial effort necessary first to transform the intellectual condition of the time and then to raise the question of economics.

Such a condition at any rate, its social and political significance, explains both the details and the recurrent nature of the type of event which, for instance, took place on 10 October 1989. What happened on this particular day is that the presence of lawyers was required to repeal a court injunction brought by environmentalists litigating against NASA's meanwhile famous Galileo probe. On what grounds? Chiefly, it seems, because men of little faith are convinced that they are blood-brothers to dolphins, whales and butterflies, or more precisely perhaps, to H. G. Wells' 'little people' to whom we have already referred and with whom they seem to have a common theme and inspiration – a sort of pygmy millennium, according to all accounts. The whole approach was one of cosmic deprecation. Before the six-year voyage to the planet Jupiter could even begin a lawsuit had to be defeated in the United States District Court of Washington DC, where it was filed on the grounds that a launch accident involving the nuclear powered space probe could easily contaminate the more heavily populated areas of east and central Florida.

Galileo, as everybody knows, is now safely on its way. More recently, however, there have been other examples. Nor, especially as an example, is the sometimes astonishing imbecility of the organized forces of conscientious objection which have proliferated into a never-ending succession of extreme and terror-stricken proclamations, quite without a certain insight into the millennial dreams and visions of the eco-apocalyptic brotherhood dedicated to marshalling active and public mass-followings. Particularly at a time when it is of the greatest importance that men should be encouraged to take a large view of the relation of their own world to others, these medieval demonstrations of the all-too-little people prove nothing, it seems to me, that could inspire a man to take more pride in his humanity than in being the relative of an ant.

None of this, of course, offers much proof one way or another for what it is difficult either to corroborate or repudiate but which, in any case, cannot be conveniently discussed here except to say that, in its very minor way, the actual risk of radioactive pollution at the hands of the Galileo probe was not only extremely improbable but, I repeat, scarcely made to seem convincing in the light of the actual issues involved. Perhaps the only corroboration really required was provided by the shuttle pilot himself: 'I can't imagine how it can hurt anyone unless it hits him on the head'. And this, in plain English – and according to the laws of probability – is obviously and inescapably true.

As I have said, there were other examples and, quite possibly, additional reasons why, in contradiction of these laws and in order perhaps to exacerbate the mathematical probability of it happening, COSMOS 1900, a nuclear-powered Soviet space probe, too, should have had no difficulty in scoring a direct hit. In this particular case, on the British Houses of Parliament! When Baroness Faithfull, a Tory Peer (who seems to have spent much of her time by the window) took the unusual step of calling on her fellow Peers not to exclude such a contingency, she appears to have been entirely convinced that a hazard so self-evident and so grave could not fail to arouse an immediate response from the House.[5] So far as I know the principal evidence she offered in support of an unexisting problem was that the 'House', and by extension presumably certain distinguished classes of men, were entirely unprepared for the full enormity of such a hazardous situation. Meanwhile, some of us may remember, the crippled Soviet satellite perished over the coast of West Africa.

'Prudence', in a phrase once coined by William Blake, 'is a rich, ugly, old maid courted by incapacity'. It is easy enough to sneer at wrong-headed old females, or more appropriately perhaps, at their incapacity to discern the point at which solicitude becomes a farce. But informally at least we are at the threshold of a new historical perspective, and an age which, at its most cathartic moment, confines itself to the extravagant dialectics of public safety, political opportunism and moral sophistry, and formally assumes the responsibility of reducing the history of the world to the plain community level because it cannot otherwise inspire, seems hardly compatible with the vanguard of historical evolution. The point is worth making because a society which has no obvious historical associations and which lacks any obviously significant development because the problem of history, once conceived on the grand and epic scale, is merely compounded as a corollary to the absurd and contradictory problems of the most narrowly conceived social responsibilities, is itself profoundly uncertain of the directions its destiny is to take.

To present a grandiose picture of the Universe as a region of refuge to escape the crush, or even worse disaster, on Earth, would be to anticipate many years of experiment and research.

Nor need one attach more significance to a cautious, even defeatist, attitude than the circumstances warrant. But, the ability to think in the very long term plays a major part and, within the limits of myth and reality, no sharp line of demarcation exists between the visible and the invisible universe, even though some hopelessly faint-hearted and paper-ridden bureaucrats who know nothing about the cosmic soul, do their best to separate the observable from the unobservable future. This argument may seem a little forced, but there is no insubstantial evidence to suggest that the shape of things to come is more completely at the discretion of those stars we never see, than dictated by a spirit of humanity which, in taking the line of least resistance, finds it more charitable to develop a strong sense of social security as an index of its functions, than to rear generations man enough to provide the future nucleus for a civilization more responsible, more purposive and more surpassing than any in the history of man.

Not unnaturally, to take up the question of travel between solar systems, all the world's experts are unanimous in asserting that a manned mission to the planet Mars cannot fail to expose the ship's company to risks that are literally incalculable. The risk is in any case that a roundabout route, requiring up to three years perhaps for a passage, and the prospect of a long absence from home under circumstances which have never been tested in all human experience, would impose almost unendurable mental strain. It can be considered as certain, moreover, that the consequences of an ill-starred mission would in any case be ruinous to the whole manned programme, for practical as well as political reasons. The problem of cosmic rays or any other form of potentially lethal radiation emitted from the depths of space, and this applies to the cumulative effects of high-energy particles of all kinds, is a particularly difficult one. Some people have in consequence denied that interplanetary travel is possible at all.

There are other aspects among the many definite and confirmed facts about the singular effects produced on the human body through long-term exposure to weightlessness which raise questions about the viability of long journeys across the gravitational limbo. But it would be out of place here to follow in detail what lies beyond the competence of this book. As Thomas Hobbes has written, 'No man can have in his mind a conception of the future, for the future is not yet. But of our conceptions of the past, we make a future.' So we would have to go back to the late fifteenth century when men like Columbus, Magellan and da Gama first proved that it was possible for a fleet of vessels to journey across the uncharted oceans without support from the land, in order fully to appreciate all of the different types of hazard to be found in the special conditions which exist in the utopian commitment to a cause which is probably as old as man himself.

Like the men who sailed the seas in their storm-scattered squadrons, the modern astronaut, once more in full action under the flaring stars, has to perform the part of a hero and develop himself psychologically and (if he is serious at all) spiritually, before he can excel in the most purifying challenge of our time – and in the most deadly one. Interestingly enough, as used here, there is another and, as I believe, more important aspect of this invocation of death as the greatest of moral and purifying powers. Some idea of the degree to which human lives have in fact become expendable and, not infrequently, ephemeral and unessential, has presumably been gathered from the lavish expenditure of blood and pleasure which has already been discussed in previous chapters. As a result human lives are at such a discount nowadays that, to use a more pertinent terminology, they can no longer be acknowledged for their true value, whatever that may be. The great majority of people, unfortunately, who know the pleasures of life, do not always stop to contemplate its value. It is not a concept that would explain anything. So the important thing is to bring out the significance of each individual life in relation to the whole. To understand, in other words, that the value of life becomes the more precious the more precarious it is going to be.

Such precariousness is no vacant stipulation. We may be a long way from it, but it is part of our vision for the future. Nor does there seem to be any reason why life should not continue to evolve even though it cannot be found anywhere else in Space. Indeed, it is to Space, if anywhere that we must turn to understand the price its existence entails. Only here will its true value become apparent. What matters is the evolutionary process which, with no accepted convention as to the propriety of living or dying, has determined what any man may determine who ponders the problem for himself: that its surrender does not constitute the refutation of life. Besides, what alternatives indeed are open to the despoilers of the earth when it is logically incontrovertible that any further limitation of its slowly decreasing circumference must somehow but irreversibly proceed towards the certain annihilation of everything contained therein?

It is unwise perhaps to dogmatize in matters of life and death, but since nothing is gained by mitigating what is not an improving situation, this might indeed be the proper moment to acknowledge what can be clearly and unmistakably inferred from its terms: that the principle which conceives of the perpetuation of maximum sustainable growth inside a closed ecological system and which admits that the number of its occupants is increasing by the amount its space is diminishing, can never be accommodated within a non-ecocidal context. It must, quite obviously, prove itself the means to its own consummation. To the certain holocaust of the whole civilized order, of everything great and small, good and bad, favourable and unfavourable, of all our likes and dislikes, all our dearest thoughts, the lowliest no less than the most sublime, as well as of all our moral profundities.

But it is not necessary for us to take so apocalyptic a view, for here, at last, is the incentive to turn to the stars. It is possible, of course, that no one expects to live long enough to witness the end of the world, not even for some hypothetical eventually. Confused, dispirited perhaps and content to fight other crusades, to some it may indeed appear that it is best to plan for ignominious survival in the hope that its inevitability does not change the nature of things overnight. But this is no time to think of fighting minor campaigns. Relative probabilities have no place in this. The issues are complementary from first to last. Or rather, there is no division of the issues requiring solution when, in this regard as in all others, they are in fact mutually and successfully (if that is the word) operating towards some final and inescapable state of absolute destruction. This is no flamboyant protestation of the wrath to come. The outcome is inherent in its logic from the very start. Even a perfunctory survey of the way in which ecological genocide is perpetrated in different parts of the world today is enough to dispel any illusion of ruefulness about the lack of vision for which a defiled and infuriated planet provides the clearest evidence. And looking at the consequences which may result from it, it is difficult not to feel a sense of bitterness towards *homo technicus* on whose shoulders must surely rest the blame for having sinned against the harmony of the universe and despoiled the splendours of the Earth, once the true isle of the Blessed, now the home of the Philistines – all but eclipsed and dying.

There she lies in all her armour, still surprisingly beautiful in all her mystery and her magic, and from an orbital survey of this blue and fragile star, in her moment of repose, it is difficult to believe that she may be nothing less than the most militarized planet in the entire universe. As the master-mariner remarked of his vessel: 'On her lived truth and audacious lies; and like the earth, she was unconscious, fair to see – and condemned to an ignoble fate'. Nor is it any the less ignoble that this fallen planet with its unholy freight and its oversaturation of arms and armed forces should now be hurtling towards Armageddon because of some intricate theory claiming that 'Only where there is life, is there also will: not, however, Will to Life, but – thus I teach thee – WILL TO POWER!'

We may therefore choose to reject it, or even damn it as the iniquitous product of politics and statecraft. But since we are here treating a species beset by Promethean torment, a fickle and inconstant species, it is only right and proper that the Will to Power should prove to be of a paradoxically wholesome significance. In plain language, it is no use admiring the virtues that keep Prometheus bound! A great deal of their strength is drawn from the very intransigence of men. Men do not live for contemplation alone. Though future generations contemplating the wreckage of their past may come to think that the prodigious human experiment has failed because every man saw himself as a champion, happy to proclaim the survival of the fittest, the plain truth of the matter is that the notion of human greatness lasted only as long as the human will to power and when that ceased to be an inspiration, greatness too had outlived its day.

The point, in any case, is that man's further and final metamorphosis – to give it the force of prophecy – depends less on a mere spiritualization of surpassing psychological states than upon the solidarity and determination of men bound together in a surpassing cause. For behind this seemingly over-literal metamorphosis – if anyone should feel bound to question the plausibility of this way of putting things – there may be found something of a vindication perhaps in the advent of a new Promethean Age. In a feeling of reverence of man for himself. For what indeed is Genius if not divine? Actually, if this reverence is not to result in a mere set of principles, a body of aesthetic doctrines such as we tend to develop in our more imaginative moments, it will have to be complemented at a new level of experience by the more substantial appearance of future astronauts – the heroic vanguard of a potentially much more conclusive migration – straining their eyes for the last glimpse they will ever get of the planet Earth.

We can perhaps imagine how, face to face with the infinite, as new worlds wax into being and then, at a leap, recede into nothingness, men with modern pressure suits and form-fitting couches in weightless metallic craft, return to question themselves, wondering anxiously whether it will ever be possible to recapture again the human view of things which has vanished from sight. After that, there is no need for words. There is only the grave and moving finality of utterly distant and receding horizons. In short, there is no place but Earth for the emotions aroused by the changing seasons or the coming of spring, by the immemorial buttercups of May, the smell of pine, or the long summer-evenings and the moonlight among the trees. Emotions too seldom memorized in tranquillity, visions the Earth alone can offer – of the autumn with its fading light, or the fall of a leaf, of the first snow, the grey-coloured ice, of that complex interweaving of psychological increments and timeless associations which cannot be found anywhere else in the entire universe but which, according to the earthly seasons of the year, provide the core of human experience from the night of passion under the June moon to the fall of ripe acorns found at the foot of an oak.

Paradoxically, in that mellow and nostalgic world, at the very moment when it has finally vanished, the evocation of human banalities takes on a new and profound significance. Suddenly the human care of human beings again seems to express something truly and maturely instinctual. It suggests the boundless, living soul of man, its indeterminate and profound spirituality, in ways which call forth indefinable and yet profuse emotions. But whether indeterminate or indefinable, the apprehension of its beauty is always timeless, archetypal and instantly recognizable – in our own minds at any rate – when seeing a young girl in a white dress, for example, or in the unknown image of a woman's face, in memories of childhood, pain or passion, even in the sight of an old man beside a shaded light, in the fire dying in the grate, in the silent somnolent night, the last moments of consciousness . . .

These manifestations, or the myriad apparently spontaneous human experiences no one seems able to explain, seem to us such an extraordinarily plausible, or rather ascertainable, representation of a riddle more profound than truth that, without requiring a clue as to what they are or where they come from we feel ourselves compelled to value them as a measure of the highest we acknowledge, as potentialities of the human soul to which we are quite unable to oppose anything rational. One of the major enigmas, it has always seemed to me, of the simple meaning of life. And yet, as the drama of a disappearing world subsides into the retrospection of its beauty, the sense of leave-taking becomes inseparable from the notion of an age in decline, of the end of an era, from the abandonment of forms of civilization once universally recognized, now diminished, denied and, notwithstanding all past experience, desperately in need of regeneration. And that, finally, is precisely why that element in man which seeks to generate anew is much more likely to find it in the direction of worlds entirely, or almost entirely, unknown and unexploited, than in the direction of a vanished Eden, of a world whose virility is diminished and whose mystery, it must be confessed, has been all but defiled and exhausted.

16

THE RIDDLE OF THE SPHINX

> The Spinx must solve her own riddle. If the whole
> of history is in one man, it is all to be explained
> from individual experience.
>
> Ralph Waldo Emerson
>
> And how could I endure to be a man, if man were
> not also poet and reader of riddles and the
> redeemer of chance!
>
> Nietzsche, *Zarathustra*

It is usually held that theoretical physics broke through a conceptual barrier somewhere in the first quarter of this century. It may well be that the decisive date was between 1900 when Max Planck announced his 'radiation law', connecting the frequency of radiation with its *quantum* of energy, and 1905, when Einstein applied it to the photoelectric effect in terms of Planck's fundamental physical 'constant'. This Niels Bohr subsequently incorporated into his model of the atom. Here, then, was the anticipation of one of the strangest theorems of science: that great epoch-making amalgam of nuclear theory and certain empirically derived relations between physical uncertainty and mathematical probability which is now called quantum mechanics. Like Einstein's theory of relativity it is the work of profound mental introspection, a breathtaking solution to the complex difficulties of interpretation which feature so prominently in the modern epistemology of science. In fact, it is precisely the combination of these two theories, together with the best currently available calculations of electromagnetism and gravitation which – depending on interactions not yet fully understood – is expected to involve the ultimate formulation of a completely unified quantum gravitational field theory with which everything that follows has to be consistent.

To those who are not familiar with the unification of physics it may be explained that ever since Einstein made his celebrated conversion equating a given amount of energy with an equivalent amount of mass, it has been the physicist's greatest ambition to devise a mathematical theory that will describe the whole of creation. What physicists call a Unified Field Theory essentially requires that the four types of fundamental basic forces which govern the material world – gravitation, electromagnetism, and the strong and weak nuclear forces, can be converted into each other. Or, in terms of its mathematical equations, into one single and unified force. One of the first results of this has been the unification of the electromagnetic with the weak nuclear force. At the same time it has to be conceded that the unified concept is largely conjectural. In fact, no one in coming to terms with the full implications of combining electromagnetism, gravitation, relativity and quantum mechanics into some kind of changeless unity, seriously imagines to find the solution in the nearby or foreseeable future.

In view of the fact that it may well hold the clue to the origin and evolution of the universe it has, of course, enormous implications. As a logically consistent, *self-explanatory* physical principle, an apparently changeless law of nature, it is, one feels, something like a ruling principle of the universe. The cause, to be exact, by which the Universe created itself. 'We burn with desire,' the devout Pascal is recorded to have said, 'to find a fixed framework of reference, an ultimate and constant base'. And whatever the apparent evidence against it, the nuclear scientist, too, is imbued with a firm conviction of the fundamental unity of all things. Indeed, the same desire is common to both. Neglecting for a moment the nature of causation in the physical world, we can even say that his direct participation in the physical universe inherently modifies that which he assimilates. His business may be reality, but participatory reality. And notions of a participatory universe have promptly begun to circulate among the more theoretical physicists, if on a much more methodical level and with the supreme object, not of attaining unity with the divine *I am* in a moment of spiritual illumination, but of reducing an almost infinite diversity into one single determining cause.

But we may leave to one side for the moment the question whether it is possible to reduce all of nature's complexity into one single undifferentiated strand of causality. For anyone who is acquainted with its correspondingly far-reaching projections and capable of following the extended arguments on which to pin a still more incisive and transfigurative hope, will also be able to see the unification of physics not only as a scientific discipline in the reductionist sense but precisely in its cultural context as an evolved form of gnosis. Nor is this special pleading. Not, certainly, in the sense that there is little real discrepancy and practically no incompatibility between the visionary and the scientist who are surely indivisible in the whole nature of our perception of space and time as some kind of inward and outward unity. Indeed, present theories suggest that the transfigurative power of his participant experience not only eliminates the distinction between subject and object, but that the only standard by which reality can now be judged is an essentially prescriptive or even solipsistic one. There is, at any rate, no such thing as a theory of perception which does not terminate in a solipsism. This even seems true, if only in an extremely attenuated sense, where the conception of a four-dimensional principle of relativity is involved. Indeed, perhaps the most significant feature of Einstein's theory of perception is the new answers it gave to the ancient problems of ontology. One might suggest, for instance, that it represents something like a synthesis of science, philosophy, and the worldview it aims to transcend and that it may, together with that other great conceptual accomplishment in theoretical physics this century, the quantum theory, even offer us the supreme contemplative achievement of modern civilization in the West.

The theory of Relativity, in other words, is by far the most profoundly conceived theory in all physics. It is the product of enormous intuitive power. Mathematically elegant, it is an altogether accomplished manifestation of the scientific genius. A triumph, and a very consummate triumph at that, of imaginative creation. Einstein's greatest merit, of course, was his emphasis on relativity as a metabolic principle. Before him the Universe had been conceived of as inherently mechanical. Now it became a dynamic, intelligent organism, in every essential alive. With Newton classical physics was at its greatest – and at its most naive. An extremely devout individual, Isaac Newton invented a perfect instrument for his own purpose: to serve his Deity no less valiantly as an intelligent, observant man, than with a mathematical description of the laws of mechanics and gravitation in which his greatness of discovery and achievement actually consisted. The nature of the universe as a function of its divine relation, has changed since Newton's day. Einstein, by implication, was probing the universe as a function of its relation to the human mind. His universe impresses the observer not by its statements of fact but rather by a strong susceptibility to the inherent characteristics of its own empirical psychology. Elementary mathematical precepts involve for us no adjustment of vision, but what Einstein envisioned in respect of a universal constant which remains consistent throughout all possible co-ordinate systems, has obvious bearings on our own conceptual self-knowledge.

So much, then, may be said of the philosophical importance of one of the most astonishing triumphs of genius in science. Though Einstein's case was at bottom only the greatest and most elementary contribution to a state of affairs which was beginning to be general, he nevertheless has an unquestionable right to a supreme place among the founders of twentieth century theoretical physics, being as true an explorer as Columbus and equally as seminal. Indeed, to fully understand the legacy of men like James Clerk Maxwell, Heinrich Hertz, H. A. Lorentz, G. F. Fitzgerald, Ludwig Boltzmann, Thompson and Rutherford to name but a few, we should perhaps remember that their natural philosophy already far transcended the purely utilitarian understanding of the Newtonian–Laplacian universe and that, apart from its new teleological and affective emphasis, Einstein's own disregard for the classical units of space and time was, in truth, the occasion of man's reinstatement into the very nature of the intelligent universe. The element of self-identification is unmistakable. So are its consistencies. Indeed, it is plain that we will, in time, come to reflect rather more critically upon the sense and general validity of the maxim that the future remains the future and the past the past.

Neither relativity nor the quantum theory distinguishes the agent from the action, and whereas it is sometimes argued that Albert Einstein always acknowledged, perhaps even insisted, that he did not wish to make the element of chance in physics the transcendental foundation of his cosmology, with all its philosophical overtones there can be little in modern science more randomly conceived of than the principle which suggests probabilities instead of stating facts precisely. For it is to Werner Heisenberg, Erwin Schrödinger and the British theoretical physicist Paul Dirac amongst others, that belongs the honour of having projected the reciprocity between the perceiving subject and the object of its knowledge into the very nature of the events themselves.

Intrinsically, like other aspects of the phenomenal world, the universe is meaningless. Nothing is of itself. There are no imperishable, let alone everlasting, standards of cosmic existence and, as for this little matter called 'the thing in itself', no possibilities of arriving at any unification with respect to the one-sided and the universal point of view. No human mind could possibly conceive of so indivisible an act, not Newton, nor Einstein. And no one summed up this inherently immeasurable state of affairs better than Albert Einstein himself: 'One may say that the eternal mystery of the world is its comprehensibility.' This was no mere figure of speech. Whether he meant to or not, Einstein was formulating a very prophetic conclusion: that the concept of an intelligent universe cannot be dissociated from that of *bona fide* reciprocity and *de facto* synchronicity of a continuous and knowing kind. Even at the risk of overstressing the interaction it can thus be said for certain that there are no facets detached from cognition for nothing static ensues. There are no facts, no 'things in themselves', nor is it conceivable that there should be.

In itself this is nothing new nor even surprising. Anyone who has studied the idealist philosophers is familiar with their denial of the existence of matter. The fact becomes remarkable, however, when one considers that the testimony of modern physics can be made to prove no less than this. This is peculiarly apparent in the fact that realities cannot produce themselves independently of the reciprocity which, on the basis of current knowledge, appears to have surfaced even at the most fundamental threshold of material analysis. And it is this combination of an apparently solipsistic perception and an inherently ambivalent rendering of it which, in terms of its subatomic specifications, gives the universe an ambiguity, a blank uncertainty, that makes even the deepest and most searching exposition of it no more than indeterminate.

Einstein, as we have said, was inclined to leave this indeterminacy undecided. Steven Weinberg, yet another Nobel laureate, contradicts his formulation almost word for word: 'The more the universe seems comprehensible, the more it also seems pointless'.[2] That, to be sure, is a sobering conclusion. There is no comprehended mystique here. His universe, we are given to understand, appears to be comprehensible but not very mysterious, rational but not animated, intelligible but without inspiration; first of all, because he relies on the intellectual effort to reduce its mystery along with its complexity and, in the second place, because the *intellectual* effort to reduce the universe till nothing remains of it but dialectical relations has obvious bearings on his own incomprehending self. He might as well be deaf and dumb.

Einstein, of course, was no intellectual. He was the archetypal artless genius. We have, at any rate, no *scientific* evidence to account for its 'significance' to ourselves. We may understand the effect but ignore the causes, ignore that such significance has an obvious if unproclaimed agenda: to enable ordinary men like Steven Weinberg to open up new perspectives on the nature of matter and consciousness and thus to impose comprehensibility upon an inherently incomprehensible and chaotic world. Comprehensibility is a generic concept like space or time. And seen thus, all we can conclude is that in that he has neglected to go further in his comprehension of the universe than a dissection of its material causes, he has been unable to treat its empirical comprehensibility as a genus in itself. And that, I am afraid, does not allow us to distinguish between the action and its agent or, in their generic aspects, between what is only a principle of efficient causality and causality as a fundamental and inseparable condition of its own mode of being.

It was Paul Valery who said that 'The mind of man can imagine nothing which does not really exist; if it could, it would create not only ideally but substantially as do the thoughts of God'. That the mind which he describes has become less deterministic, and at the same time more substantially transfigurative in helping to provide a new psychological dimension in theoretical physics, owes much to the tireless efforts of Werner Heisenberg and the Uncertainty Principle which upset all previous concepts of scientific determinism. Physicists call it the Indeterminacy Principle. One may prefer to call it the restoration of the alienated dualism between science and philosophy which dates back to the early Greek cosmologists. For one thing is certain. If, as Bishop Berkeley said, 'to be is to be perceived', then, in a subjective sense, the universe is a solipsistic creation, a self-perpetuating riddle, which can never, even in principle, be adduced in proof of itself.

For the first time in the history of science a physical theorem is pervaded with a genuine ontological element. As we have noted, the substance of it is strange enough, indeed, weird enough; while the mathematical rendering of it is uniquely determined by an inherently limited predictability. Because it qualifies the physicist for an essential function in his representation of reality, the Indeterminacy Principle is to some extent a metaphysical equation, even though it has no ethical content whatever. Nor is it susceptible to classical logic. It can only be stated empirically and left to challenge one's judgement. It may be expressed mathematically or, proceeding on the first assumption, at the level of the new psychological and solipsistic explanation. But it has to be accepted as an ontological principle, as the result of a 'divided mind', or not at all.

In any case, it is the consensus of virtually all natural philosophers that many of the features of the observable universe can be explained by processes that occur in the human brain. Processes that have nothing to do with either the actual or the 'primary' but with sounds, colours, odours and their effects, to name but 'secondary' qualities, upon the retina and the optic nerve. One plausible result of this may well be that it is pointless to discuss the nature of the universe with men of sceptical intelligence who continue to use their own neural sensations as their material evidence. On the one hand they understand a great deal, in another sense they comprehend nothing. In fact, we shall probably get nearest to the truth if we assume that the conceptual component in knowledge merely renders coherent what attains to consciousness of itself. The mystery of universal comprehensibility is not an esoteric request nor the work of any particular agency. It is an aspect of its experience, the meridian from which all measurements are taken. Nor am I insisting that the nature of the universe is best understood as some kind of contemplation of its own incarnation. But I am not so sure that it would be wrong to insist that because the intelligent character of the universe cannot be effectively distinguished from the cognitive or inquisitive mind, that to understand the universe is consequently in some measure to understand ourselves.

Thus, while the comprehended universe may justifiably be

302

characterized as mystical, it cannot be defined as objective. And the vital question, therefore, to which we must address ourselves is not whether, if ever, the world can be explained by the world, but whether the riddle of existence can ever be solved by anything other than itself. And what that consists of is best, perhaps, described by reference to a quotation from one of Edgar Allan Poe's 'ratiocinative' essays. 'Every work of art,' he remarked, 'should contain within itself all that is requisite for its own comprehension.'

The words of a man of supreme lucidity, and very plausibly offered. In fact, the attempt to expound a work of art is an experiment in creativity to which many a reader of riddles may consecrate the intellectual labours of many an infinite year. But to prove or disprove the riddle which the Sphinx can only propound by subjecting it to strictly rational modes of extrapolation is to be guilty of the paltry error of reducing the creative artist to the level of a cerebral automaton. On this level the universe operates with perfect self-consistency: unless they appeal to something within themselves, ratiocinating men can never reveal the final meaning of the riddle. While it may be rendered, nothing can be solved. Nor can it be known or conceived of in any terms other than its own. This is neither a defence of idealist philosophy nor of the empiricism of Locke and Berkeley (though its unexpectedly late fulfilment perhaps). The irony of it, in any case, is that when the process of induction is confronted directly and facts are allowed to speak for themselves, they are found to be nothing. More precisely, the atom is empty. Not merely is there no *material* evidence for non-associate physical occurrences, but we are apt to question whether it exists at all.

The concept of the atom strikes one today as an almost purely arbitrary construction, a functional mathematical instrument which the physicist, with the scanty furnishings of fact, has adapted to the specifications of a carefully conceived design. But is it real? The question scarcely has any application except to suggest to us that even though the atom intrinsically aspires to a condition of vacuity, it is still rooted in the reality which derives from it. 'Unreal, perhaps, but not illusory', as Leibniz said of another matter. Its failure to convince is not something for which the scientist can be blamed, therefore. Because the process of induction proceeds suggestively, it is safe to maintain that a certain suggestiveness or 'ideality' is one of its increments. Consider a quantum of electromagnetic radiation, for instance, or the use of probability waves in order to explain energy levels within the atom. The atom, here, is not a fact, not the thing in itself, but, like everything else that exists, readily susceptible to the reduction of its component parts into terms of the abstract, such as energy fields or electric charges. And since the subdivision of individual particulars precludes any vantage-point of the universal whole, it is obvious if we are not misreading the evidence that the relation of the particular to the universal is connected indirectly, and quite often directly, with our vision of time and space, beginning with precise microscopic theories about the earliest instant of creation and leading to relativistic forms of geometrical space as empirical categories of intelligent homocentric activity.

And so one wonders – naturally enough rather self-consciously – if science knows nothing of the unifying primordial cause beyond a multiplicity of physical co-ordinates, whence derives the continuum that binds the universe together? There certainly is something unsatisfactory about the evocation of something shadowy, vast, vertiginous, omnipresent and ubiquitous which yet appears to have no purpose of its own. For if it is said to be 'unknowable', suggestive of mind without matter, it is nevertheless commandingly real. We may, and perhaps we ought to, reject the comparison of cosmological projections of the ideal with geometrical representations of the material. But since there are powerful and persuasive theoretical arguments that arise from the findings of condensed matter physics for instance, which imply that those mathematical theorems which have given a geometrical framework to the material nature of the universe may not always correspond directly with empirical reality, we might also be persuaded that it is convenient for the construction of cosmological theories not to have any absolute significance.

This, as we have already seen in the first chapter, is particularly well illustrated in the case of what mathematicians have denominated a Black Hole. The central fact about the black hole is that it has no empirical status of its own. It is so remote from the classical physics of gravitation that one cannot exclude the possibility that, once posited as independent of the observer, it is neither real nor even rational. This is in fact an accurate statement of the case. Black holes manifest themselves not only in terms of absolute density comprising the irreducible, but quintessentially as conceptual phantoms, and may even set the future frame of reference for conceptual debates about 'space-time bridges' through which men might extend and improve their senses of the here and now, as well as being brought face to face with their own inverted image of gravity, space and time.

The reason for this is that the physicist, as a wholly engaged participant, has been subjected to the difficulty of dissociating his mathematical perception of the real from its physical representation as a matter of observable fact. While the black hole may be empirically verifiable, it nevertheless needs to be distinguished from empirical events. What has happened is that the elimination of chronological discontinuity from one level of perception to another has had the effect of producing a paradox: the simultaneity of two mutually contradictory frames of reference. The clash between reality and illusion. Which may help to explain why the difference between reality and illusion is not that the one appears to imply a consistent geodesic universe and the other a hypothetical set of equations, but that the black hole has offered itself as a dialectical relation – as distinct from the personally certified fact of the observer – beyond which further considerations of real and unreal are in fact null and void. Hence, it is precisely because they are mutually illusive that questions of being and non-being are irrelevant in the epistemology of physics. They are in fact dictated as much be the necessity of dissociating subject and object as by the physicist's commitment to find some means of sustaining both until he comes to the most sustained discontinuity of all: the Singularity.

Principle primordial of negative energy, the Singularity is the mechanism behind the illusion. It also represents a conscious endeavour to satisfy the conceptual requirements of the astrophysical theorist. Yet it is true creation. The Singularity, in other words, is not unreal. In a certain sense, it is the outcome of a clash between two mutually exclusive frames of reference. A symptom of conceptual conflict. And the physicist is the middleman who creates it. Though there is no conceivable way of unifying these two facets of his art, there are in fact persuasive arguments on both sides of the conceptual horizon debate. One is the conception involved that because it introduces a principle that appears to lie 'outside' of the sidereal universe, the Singularity cannot be said to *exist*. That since all experience is in time, and the Singularity is timeless, it cannot, according to this logic, substantially be 'there'. It merely represents, not a materially concrete presence, but a fundamental intellectual difficulty facing any effort to take the concept of physical continuity beyond the proper limits of its application. Nor is it easy to ascertain which of what are in any case two temporally relativistic frames of reference can really be held to exist. As I have said, the question is null and void, except to remind us that there is no such thing as absolute relativity. But if, because of its relativistic dimensions, the Singularity is forever to elude any conclusive test for its reality, nothing that has been said so far about the conceptual function of knowledge as a materializing force specifically maintains that, as a result of such function, it may not also '*create not only ideally but substantially as do the thoughts of God*'.

Compare with this what Einstein has to say. 'Experience remains, of course, the sole criterion of physical utility of a mathematical construction. But the creative principle resides in mathematics. In a certain sense, therefore, I hold it true that pure thought can grasp reality, as the ancients dreamed'.[3] What Einstein seems to be referring to is the conceptual power inherent in the human mind to grasp the *invisible* universe. An indication of this power is of course the way in which the universe has come to be the object of its own attention. Nor does it escape one's attention that its apparent grasp of itself can be asserted only through a mathematical theorem. But whilst one neither presumes nor precludes the general validity of the theorems the physicist has introduced, they are interesting, as I see them suggested, precisely for what they reveal about the evolution of the human mind rather than the universe.

In considering this subject one may recall the famous fifth paradox of Zeno of Elea, where a person or a 'body' runs into theoretical difficulties trying to reach a given point. Zeno, philosopher, mathematician and an eloquent propagandist of certain relativities of his own, contended that before a person may pass from one given point to another he would first have to cover an infinite number of imaginary subdivisions, but that because of a complicated hypothetical interaction between the finite distance and an infinite number of divisions it cannot be traversed in a finite time. Try and cover the whole distance, he said, and you would first have to traverse the half. Try and cover the half and there is the quarter. Try and cover that – *ad infinitum*. The inference is unmistakable, and here, certainly, it can overtake plausibility: one's goal can never be reached because every fraction of the distance, regardless how minute, can always be sub-divided.

Though there is no suggestion in Aristotle's account of the plausibilities used by Zeno that anyone found them persuasive, the Elean's proposition could easily be mistaken for a theorem computed today about the slowing of time for observers in relative motion vis-à-vis the event horizon, which also implies an apparent paradox. I say apparent because, as I have explained, since distinctions between real and apparent are just a consequence of one co-ordinate system set against another, it is useful to imagine the event horizon as the simplest mathematical description consistent with this general idea rather than try and explain it in terms of the actual and the ascertainable. If this were not the case it would be as hard for a body in (relative) motion to pass right through the event horizon as it is hard to take seriously Zeno's finite distance infinitely and arbitrarily divided into imaginary units. The truth in any case is that in addition to being moving observers we are also imagining subjects for it is exclusively out of this connection that relativistic objects in terms of fractioned time and geometrical units are born. Nor is it necessary to assert that outside the sidereal universe there is no measurable distinction in terms of quantifiable standards. Once the gravitational collapse has exceeded the escape velocity of light relative to the observed universe it interacts only with itself, whatever that may be. And we must either grant this assumption or resign ourselves to the fact that observers in relative motion may never agree on frames of reference whose mutual maladjustment is not only in conflict with those fundamental constants of nature which are the same for all of us, but whose central discord, speaking teleologically, produces a *tangible* incongruity. Incongruity I say, but the incongruity of a tremendously, indeed paradoxically, concrete presence.

Perhaps to the physicist there is a difference between the observational consequences of the unimaginatively small and large-scale problems of astronomy and cosmology, though it might be a serious mistake all the same to conclude that the end result of the former differs from that of the latter in anything but in scale. This notwithstanding, the man of science has an important point. Science clearly needs reason in order to render comprehensible the nature of the causal relationship between itself and the object of its knowledge. This relationship, moreover, may seem precarious. But when the particle physicist studies the fundamental structure of matter with its nuclear and electromagnetic forces and, in laboratory processes involving quantum field theory, abstracts material from energy, not only may particles be artificially created and eliminated but, by means of correlates such as 'messenger' or 'virtual' particles, determined solely and exclusively by their material usefulness as of one energy state relative to another.

A virtual particle, it may be noted, is one so evanescent that it leads only a phantom existence. Its presence, in other words, can only be inferred or discovered indirectly. But whether we call it virtual or comprehensible, we may equally misrepresent its meaning. To begin with, until it ceases to be virtual the name stands not so much for a peculiar kind of materialized entity as for a particular type of mental operation. Further, I have met with no evidence to convince me that these two principles might not exist side by side, if on two separate and at times complementary planes. Interestingly, what is true in the sphere of perceptivity is no less true in the sphere of experiment. Nor is this especially surprising, since the hypothetical nature of matter can be observed in the laboratory. Indeed, what has long become a standard part of a wide range of laboratory processes may not only involve the creation of entirely new forms of matter out of 'nothing', but even lead to the prediction of its requisite properties – and hence to the 'discovery', as it is termed, of certain new types of particles – even before these can be observed 'in nature' or measured in the laboratory. It is almost as though our first introduction to it is as to some kind of disembodied knowledge. To a form of knowledge whose substance, in distinguishing between 'discovering' and 'inventing' it, is primarily dynamic, conceived of at ever increasing degrees of self-perpetuation.

'How many more layers are there yet to be: atom to nucleus to proton to quark . . . ?' Thus Professor Wolfendale, the Astronomer Royal.[4] But it is pointless to speculate. There is no final solution to this problem. Nor is it a reasonable objection to point out that there is a pre-existing cosmic principle at work which requires the universe to have possessed itself of all the properties which are intrinsic to it. The significance of what John Wheeler of Princeton called 'a participatory universe' cannot be evaded simply by replacing one difficulty with another. I think it unlikely that the universe was the work of a deliberate craftsman, the outcome of a single premeditated experiment, or that it was plotted prior to its composition. On the contrary I am persuaded that rather than presiding over the presented action, the craftsman resides in the creative process and its complementary empirical workmanship, being its chief agent in exactly the same way for example as momentum is the product of mass and velocity or the mass of a body the function of both. Which is precisely why one may say without being unduly literal, that if velocity is the ratio of distance to time, and time is a phenomenon inseparable from the idea of space and from the presence of movement and dimension, the sum total of, time, space, movement and dimension is, of course, the essential meaning of *mind*. Not, one should add, because it is possible to abstract the primary from the secondary, which clearly it is not, but because so far from being fundamentals, neither matter nor mind can be anything but reciprocal.

At our present state of knowledge we simply do not know what combined characteristics, if any, are innate in the consummation Einstein foresaw. The unification of the gravitational and electro-magnetic field-forces has not advanced nearly enough for that. But, given the apparent difficulty of finding a solution to the problem of reducing all physical causes to a single common denominator, it may well be that the great mistake of the theo-retical physicist has been to suppose that the nature of the physi-cal universe was consistent in itself and conforming to the material laws which govern it. All the evidence suggests that the values of a universal self-explanatory principle will, like every other effect of a measurable or quantifiable character, vary with the intention of the conceptual factors involved. The fundamental, in other words, can never be ascertained; to ascertain it would be to subjectivate it to the relativistic, and that is its mere derivative.

Instead a different proposition had better be made; that a single principle capable of explaining the nature and origin of every-thing in the material universe, is more likely to be the measurable effect of opposite if complementary forces, than the cause which determines its own identity as an isotropic *a priori*. Inevitably, for an association of identities can be established throughout. Not altogether unlike the man who is searching for his glasses all the while he is looking through them, the modern physicists's situ-ation, too, corresponds to a state in which no *apparent* causes act. There is nothing new in that, of course. As Aquinas said of causes, 'we never observe, nor ever could, something causing itself, for this would mean that it preceded itself, and this is not possible.'

On the logic of this there is no need to expand. The difficulty arises when we decide that creation or causation is something we do arbitrarily, as though it were not a purely formal exercise of our theory of perception, but a cerebral transfiguration of the 'thing in itself'. For this, in fact, is just what it is not. There is no distinction between subject and object at the pre-conceptual level, no sensory experience which will corroborate their mutual correspondence. Where the grounds of knowledge happen to conflict, it is all we can do to inquire and search after the truth. Necessarily. And I am referring not only or even primarily to the considered and implemented effects of knowledge, nor, as a special case of this, to information as a conceptual mechanism producing effects in inherently material ways. What I am referring to is precisely the manner in which the selective involvement of information has mutated, and – I should very much like to insist – is going to mutate, the traditional universal relations.

The complexities of the conceptual descent into the unconscious therefore, are those of men on the threshold of constant self-discovery. Men learning at the symbol-inducing level rather than unconsciously and reproducing it as their own. But this involves much more than mere words can convey. It amounts, in effect, to a new view of causality, to the triumph of mind over matter, indeed, of the dreamer over the dream. The dream which today proceeds in quantum jumps, or quantum leaps and bounds, rather than by geometrical progression, for if the evidence available permits of such a general statement, then the destiny of the whole of mankind, and indeed of the Universe itself, is bound up with its implementation, and never more so than when it is presented according to laws which are said to be objective.

But first things first. If, at least from the spiritual and psychological point of view, the great problem of the years lying immediately ahead will be the problem of motivation – and there is no doubt that *homo natura* is on the brink of catastrophe because our technocratic universe has driven him to the ultimate disbelief in a living mythological reality – the third millennium, as I suspect is recognized, will be a key period of conceptual development in the evolution of the human mind. It is true, human science and technology may possess very little mystic of their own. Yet, though we may not think of modern physics as an exercise in the supernatural, no one who seriously considers the way in which men have transcended what are more commonly thought to be their limitations, is likely to dispute the existence of the supernatural in the natural. For as another form of *gnosis*, it is also capable of great metaphysical accomplishment. Or, to point the moral more clearly, sooner or later, in the inevitable progress of things, the future metaphysicist may not only provide the answer to that ancient ontological enigma, the perennial theodicity problem of which, under all kinds of recondite formulae, an entire philosophical tradition has been looking, but to the problem of human nature itself – and there is nothing irreligious about that.

Heaven forbid that I should make inference beyond the consciousness of our own powers. But, in the sense that it seems to be self-amplifying, one day perhaps to pervade the entire universe, there is no reason for supposing that gods are superior to men. In particular it seems to me that, following an infinite chain of causes like a great wheel moving within its own circle, men are poets also, readers of riddles and the dreamers of dreams; and their dream distinguished as much by its qualities of imagination, its perception of beauty, its sense of awe and prophecy, of proportion and harmony, as through its scientific acumen and the synchronicity of the cosmic consequences it continuously foreshadows. The only flaw in this recapitulation is that it is incomplete, too inconsiderable even or, at any rate, insufficiently ecstatic. In fact, even this reservation needs amplification. For although man seems insignificant, inconsiderable and at times even inconsistent, and his world an almost excruciating mathematical abstraction, his is the mind that binds the universe together, the principle of equilibrium on which the cosmos turns and evolves.

One way of amplifying this further is to consider that everything in the universe conspires to form a coherent unity, an interconnected whole; the geometrical planes, the gravitational equations, the kinetic action that furnish the whole timescape and chronology without ever becoming static. For it is precisely the pervasive nature of what physicists call the anthropic principle which makes it so utterly incapable of precise definition, an abstract ideal it would seem rather than a workable concept. I shall, however, make an assertion of fact and a scriptural analogy. I may be right or wrong about the next evolutionary cycle, but there is every indication that its impact, during the past quarter of a century or so, on the way physicists think, has been so powerful and compelling and its growing preponderance so potent since, that, in an era of profound transfiguration, it would be quite

311

unthinkable to take away the human factor, its principle of coherence, from science and especially from physics. There is, moreover, a perfectly good sense in which scriptural vision is not only one of man's essential puniness but also of his divinity – the kind of sense, I am sure, which corresponds to something analogous to the findings of human intuition into the nature of the physical universe or, indeed, into the uncertainties of its being.

Although the uncertainties are indeed ambivalent, this is perhaps the most appropriate place to suggest what has already been suggested before; that 'true miracles never contradict and defy nature, they rather restore nature to its first and unfallen state'. Therefore, if there were no more solid evidence than that miracles are usually, perhaps inherently, unamenable to scientific treatment, the one *fact* to be communicated about the supernatural is precisely that it offends nothing but logical understanding, and not even Christ would pretend otherwise. Nor do I believe that Christ was attributing to himself unreasonable abilities. If anything, he was a master-craftsman, a reader of riddles and the redeemer of chance. To put matters bluntly, all it really meant for him was that from the moment you learn to walk on water you are no longer under the necessity of getting your feet wet, and on the basis of this ascertainable fact I find much in it which is powerful and much which is imputable. Unfortunately, as we have remarked before, the observed and experienced fact is seldom being taken very spiritually. And lest it be thought presumptuous of scientists even to attempt to solve the riddle of creation, the only comment, I think, to be made is that it is not expected, in view of men's manifest aversion to obvious truths, that the spell will be broken or the secret compromised, let alone confuse logicians.

However, Christ never told all. And that can best be appreciated, perhaps, by examining His own cryptic words: 'I have yet many things to say unto you, but you cannot bear them now' (John 16:12), for which, moreover, I do not propose to suggest an explanation. I can only suggest this: if truth is the ultimate criterion for judging the nature of the universe, there is no valid reason, in adhering to universal principles which in turn reflect the true nature of man, why Christ should have been capable of achieving what we, in entering upon His existence, may not achieve ourselves. What, in the nature of things, is more natural than that? At all events, to transform his sense of divine omnipotence into a mere condition of faith is not to honour Christ, frankly, but to offend against his genius. Nor is it unreasonable, perhaps, in following the logic of this view, to believe that his words may at length be revealed as a wonderfully auspicious statement, provided we at last comprehend how remarkably simple the plain truth really is and that, in the blessed simplicity of its universal spirit, it involves our participation and our causation as a complete and indivisible embodiment of something much more fundamental than physical laws.

And a last thought. If men cannot control the fruits of their own imaginings, they will have to carry with care the burden of the riddle which they can neither penetrate nor possibly control. 'Men thought for many generations that they had answered the riddle of the Spinx.' – as someone said on another occasion – 'They misconceived the meaning of her smile.' Fortunately, for an answered riddle ceases to inspire! There is no other solution conceivable, perhaps no salvation at all outside that very riddle, except for the Will of the Willers that it shall continue to shape the universe in the most unconscious of ways. And to what end? That unchanging end, finally, is my real objective and, if I can help it, the setting for much of a subsequent and concluding book, 'a book' – to close with the words of a more lucid witness of the eternal, shall we say, supernatural transfiguration – which 'belongs to the very few. Perhaps none of them are alive yet.'

O Will, my essential, *my* necessity, dispeller of need!
Spare me for one great victory!

NOTES AND REFERENCES

INTRODUCTION

1 Nietzsche, F., *Beyond Good and Evil. Prelude to a Philosophy of the Future*. Transl. by R. J. Hollingdale. Penguin Books, 1990, p. 31.
2 'Even God has his Hell: it is his love for man'. *Zarathustra* Pt. II/3.
3 Huxley, A., *Do What You Will*. Watts & Co., London, 1936, p. 178.
4 Ibid., p. 180.
5 Ibid., p. 70.
6 Nietzsche, op. cit., p. 52.
7 Quoted in Churchill, W. S., *A History of the English-Speaking Peoples*. Vol. 1., *The Birth of Britain*. Cassell & Co., London, 1956, p. 24.
8 *Disturbing the Universe*. Pan Books, London, 1981, p.112.
9 May 22, 1884. In a letter to Freiherr Dr von Stein: '. . . und wenn ich Alles von mir erlange, *was ich will*, so werde ich mit dem Bewusstsein sterben, dass Künftige Jahrtausende auf meinen Namen ihre höchsten Gelübde thun.' PAN Heft III. 1898, p. 169.

PART ONE

1

1 *Against all Odds*; Greenpeace leaflet issued in 1988.
2 *The Sunday Telegraph* 3.6.90, p. 11.
3 Sullivan, W., *We Are Not Alone. The Search for Intelligent Life in Other Worlds.* Signet Book, 1966, p. 253.
4 Asimov, I., *The Universe. From Flat Earth to Quasars.* Penguin Books, 1971, p. 63.
5 Davies, P., and Gribbin, J., *The Matter Myth. Beyond Chaos and Complexity.* Penguin Books, 1992, p. 36.
6 Huxley, op. cit., p. 59.
7 Ibid., p. 54.
8 Wells, H. G., *The World Set Free.* The Hogarth Press, London, 1988, pp. 7 and 9.

2

1 Marx, K., *Capital.* Allen & Unwin, 1949, See Author's Preface p. xxx ff.
2 *Encyclopedia Britannica* 1929, Vol. 14, p. 995.
3 Crankshaw, E., *The Shadow of the Winterpalace.* Macmillan, London, 1976, p. 124.
4 Weber, M., *The Protestant Ethic and the Spirit of Capitalism.* Unwin, London, 1985, p. 53.
5 Ibid., p. 17.
6 Kochan, L., *The Making of Modern Russia.* Penguin Books, 1971, p. 266.
7 Ibid., p. 164.
8 Ibid., p. 96.
9 Hugo Grotius (1583–1645). See Mazzarino, S., *The End of the Ancient World.* Faber and Faber, London, p. 100.
10 Marx, op. cit., Editor's Preface p. xii.
11 Ibid., Autor's Preface p. xxii.
12 In a letter to Lassalle; see Clark, R., *The Survival of Charles Darwin.* Weidenfeld & Nicolson, London, 1985, p. 212.
13 Spengler, O., *The Decline of the West.* Allen & Unwin, London, 1961, p. 181.
14 Quoted in Ryan, A., *Bertrand Russell. A Political Life.* Allen Lane. The Penguin Press, 1988, p. 28.

3

1 Rowse, A. L., *The Expansion of Elizabeth England.* Macmillan, 1981, p. 192.

2 It is possible already to think of a number of US–Russian joint stock companies. International Space Enterprise (ISE), for example, a US corporation established in June 1992, is leading an international consortium that will undertake mankind's first privately financed robotic missions to the Moon. Another US company, Rimsat, is the major foreign partner of Informocosmos, an association of leading Russian space enterprise which is responsible for commercializing Russia's space technology and developing its satellite communications. See *Spaceflight* Vol. 36, July 1994.

3 Hoyle, F., *The Nature of the Universe.* Blackwell, Oxford, 1950, p. 8.

4 Clark, R. W., *Benjamin Franklin.* Weidenfeld & Nicolson, London, 1983, p. 386.

5 Smith, D. C., *H. G. Wells. Desperately Mortal.* Yale Univ. Press, 1986, p. 47.

4

1 Quoted in Morris, J., *Heaven's Command.* Faber & Faber, London, p. 74.

2 Quoted in Dudley, D., *The Romans.* Hutchinson, London, 1970, p. 35.

3 Grogan, E. S., *From the Cape to Cairo. The first Traverse of Africa from South to North.* Nelson & Sons, London, p. 293.

4 Najder, Z., *Joseph Conrad.* Cambridge University Press, 1983, p. 140.

5 *Macaulay, Lays of Ancient Rome. With Selections from the Essays: Lord Clive.* John E. Stafford, Brighton, p.37.

6 Quoted in Edwardes, M., *Red Year. The Indian Rebellion of 1857.* Hamish Hamilton, London, 1973, pp. 39 and 15.

7 Nietzsche, op. cit., p. 195.

5

1   Lord Milner: 'My patriotism knows not geographical but only racial limits. I am an Imperialist and not a little Englander, because I am a British Race Patriot'. *The Times* 27.7.1925; Quoted in Stewart, D., *T. E. Lawrence*. Hamish Hamilton, London, 1977, p. 41.

2   Connolly, C. *Enemies of Promise*. Penguin Books, 1961, p. 32.

3   Shaw, B., *Plays: Pleasant and Unpleasant.* Vol II. Constable & Co., London, 1903, p. 200 ff.

4   Thucydides 1.70.7; transl. Rex Warner. Quoted by Bowra, C. M., *Periclean Athens*. Weidenfeld & Nicolson, London, 1971, p. 247.

5   Battiscombe, G., *Shaftesbury, A Biography of the Seventh Earl*. 1801–85. Constable, London, 1974, p. 170.

6   Brod, M., *Heinrich Heine*. Greenwood, Westport, Connecticut, 1976, p. 77.

7   Thucydides 2.64.5; Quoted by Bowra, C. M., op. cit. p. 131.

8   'Asia is waiting for us', says the King of Pontus, 'and cries out for help; the Romans have succeeded in making themselves hated because of the greed of their Proconsuls, the extortion of their tax-collectors, the injustices of their magistrates . . .' (Sallust, Ep. Miths. 18) Quoted from Mazzolani, L. S., *Empire without End*. Harcourt Brace Jovanovich, New York, London, 1976, p. 61.

PART TWO

6

1   Jung, C. G., *Civilization in Transition*. Collected Works, Vol. 10, pars. 148–196: *The Spiritual Problem of Modern Man*. See *The Portable Jung*. Penguin Books, 1976, p. 467.

2   Schnabel, J., *Dark White. Aliens, Abductions, and the UFO Obsession*. Hamish Hamilton, London, 1994, p. 137.

3   Gay, P., *Freud. A Life for Our Time*. J. M. Dent, London, 1988, p. 179.

4   Quoted by Harrington, M., *The Accidental Century*. Penguin Books, 1965, p. 11.

5   Clark, J., and Coleman, L., *The Unidentified*. 1975, quoted in *Project Blue Book,* Ed. B. Steiger, Ballantine Books, New York, 1976, p. 343.
6   Sullivan, op. cit., p. 282.
7   Hawking, S.W., *A Brief History of Time. From the Big Bang to Black Holes.* Bantam Press, London, 1988, p. 174.
8   Connolly, op. cit., p. 111.

7

1   Spengler, op. cit., p. 48.
2   Gibbon, E., *The Decline and Fall of the Roman Empire.* Chapter 38; Appendix. Quoted by Johnson, P., *Enemies of Society.* Weidenfeld & Nicolson, London, 1977, p. 44.
3   *Satires* III:62.
4   Herder, J. G. von, *Reflections on the Philosophy of the History of Mankind.* University of Chicago Press, 1968, p. 249.
5   Kingsmill, H., *The English Genius.* The Right Book Club, London, 1939, p. 26.
6   Barrow, R. H., *The Romans.* Penguin Books, London, 1975, p. 204.

8

1   Mazzarino, S., *The End of the Ancient World.* Translated by George Holmes. Faber & Faber, London, 1959.
2   Ibid., p. 26 (Cicero, De Re Publica, V. 1/2).
3   Glover, T. R., *The Ancient World.* Pelican Books, London, 1948, p. 278.
4   Mazzarino, op. cit., p. 135.
5   Herder, op. cit., p. 236.
6   Kingsmill, op. cit., p. 143.
7   Stern, J. P., *Nietzsche.* Fontana, London, 1978, p. 13.
8   Pakenham, T., *The Boer War.* Weidenfeld & Nicolson, London, 1979, p. 230.
9   Shirer, W., *The Rise and Fall of the Third Reich.* Pan Books, London, 1965, p. 1044.
10 Trevelyan, G.M., *British History in the Nineteenth Century and After (1782–1919).* Penguin Books, London, 1979, p. 123.

11 Shirer, op. cit., p. 896.
12 Clark, R. W., *Benjamin Franklin.*Weidenfeld & Nicolson, London, 1938, p. 39.
13 Solzhenitsyn, A., *The Gulag Archipelago.* Collins-Fontana, London, 1974, p. 272.
14 Connolly, C., op. cit., p. 272.
15 Spengler, op. cit., pp. 328 and 364.
16 Kingsmill, op. cit., p. 141.
17 *The European* 5–8 Nov. 1992; p. 8: J. Enoch Powell, former Conservative and Ulster Unionist MP: 'Praise be! My world has come to its senses'.

9

1 Quoted in Shirer, op. cit., p. 131.
2 Ibid., p. 128.
3 Ibid., p. 130.
4 Ibid., Book I, Chapter 4; p. 128 ff.: The Intellectual Roots of the Third Reich.
5 Holden, G., *The Second Superpower. The Arms Race and the Soviet Union.* CND Publications, 1985, London, p. 17.
6 Arbeitsgemeinschaft Kriegsursachenforschung, Hamburg, Dec., 1993.
7 *The Independent* 10.7.90; p. 1.
8 *The Daily Telegraph* 7.8.88: ' "Skinhead" violence hits France.'
9 Palmer, R. R., *The Age of the Democratic Revolution.* Vol. I. Princeton University Press, 1959, p. 191.
10 Battiscombe, G., op. cit., p. 174.
11 Stone, L., *The Causes of the English Revolution 1529–1642*, Ark Paperbacks, 1986, p. 60.
12 Woodcock, G., *Anarchism. A History of Libertarian Ideas and Movements.* Penguin Books, 1962, p. 44.
13 Colin Ross, *Multiple Personality Disorder.* Quoted in Schnabel, op. cit., p. 296.
14 'The killing of children where they are seen as a social problem and dealt with accordingly, could happen in Europe. No country yet has solved the problem of street children.' From a report on the phenomenon of street orphans in Eastern Europe comissioned by the European Community. *The European* 10–13.9.1992, p. 5.

15 Morris, D., *The Naked Ape*. Triad/Mayflower, 1977, p. 111.
16 Deutsche Presse Agentur, June 1993.
17 *The Daily Telegraph* 17.12.85.

10

1   Tate, A., *Our Cousin, Mr Poe*. From: *Poe. A Collection of Critical Essays*. Ed. R. Regan. Prentice Hall, Inc., Englewood Cliffs, N.J. 1967, p. 42.
2   Rowbotham, S., *Hidden from History. 300 Years of Women's Oppression and the Fight Against it*. Pluto Press, 1974, p. 49.
3   *Independent on Sunday* 17.10.93, p. 24. 'Family devalues'; A University of Maryland sociologist found that in 1985 parents spent an average of 17 hours a week with their children, against 30 hours in 1965.
4   *The European* 4–7.2.1993, p. 8.
5   Maurois, A., *Victor Hugo*. J. Cape, London, 1956, p. 212.
6   Allen, W., *The English Novel*. Penguin Books, London, 1970, p. 268.
7   'Gay genes do not exclude choice'. *The Independent* 16.7.93, p. 19.
8   *Economic and Philosophical Manuscripts,* 1844, quoted in Rowbotham, op. cit., p. 65.
9   *The Daily Telegraph*, 12.12.1987, p. 48.
10 Kingsmill, op. cit., p. 15.
11 Hoyle, F., *The Intelligent Universe*. Michael Joseph, London, 1983, p. 71.
12 Ibid., p. 49.
13 Connor, S., and Kingman S., *The Search for the Virus*. Penguin Books, London, 1988, p. 1.
14 *The European* 28–30.6.1991: p. 15. Ustinov at Large: 'Coming Home is a Liberation'.
15 Freud, S., *Totem and Taboo*. Routledge & Kegan Paul, London, 1950, p. 20.

PART THREE

11

1   This and all other quotations from Francis Bacon are taken

from Daphne du Maurier, *The Winding Stair. Francis Bacon. His Rise and Fall.* Pan Books, London, 1976.

2   Hoyle, op. cit., p. 8.

3   A contemporary of H. G. Wells, Edgar Schuster used this term in proposing that mental characteristics follow the same rule of inheritance as physical ones. Schuster, E., *Eugenics.* Collins, London, 1922, p. 35.

4   Darwin, C., *The Descent of Man.* 1871, 2:405; quoted in Clark, R. W. *The Survival of Charles Darwin.* Weldenfeld & Nicolson, London, 1985, p. 180.

12

1   Quoted in Dickson, L., *H. G. Wells. His Turbulent Life and Times.* Penguin Books, London, 1972, p. 357.

2   Ibid., p. 357.

3   Ryan, op. cit., p. 174.

4   Ibid., pp. 128 and 145.

5   Ibid., p. 179.

6   *The Autobiography of Bertrand Russell. 1872–1914.* Allen & Unwin, London, 1967, p. 147: 'Cantor had a proof that there is no greatest number, and it seemed to me that the number of all things in the world ought to be the greatest possible. Accordingly, I examined his proof with some minuteness, and endeavoured to apply it to the class of all the things there are. This led me to consider those classes which are not members of themselves, and to ask whether the class of such classes is or is not a member of itself'.

7   'It is, perhaps, interesting to point out that nuclear physics was one of the few branches of modern physics to which Einstein did not contribute, no doubt because when it began, in the modern sense, in the 1930s Einstein was almost entirely preoccupied with his unified field theories.' Bernstein, J., *Einstein.* Fontana Press, London, 1973, p. 130.

8   Clark, R. W., *The Life of Bertrand Russell.* Penguin Books, London, 1978, p. 648.

9   Johnson, P., *Intellectuals.* Phoenix Paperback, 1988, p. 246.

10   Hoyle, F., *Energy or Extinction. The Case for Nuclear Energy.* Heinemann, London, 1979, p. 35.

11   Wells, op. cit., p. 173.

13

1 Quoted in Palmer, op. cit., p. 54.
2 Chesterton, C., *A History of the United States*. J. M. Dent, London, 1940, p. 101.
3 Buckmann, P., *Lafayette. A Biography.* Paddington Press, New York, London, 1977, p. 43.
4 Churchill, op. cit., p. 74.
5 Douglas, D. C., *William the Conqueror. The Norman Impact upon England.* Eyre & Spottiswoode, London, 1966, p. 84.
6 Ibid., p. 6.
7 Nietzsche, op. cit., p. 127.
8 Connolly, C., op. cit., p. 279.
9 Wells, H. G., *The Food of the Gods and How it Came to Earth.* Thomas Nelson, London, p. 281.

14

1 Herder, op. cit., pp. 253–54.
2 Macaulay, op. cit., p. 171.
3 *The Daily Telegraph*, 31.8.90, p. 17.
4 *Independent on Sunday* 17.10.93, p. 13. 'The day the new world order died'.
5 Johnson, op. cit., p. 306.
6 John F. Kennedy Library interview with Wernher von Braun, 31 March 1964; Quoted in *Spaceflight* Vol. 36 July 1994, p. 229.
7 'World Priorities', Washington; June 1991
8 Hoyle, F., The Intelligent Universe. op. cit., p. 223.
9 Jung, K. G., The Relations between the Ego and the Unconscious. Two Essays on Analytical Psychology. *The Portable Jung*. Penguin Books, London, p. 104.

15

1 Dyson, F., *Disturbing the Universe*. Pan Books, London, 1981, p. 116.
2 We may let that argument stand. But I am indebted to Duncan Lunan for the reservation that it was 'Kennedy's hidden agenda to stimulate the enconomics of states where

his support was weak, and revive the economy of the US as a whole.'

3 Lunan, D., *Man and the Planets. The Resources of the Solar System.* Ashgrove Press, Bath, 1983, pp. 33–34.
4 Rorvik, D. M., *As Man Becomes Machine. The Evolution of the Cyborg.* Abacus, London, 1975, p. 15.
5 *The Independent* 30.7.88; 'Baroness Faithfull, a Tory Peer, challenged ministers about what precautions had been taken in case COSMOS 1900 landed on the Houses of Parliament themselves.'
6 1990: According to 'World Priorities' (Washington) there were 26 million enlisted men in regular armed forces, plus another 40 million unenlisted reservists. 1994: An estimated 100 million live landmines in some 60 countries of the world are still uncleared, while the world's manufacturers, led by Italy, Russia, Brazil and China, produce more than 500,000 landmines a year. 2000: American Intelligence predicts that there will be 24 developing nations with ballistic missiles, nine of which will have, or be near to acquiring, nuclear capabilities.

16

1 Quoted in Dyson, op. cit., p. 50.
2 Ibid., p. 258.
3 Bernstein, op. cit., p. 105.
4 Wolfendale, A., The heavens help us. *The Times* 3.8.94, p. 15.